In The Wings
A Memoir

by Diana Douglas Darrid

Barricade Books/New York

Acknowledgments

My thanks to my dear friends Mickey and Walter Seltzer, who first urged me to publish these pages, and to my two sons, Michael and Joel Douglas, who read them and concurred. And to Tristine Rainer, whose excellent book *Your Life as Story: The New Autobiography* helped give a final form to the piece.

Barricade Books/New York

Published by Barricade Books Inc.
150 Fifth Avenue
Suite 700
New York, NY 10011

Copyright © 1999 by Diana Douglas Darrid
All Rights Reserved.

No part of this book may be reproduced, stored in a retrieval system, or transmitted in any form, by any means, including mechanical, electronic, photocopying, recording, or otherwise, without the prior written permission of the publisher, except by a reviewer who wishes to quote brief passages in connection with a review written for inclusion in a magazine, newspaper, or broadcast.

Library of Congress Cataloging-in-Publication Data

Darrid, Diana Douglas, 1923-
    In the wings : a memoir / by Diana Douglas Darrid
    p.   cm.
    ISBN 1-56980-151-7
    1. Darrid, Diana Douglas, 1923- . 2. Actors–United States
  Biography. 3. Douglas, Kirk, 1916- . 4. Douglas, Michael, 1944-
  . I. Title.
PN2287.D283A3   1999
792'.028'092–dc21
[B]
                                              99-27885
                                                  CIP
Printed in the United States of America.
SECOND PRINTING
10 9 8 7 6 5 4 3 2 1

Contents

Preface		7
Prologue		9
1.	Bermuda	13
2.	London	25
3.	Upper Chine	31
4.	America	61
5.	Hollywood	73
6.	New York	87
7.	Marriage	97
8.	Hollywood Redux	117
9.	Divorce	147
10.	New York Redux	153
11.	California Once More	199
12.	Westport	215
13.	Broadway	223
14.	The Sixties	243
15.	The Seventies	265
16.	The Eighties	293
17.	The Nineties	315
18.	After	331
19.	Back Home	363

For Cameron

Preface

It was the spring of 1994, and I was filming *Disclosure* at Warner Brothers. studios in Los Angeles. I shared a house in Beverly Hills with my mother, Diana, and my brother, Joel. Mom's old house in the San Fernando Valley had been extensively damaged in the L.A. earthquake, and Joel was recovering from surgery. It was the first time in more than thirty years that the three of us lived together. The experience proved to be a wonderful opportunity for us to spend many evenings together reminiscing about earlier years, sharing stories we had never told each other before, and most important—laughing a lot.

Much has been written about my father, Kirk Douglas, over the course of his fifty-year career, including his own best-selling autobiography, but I knew little about my mother's past. Having this chance to hear about her early life and the history of the Dill family, I discovered that Mom had a great story to tell. Her recollections were not the usual scandalous celebrity "kiss-and-tell" adventures one has become accustomed to from Hollywood. The stories of her family, Bermudian childhood, and years in the theatre and the movie business were fascinating; peopled with great characters. They were packed with love, humor, and tragedy.

I asked her if she would put her story in writing so that my son, Cameron, would have the chance to discover and enjoy his grandmother's heritage. The next time we had a discussion about my request was in 1998 when she presented me with a manuscript entitled *In The Wings*.

I am extremely proud of the great dignity with which

my mother has conducted her life. I am deeply grateful for the knowledge and upbringing she and my stepfather, William Darrid, gave me and could not be more pleased with her decision to publish her own story.

—Michael Douglas

Prologue
—1949—

The door slammed.

Through the panes, I watched the beam of the headlights as the car threaded its way down our narrow driveway. A final blink of the red taillights and it was gone. My husband was gone.

I went upstairs to our bedroom, stumbling over something soft. It was one of his shirts that I had kicked into a corner in a fury during one of our final arguments. I picked it up. The smell of him still clung to it, and I threw it on a chair, sat down on the bed, trying to sort out my jumbled emotions.

The events of the past evening still made me boil.

Warren Cowan, Kirk's publicity manager, had been with us attempting to stage-manage what should have been a completely private affair. A painful separation.

It was explained to me that I was impossibly naïve about the ways of Hollywood, and that if I didn't speak first to Louella Parsons and then to Hedda Hopper, it could have a detrimental effect on Kirk's career.

"Godammit, I won't!" I swore. "It's absolutely no one's business, but ours."

"Honey, he's a star now. Anything that affects him is everybody's business."

"Doug?" (I had called him that ever since our days as students at the American Academy of Dramatic Arts when his stage name, Kirk Douglas, was newly acquired) His head was down, and he seemed to be studying his hands intently. He didn't answer.

"Is that what you want? Do I have to talk to those stupid, gossipy women? What's the matter with you?" He looked up then and shrugged.

"That's the way things are in this town, dear. I didn't make the rules."

"You don't want to hurt his career, now do you?" chimed in Warren.

"Oh, shut up, Warren! What about our life? What about our kids? They didn't ask to be splashed all over the headlines!"

"Honey, they're only five and two…"

"I don't give a damn. I think it's disgusting."

"It's the price of fame. It's the price of celebrity," said Warren. "As an actress, you'll probably have to deal with it too, one of these days. Better get used to it."

"Not on your life!"

Warren stood up.

"Okay," he said. "I guess nobody can force you. But it seems a pity that after he's worked so hard, got such great notices in *Champion*, and needs the publicity, now you'd go and pull the rug out from under him." There was a silence as they both stared at me.

I stared back. The silence lengthened. Finally, I spoke. "Is it really true? They have that much power?"

"They can make or break a career. They've asked to talk with you, and we can't afford to alienate them. It could look bad, like we're covering up something. And they never forget. Never."

"Shit," I said. Then, "Okay, I'll do it."

"Don't cry," warned Warren.

"Don't worry, I won't."

"Remember…'Irreconcilable differences,' nothing else."

"Irreconcilable differences. Got it."

They watched me as I picked up the phone and dialed.

I stuck to the party line while Miss Parsons expressed

her sorrow for "those dear little children," how Doug and I had seemed "the happiest couple in all of Hollywood," and dropped delicate hints about my husband's leading ladies.

I hung up.

"Now, would you please get out. Now."

Warren left immediately. Doug and I exchanged some information about the children's plans, then he moved to the door. His eyes never met mine.

I sat up most of the night, smoking and cogitating. I was trying to make some sense out of our history. How two people, who had been passionately in love, both gifted with senses of humor and intelligence, could end up six years later at such a ruthless impasse. The pressures of new-found celebrity were just the final wedge. "irreconcilable differences" was not so far off the mark, I decided.

We had brought to marriage such different concepts of what it constituted, what was expected due, in a great part to our different upbringings, our different approach to life.

Doug had fought his way up out of grinding poverty.

He had been born in 1917 to a Russian immigrant couple, Bryna and Harry Demsky, in the upstate town of Amsterdam, New York. His father was often absent and sometimes abusive, but his mother and all of his six sisters were endlessly supportive of his hopes and ambitions, helping him develop self-confidence and a drive that was to serve him well all his life.

I, on the other hand, had been born in Bermuda in 1923 to a family who had lived there since 1620, whose roots went deep into island life, who were fairly well-to-do. Money was mentioned infrequently as it was considered vulgar to dwell on the subject. My father was attorney general of the island for eighteen years.

I lit another cigarette as I pondered.

I knew I should try to get some sleep as I was due in makeup at six. I was in the midst of shooting *House of Strangers*, a film directed by Joseph Mankiewicz and starring Edward G. Robinson. Sleep was impossible.

12 In The Wings

A childhood memory flashed into my brain. A memory of deep anger with my father.

Could that be a clue, a key to understanding the foibles of the adults we had become? Had it affected how we dealt with one another?

Much, much later when my son Michael asked me to recount my memories as honestly as I could for his son Cameron, my mind flashed back to the 1949 scene just recounted. Although it's certainly not the usual information that grandparents choose to give their grandchildren, perhaps following the trail back to its inception might give some inkling as to how the choices I made led to a life full of incident.

Chapter 1
BERMUDA—1926

My earliest memory is of standing, holding the bars of my crib in the dark.

Something had awakened me. Some noise beyond the pounding of the waves below my parent's bedroom. Something that seemed to come from the fireplace.

I heard it again. A faint tinkle. Then a louder jingling of bells. I gripped the bars tighter. Then footsteps stamping on the roof and a loud, hoarse male voice echoing down the chimney.

"Ho-ho!" it bellowed. "Ho, ho, ho, ho, ho!"

I screamed loudly.

"Oh my God," said the voice.

I kept on screaming till my mother's footsteps came pattering up the hall. In vain she tried to comfort me while my teenage brother, Laurence, stood red-faced and apologetic. He had decided, with his flair for the dramatic, to reinforce my belief in Santa Claus by acting out the part, shaking sleigh bells, and shouting down the chimney.

I viewed both Laurence and Santa with suspicion from then on.

I don't know why I was in my parents' room that night. Some relative or guest must have been occupying the bed in my nursery. The nursery was painted a vivid shade of pink with the high, white-tray ceiling typical of Bermuda houses. Sometimes a lizard or land crab would cross the beams, and the large bed was draped in gauzy mosquito netting. Stuffed animals and long-legged dolls lolled in the pillows, sometimes sharing the bed with friends of my brother's, sleeping off hangovers.

There was a bookcase with all the Christopher Robin books and a large dollhouse that my sister, Fan, would decorate with tiny, white lights at Christmastime. On the wall were two pictures of a sailing ship,"The Seeadler", autographed to "My dear little Diana, from Erich Von Luckner." I don't remember meeting the infamous Count Von Luckner (known for his piratical raids on British ships during World War I), but I gather, as a baby, I made quite a hit with him when he was visiting.

Our house was always an open and hospitable one. Guests came and went in bewildering profusion. One young man, a Scottish laird named Lord Dundas, hung around for several months, claiming to be a Cambridge classmate of my brother Bayard. I would see him in the morning, scurrying out of the bathroom past me wrapped in a sheet, looking terminally anxious.

Mother kept mentioning him in her letters to Bayard and finally got a response that he barely knew the guy and, furthermore, could not stand him. Nevertheless, it was hard for my kindhearted mother to ask him to leave. It wasn't until Laurence came down with pleurisy, and Dundas, raiding the fridge, ate up the last of the eggs she had been saving for the invalid's eggnog that she hit the roof and ordered him gone. By that time he had been with us almost four months.

Once, I found the entire Edwards family in my bed. They had recently moved into "Winton," a house on the hill behind ours, and we knew them only slightly. Their father had gotten drunk and chased them out of the house with a shotgun. Mother took them in, with warnings to me not to talk about the incident as it might upset them.

Life was full of adult secrets that must not be discussed and, though a sunny exterior was maintained for the most part, the difference between things as they were purported to be and things as they actually were puzzled and fascinated me.

So I watched the Edwards family in church. Father, mother, and children all singing lustily together, praising the Lord, and I wondered. I watched a friend of my brother's sleeping in my bed in a fume of alcohol, his face innocent as a baby's. I remembered how cruel and sarcastic he was when awake. And I wondered.

I would hear slurred and angry voices coming from the library at night, but when my father's bugle wakened us in the morning, I was told that they were merely discussing points of law. I would hurry by the library door with its smell of cigar smoke and whiskey.

Still, by and large, those days were sunny and blissful. Barefoot, I would squat on the rocks, watching the tiny sea creatures in the tidal pools, feed hibiscus buds to my pet turtle, dress my patient Airedale in my doll's clothes and wheel him in a pram, and drag a stick behind me, explaining to my black nanny that it was a prancing steed. And sometimes I would run away.

I remember my forays being based on curiosity, not unhappiness, a wish to see what was around the next bend, what new interesting friends there were to be made. Once, I slipped away from my mother at the Agricultural Exhibit and hitched a ride home with a farmer, his cart piled high with produce. We had an interesting discussion about frogs.

Later, I was told of the anxiety I had caused by my wanderlust. My father had recently proposed legislation in Parliament limiting immigration to the island, and this had caused some families to be separated. He had been receiving threats, to him and the family, but none of this was imparted to me.

I loved the hurricanes. The preparations as the waves grew higher and the sky grew darker, the outdoor furniture brought in, the last phone calls before the line went dead, the candles and hurricane lamps brought out. It was a time when the family was closest, huddled round the fireplace in the dining room. Mother sang softly as she massaged our scalps and we sipped cocoa. Beatrice and Israel, the cook and groom, sang hymns from their native Antigua, and Father and the boys made occasional forays to check on the storm shutters while the wind shrieked outside.

The curious look of everything after the storm. Boats high on the pasture land. New vistas across the hill where the trees had been toppled. The oleanders smelled like ice cream tasted, and dew shone on the cedar berries. Fan's marmoset rode an upturned table floating in the garden. Big fronds, fallen off palmetto trees made fine sleds for racing downhill, and we bumped them over the ha-has on Granny's lawn.

My father was descended from two brothers born in Northern Ireland in the early seventeenth century. They were on their way to Virginia, but stepped off the boat in Bermuda and decided to stay. They were ardent royalists and remained so all during the tenure of Oliver Cromwell, one of them reportedly fighting a duel in Devonshire churchyard defending the king's name.

Their descendants were mostly sea captains, building their barques out of Bermuda cedar grown on their properties, sailing them to England in the good weather to have the iron ribs put in, then doing commerce from Newfoundland to the Caribbean. From letters my father unearthed, it seemed likely that some of the business in the Caribbean included privateering, but they maintained their churchgoing respectability at home.

The last of the sea captains was my great-grandfather, Thomas Melville Dill, who sailed one of his ships, the *Sir George Seymore*, from Bermuda to Ireland in thirteen days, a record I believe is still unbroken. His last ship, the *Cedrene*, was wrecked off the Isle of Wight on her maiden voyage. but all hands were saved.The vessel had an afterlife as the ceiling in the chapel at Mottistone where it remains to this day, filling the air with the aroma of Bermuda cedar. Sadly, Captain Dill contracted cholera at the East India docks in London, his signet ring was mailed back to his wife in Bermuda, and he was buried in the Bows Lane cemetery, in London, crossed anchors on his headstone. That signet ring had five cuts on the back of it where it had been cut off the fingers of five deceased Dills. It was reputed to be cursed so that any male member of the family wearing it off the island would die abroad, and the ring mailed back.

His son, my grandfather, Thomas Newbold Dill, was mayor of Hamilton and, I gather, of somewhat liberal persuasion politically, something that my father rebelled against. My father was fiercely and dogmatically Tory with a strong militaristic bent. "Might makes right!" he would pronounce with a triumphant grin, silencing all opposition.

My mother, Ruth Neilson, was an American who traced her ancestry back to Peter Stuyvesant, the last Dutch governor of New York. Livingstons and Van Rensselaers were also in the family tree, along with presidents of Columbia and Rutgers. However, she grew up in relatively modest circumstances, living with her parents and two sisters on the banks of the Raritan River in Perth Amboy, New Jersey.

She described her first sight of my father, Thomas Dill, climbing up the hill from his sailboat, with a watermelon tucked under one arm as a house gift. She immediately lost her heart. She was then fifteen. When she was twenty-one, she persuaded my grandmother to take a trip to Bermuda, where she and father met again, and he proposed to her, sitting on the High Rock, the rock where all their children learned to dive.

She was a merry soul, optimistic and pliable, traits that she certainly needed in dealing with my autocratic father.

"You are much too lenient!" he would say.

"I have to be since you are much too strict!" she would retort.

Nevertheless, they were a deeply devoted couple, complimenting each other with their differences, both with a curiosity and relish for life that made them lively companions. They were also both incredibly handsome.

Granny Dill lived in the house across the way, and she

kept a severe eye on all the comings and goings at Newbold Place. She heard our catechism on Sundays and laid down the law as to what could and couldn't be done on that holy day. No tennis on Sundays. No jazz music on Sundays. No red to be worn on Sundays. And definitely no dancing on Sundays. She looked a bit like Queen Victoria and always had a tin of licorice at her side. One of the grandchildren was always delegated to ride in her carriage with her to church, something we always tried to avoid, as we got our knuckles rapped if we missed a part of the catechism.

For the first few years of my parents' marriage, she had insisted that they live in her house in an apartment she had built over her living quarters. But when the third child, Bayard, was on the way, my usually docile mother delivered an ultimatum to my father. They had to move to their own house…or else. With that, Newbold Place, a family holding directly across the way and on the seashore, was made over to them, and the rest of their six children were born there.

Ruth was the oldest. She married Seward (Johnny) Johnson, when she was twenty-one, in 1924, the year after my birth, so I have no early memories of her. Then Tommy, sweet natured, awkward, and unpredictable when drunk. Bayard, away at Cambridge until 1928, sending pictures of himself on the tennis team looking dapper in a striped blazer, racquet tucked under his arm. Laurence, red-haired and musical, an incorrigible tease and prankster. And Fan, almost eight years my senior, busy with her girlfriends and school.

"Remember," she would say to me, "you're not the only drip in the ocean!" Perhaps, my being the youngest, she was afraid that I might be spoiled.

I was born late in my parents' life. Mother was forty-three and Father close to fifty when I arrived, unplanned. Father seemed in a continual state of chronic, middle-aged irritation through my childhood, but my mother was comforting and protecting always. The only time she lost her temper was when confronted by dishonesty or lying, resulting in a swift whack with her hairbrush across one's bottom.

My father's punishments were always more deliberate. One waited in trepidation for the razor strop. At the age of about five or six, I announced that I was too old to bare my bottom and asked that my hands be whipped instead. Father complied on the condition that I not weep. I didn't, but fixed him with a steely stare.

I don't remember getting the razor strop again.

The nannies came and went, not making much impression, but I loved Beatrice and would hang around while she was ironing and listen to wonderful, scary stories about Antigua. One day we were watching the boys on the dock hang their feet in the water to catch octopi (scuttles they were called locally). They waited for an octopus to wrap its tentacles around their ankles, then lifted the creature out, biting between its eyes and turning it inside out where it lay, paralyzed but still alive, waiting to be cut up for bait.

"In Antigua," Beatrice said, "I did that, and you know what happened? Damn octopus go right up my arm. Up, up my throat. Tentacle up my nose. Israel cut off the tentacle, but it kept wiggling up...up..."

"Did you ever get it out?"

"I don't know. Take a look up there. See anything?"

I peered up the broad nostrils, and she grabbed me, laughing and rocking me back and forth. She sang wonderful Calypso songs about crime and death and voodoo. Later, when Calypso became popular and was played in nightclubs, it always seemed out of place to me. It belonged with Winnie the Pooh and nursery rhymes.

My brother, Bayard, came home from Cambridge when I was five, bringing with him a fellow law student who later became his partner, Jim Pearman. I fell desperately in love with Jim, and asked him to please wait until I grew up before making any plans to marry.

"But can you cook?" he asked seriously.

"I can make great tomato sandwiches," I answered with

equal seriousness.

"Well, then…"

He seemed to be considering it, but married the first year I was in boarding school.

The fifth of November, Guy Fawkes Day, was always the cause of a big celebration. Preparations would start weeks earlier. Stuffing a rag dummy (lifesize), painting its face with curly mustaches, and finding the right clothes for a seventeenth-century plotter (black cape and plumed hat were best, but once we made do with my father's riding breeches), assembling firecrackers, rockets, sparklers, and little red spitters that wriggled through the grass spitting blue flame.

Then the pyre was built. Cedar branches and palmetto fronds were stacked to a height of about twenty feet and soaked in kerosene.

On the night of the fifth, the effigy would be strapped to a chair and carried up the hill to the bloodthirsty chant of: "Guy Fawkes Guy!/Stick him up on high/Stick him on a wood pile/And there let him die!"

Then someone would climb up on a ladder and rope him to a stake. Someone else would plunge a torch into the pyre, and the flames would roar up into the sky while everyone cheered. Rockets flew and sparklers danced.

One fifth, someone set off a rocket too close to me, and I took off running down the hill in the dark. I ran into a barbed-wire fence and tore a corner of my mouth open. There were family discussions about whether stitches should be taken, but Mother, with her instinctive knowledge of home medicine, knew that stitches would leave a scar. Instead, she applied bread poultices, letting it heal slowly. Bread, we now know, is the basis for penicillin and ,there is no scar. Only occasionally will a studio makeup artist remark that one side of my mouth doesn't match the other.

At this time, there were no cars in Bermuda (they didn't arrive until the 1940s). Most families owned a horse and carriage, and those who didn't got around by pedal bike. We had a horse and carriage and also a pony trap with a vile-tempered pony named Joe. He would kick and bite anyone who came within range while being harnessed, but once between the shafts, behaved quite sensibly and would transport me to Woodside when I started school.

Woodside was the Watlington family home over on the Middle Road, and one of the daughters, Clare, had started teaching a few children. Some people are natural teachers, and she was one. She never talked down to her charges, listened well, and made learning an exciting adventure. She was disciplined and brought us along at a smart pace. We were doing long division by the time we were six, and we had a good start in geography and history.

There were about ten boys and as the only girl, I was a natural target for their teasing. After pouting a bit, I discovered that if I told long and outrageous stories, they would leave off baiting me and listen. I was the Scheherazade of Devonshire Parish, weaving ever-more elaborate tales, some with a tiny kernel of truth, but mostly sheer fabrication.

I took one little fellow under my wing. His mother made him wear pastel knitted suits, and he took a lot of ribbing from the rest of the boys. When they taunted him, he would get nervous and pee, and this aroused all my maternal instincts.

Clare remembers coming into the classroom, seeing a large puddle on the floor, and hearing me claim, dramatically, "Miss Clare, I've been crying and crying. See what a big puddle I've made." That little fellow is now one of the directors of the Bank of Bermuda. I haven't reminded him.

Bayard began courting Clare at around this time, and sometimes he would ride me over on the bars of his bike with Fan pedaling beside us on her way to Bermuda High School.

One day, as Fan was on her way up the North Shore, cycling alone, a dog leapt on her from a high wall, and she was badly bitten around the neck and shoulders. I lay on her bed while she was home from school and had her relate every grisly detail. Thereafter, I had months of nightmares involving bulldogs and would run, whimpering, up to my parents' bed and leap in beside Mother.

She would pat me, making a comforting sound we called the motherly neigh.

Father would say, "Jesus Christ, not *again*!" as he flopped over.

Living on the water, it was important that we all be able to swim, and we all could by the age of three. Father would blow reveille on his bugle at about five-thirty in the morning, and we would all pile out as he came bellowing down the hall.

"Show a leg! Show a leg!" Some sort of naval term which galvanized us into action.

We would leap into the water from the dock, swimming year-round. (He had a theory that cold water prevented colds.) Then up to the lawn behind the house for calisthenics, then the flags were hoisted: the Union Jack up the main flagpole, the red ensign up one adjacent, and the house flag on the tower. Then we were allowed to have breakfast.

One family I loved to visit were the Tites, who rented one of the Devonshire Dock houses from my father. The grandfather was a carpenter with a great, white walrus mustache and a deft hand at turning cedar. I loved to watch him at work, the cedar shaving curling up around his feet, his blue eyes concentrated, the rich sharp smell of the wood filling the room. The Tites had five children and the eldest, Alice, was about my age. The others were a year apart, stepping down to the baby whose diapers were always full.

Mrs. Tite was tired and harried, her hair stringing loose from a skimpy bun. Mr. Tite was a shadowy figure, seldom seen, until one memorable day.

Alice had been playing with me in my nursery and had admired a dress I had. I had insisted she take it. The next day, I dropped over to the Tites and was met outside the back door by a furious and tearful Mr. Tite. He threw the dress at me.

"Take it!" he yelled. "We don't need your charity! We may be poor, but we're proud!"

It was the first time I had seen a grownup cry. I was aghast and ashamed, but still not sure what I had done wrong. The Tite children stood behind the screen door and didn't come out. Mr. Tite's eyes were red and full of hate as he glared at me.

I picked up the dress from the dirt and backed away.

I supposed I played with the children again, but I don't remember it or any reconciliation. I know that I didn't tell my parents as I sensed that they were implicated in some way.

Mother sometimes took me along when she went calling, an excruciating experience for an active child, but one that she felt was helpful in terms of discipline and the social graces. Cards were left on a silver platter if the recipient was not at home, and tea was taken if she was. I would stare at my black patent-leather shoes and will myself to a land of castles and pirate ships while the grownups spoke of dinner parties and charitable organizations, dropping their voices and darting sidelong glances at me when anything scandalous was in the air.

Scandalous. Sex was interesting, fascinating, there was no getting around that. Fan and her best friend, in their early teens, would closet themselves in our bedroom, locking me out, while they discussed delicious secrets, told smutty jokes and otherwise exchanged information. Infuriated, I told them that I would chop down the door if they didn't let me in. They didn't believe me, and to this day, there are deep hatchet gouges in the cedar door of the bedroom.

Alice's brother, Sonny Tite, proposed one day, "I'll show you mine if you show me yours." Alice and I took off our pants with alacrity and pulled our skirts above our waists. A sideways glance reassured me that Alice's hairless pubis was identical to mine, and Sonny stared to his heart's content, blue eyes glittering, but when it came time for him to reciprocate, he refused and ran off laughing while Alice and I pelted him with stones. I remember tears and anger at having been taken advantage of and a fear of parental discovery for, though sex had never been discussed, there was a consciousness of shame.

In 1929, when I was six, we spent the summer at Bayhead, New Jersey. The musical *Whoopee* with Eddie Cantor was a big hit that year, and one saw it everywhere. Laurence had a *Whoopee* shirt that he wore until Mother insisted it be laundered. He then sat on the beach sulking, getting the deadly sunburn that only redheads seem to get. I remember peeling sheets of skin off his back, putting them carefully into a tin lozenge box.

Bobby Johnson, Ruth's nephew about my age, tried to interest me in another bout of "show," but I was too canny this time and suggested it would be more fun to set fire to an abandoned house instead. Luckily, some adults intervened before we could carry out our plans, and for the rest of our stay, I was bedded with whooping cough.

Back in Bermuda, plans were afoot. Steamer trunks came out and Snapper, our Airedale, sat on them and howled. Last minute trips to the dentist (a woman, as I recall—fairly unusual for those days) and being fitted for shoes, lace-up oxfords which felt strange after bare feet or sandals but were, I was told, de rigueur for…London.

Chapter 2

LONDON

Cold. Drizzle. Fog. Bleakness. Alien faces, pinched and pale. A somewhat alien tongue. Being corrected by sweetly acid teachers…

"We do not say pajama *pants*, dear. We say pajama *trousers*."

And in answer to my madly jigging request…

"But why do you want to see the *bathroom*, dear?"

And after the inevitable accident…

"But why didn't you say that you had to go to the lavatory? Really!"

The school, the Doreck School, was at the far end of Kensington Garden Square. It had day pupils and weekly boarders. I think I began as a day student and graduated to weekly boarding, though why this was done I cannot fathom, as the Kengar Hotel, where my parents were living, was only at the opposite end of the square.

I found the weekly boarders and the dormitory quite spooky; gaslight was still being used. I watched the teacher light up with trepidation. First the hiss, then the pop, then the wavering blue flame. Then, at lights out, I was left to ponder my roommates. One was quite seriously retarded and would rock back and forth on her bed droning a mysterious mantra.

"Hans hanuris," she would mutter endlessly. "Hans hanuris."

"What does she mean?" I asked Hermione, my other roommate.

"Who knows," she replied. And then swearing me to secrecy, said that God had come to her and told her that she was the Queen of Beauty. I lay in the dark, silent and wide-eyed, and yearned for deliverance from this weird place and for Bermuda.

Weekends at the Kengar Hotel were uneventful. The grownups played whist in the lounge while I lay on the floor drawing fanciful pictures of knights and ladies on horseback.

Sometimes I hung out with the Welsh maids below stairs, who were friendly and who had lilting laughs and terrible body odor. When I saw their primitive sanitary conditions, I understood why, but still found it hard not to recoil when they hugged me.

I saw some boys playing in the square and made overtures to join them, which were at first rejected…

"You don't know how to play *boys'* games!"

Eventually they let me in to their cadre, and I climbed fences, threw stones, and ran as fast as any of them and was accepted as one of the guys. I suffered an unrequited crush on Trevor, the oldest, and his younger brother, Basil, followed *me* around like an adoring puppy dog. Unrequited love's a pain to the loved or the loving.

Wintertime in Kensington Gardens. Thin ice on the black waters of the Serpentine. Vapor rising in the air as I reined in my imaginary steed and cantered across the park to the playground.

This is where the Cockney kids played. Trevor, Basil, and their ilk would never venture to this rough spot, nor would their parents let them as they would be jeered at and possibly beaten up for being little "toffs," but as a girl, I posed no challenge to the street toughs, and so they let me alone.

The seesaws were splintered. Many swings were without seats, their chains creaking in the wind, but that didn't deter me. My goal was always the maypole with its cargo of joyous, runny-nosed kids, their arms stuck through the leather loops whirling like crazed bats, their steel-tipped boots striking sparks on the tarmac.

I ran alongside, keeping pace until I spied an opening and then darted in, arm through loop, racing toward that first wild magic leap into the air. The park tilted on its side. The trees grew upside down. Steel-tipped boots flashed close by my head, but how could I care when I was flying like an eagle, shouting and singing, the wind whipping my hair? Three short steps, then off again, whirling out, higher and higher.

One day it jerked to a halt, and one of the boys rolled off to the side, nursing a wounded knee.

"Ooww, fuck!" he yelled.

I squatted down beside him.

"Can I help?"

"No."

"Oh. What was that you said?"

"What?"

"That word. It sounded like 'fuck.'"

The playground exploded in laughter. The boys pounded each other on the back and fell about, holding their bellies and gasping. It seemed I'd hit upon some magic formula. I smiled and tried it again.

"Fuck?"

Total pandemonium. The boys whooped with delight, tears running down their faces while I danced on the seesaw, relishing my newfound popularity, chanting the magic word.

"Fuck…fuck…fuck!"

My mother snatched me out of the playground and walked me back to the Kengar at a fast clip. As I remember, she suggested to my father that it might be better that I not frequent that playground in the park as I was picking up a "rather dreadful Cockney accent."

It was around this time that Fan came back from her finishing school in Switzerland. I learned later that Father had suffered financial losses when England went off the gold standard and could no longer afford to keep her in that expensive school. Being away from our home grounds in

Bermuda, Fan and I became more intimate, which was going to stand me in good stead.

One of the boarders at The Kengar was a Captain Wareham, a shy man with a tic that twitched his eyes. My parents said that he had been "shell shocked" during the Great War. He would ask me to come and sit with him at his table and treated me with grave courtesy, weighing my opinions as seriously as he would that of a grownup. Naturally, I was enchanted and expounded on every object under the sun, and when he asked me up to his room to have some fairy tales read to me, I accepted with alacrity.

He would sit me on his lap in front of the little gas fire, his hand patting my thigh as he read the stories. I would nod sleepily, my head on his shoulder. One evening his breathing became heavy and his hand slid up past the elastic leg of my panties. I sat bolt upright.

"What are you doing?"

He stood up. "Oh, I mustn't, must I? I mustn't, must I?"

"I don't know. I think I better go—now."

I ran downstairs and told Fan.

"Don't tell Mother or Father. They'd be so upset, they really like him," she said. "But if he asks you to his room again, say you'll be there if I come, too. That should fix him."

How children protect their parents.

Shortly after this, boarding-school brochures started showing up in the mail. It had been decided that Fan must have another year or so of formal schooling and that I would accompany her. I pored over the pamphlets with great delight. Fan glanced at them ruefully, knowing she would never have the freedom and sophistication that she had enjoyed at Le Manoir, skiing and dating Swiss fellows. But for me, they represented a gateway to be with my peers, and I fantasized about having good girlfriends to giggle and share secrets with. I turned the pages with relish. Once, I caught my mother looking at me, her expression wistful.

"Anxious to leave us so soon, darling?"

I was embarrassed and did not know how to reply, so I hugged her and made a joke.

We had a house that summer in Ryde, on the Isle of Wight, across the island from where the school Upper Chine was located. My eldest sister, Ruth, arrived with her children, Mary Lea, Elaine, and the baby, Seward. They were only a few years younger than me, so I had a fine time playing with them, dressing them up, and bossing them around. I was conscious that their family was a great deal wealthier than ours, and I remember being bitterly jealous of a set of miniature golf clubs that had been given to Elaine.

Captain Wareham came down one weekend, and we eyed one another warily and barely spoke. I think my parents were puzzled at the sudden coolness between us. Fan gave me a knowing nod and stuck close.

During the summer, a band played on the esplanade, Gilbert and Sullivan, *Floradora*, and martial tunes would drift over to us while on the putting green or up on Ryde pier with its bagatelle machine and peep shows. We went to the movies—*Love Parade* with Maurice Chevalier—and we ate ice cream and swam in the waters of the Solent which lapped at our back wall.

It wasn't Bermuda, but it was a darn sight less bleak than London, and I thought it possible, just possible, that I could get used to living in this strange country. That September I started at Upper Chine.

UPPER CHINE

"Upper Chine School for Girls" said the bronze plaque on the granite gateposts. A gravel drive swept in a semicircle to the front door.

I peered out of the cab window hoping to see a crowd of happy youngsters chasing around the grounds, but there was no one in sight, only the soft rain of southern England falling steadily. There were false smiles on my parents' faces, and Fan stared out the window.

A maid, or "domestic" as we were encouraged to call them, answered our knock and led us into the study of the headmistress, Miss Damon. She had the nose of a Roman senator, icy green eyes, a formidable bosom, rigidly marcelled gray hair, and swollen ankles to which I kept my eyes fixed after one terrified look at the rest of her.

"Colonel Dill. Mrs. Dill. Frances. And *this* must be Diana. Don't you shake hands, Diana?"

A poke from my mother and I reached out and took the white, soft hand, still a little sticky from lavender hand lotion.

"That's better."

All during the pleasantries exchanged with my parents, I was conscious of her cool, appraising gaze, and my spirits sank lower. I shot a glance at Fan, but she sat forward on her chair, looking interested and flashing her "charming" look around the room. My parents both seemed to be nodding a lot. I knew a terrible mistake had been made.

When we went back out to the hall and I saw the waiting taxi through the window, it was all I could do not to hurl myself sobbing into my mother's arms, scream, and beg them to take me back with them. But I knew that to do so would be to disgrace me forever in my father's eyes, and I wanted his recognition and respect more than anything in the world.

Mother's eyes were red as she held me close, and, when they got into the taxi, she buried her face in my father's shoulder while he patted her awkwardly, his chin held high. I looked around for Fan, but she was chatting with a woman in a nurse's outfit who was introduced to me as "Sister," the senior matron.

They started up the stairs, and, as I started to follow them, a hand fell on my shoulder. "No, Diana. Only seniors are allowed up there. You're just a junior."

"But…she's my sister…"

"That makes no difference. Rules are rules. Come along now."

Miss Damon turned on her heel and left as I was led away by the junior matron.

The dormitories slept eight to a room with twin sinks at one end, iron bedsteads, and bedside chests that were inspected daily for any infractions of tidiness. The rooms were called Wynken, Blynken, and Nod.

The youngest of the boarders were five or six, all dependents of the Indian Army. In the last days of empire building, it was felt that India was too rife with diseases to chance exposing small Anglo-Saxons to the dangers, and we all had to be properly schooled to be the next generation of Empire Builders. It is amazing to look back now and recall the supreme self-confidence, one could say "smugness," of the upper and upper-middle classes in England at that time.

As a colonial, I was viewed with faint curiosity, and the fact of my having an American mother made me even more of an exotic. My roommates quizzed me about American gangsters and film stars, decried the practice of chewing gum as "frightfully vulgar," and asked if my mother indulged in it often. Homesickness was just "too soppy for words," so the Indian Army children and I soon learned to disguise our feelings, though sometimes one of them would cling to the hem of seniors' tunics, calling them "mummy."

My Scheherazade storytelling cut no ice here, and my attempts to be fascinating met with cool contempt. I was bewildered and sad. Someone seemed to have changed all the rules of the game, but kept them from me. Nothing I knew applied anymore. I seemed to have become unlikeable.

I remember hiding on my eighth birthday behind the curtains of a window seat, watching the rain come down and weeping quietly, wondering if anyone would remember that today was the day. At teatime, I found out that a chocolate cake had been arranged by my parents, and I basked in a few minutes of popularity, but it soon passed.

I approached Fan once during "break," or recess (a fraternizing strictly frowned upon) to suggest that we both take all our pocket money out of the bank on Saturday and hightail it away from this grisly place as fast as possible.

"Mother and Father have just gone to Venice for the first time. Do you really want to spoil everything for them?"

I guessed not.

I stared at her. She was being logical. She had joined the adults—the enemy.

I retired again into my watchful melancholy.

The winter seemed endless, but with the spring a marvelous new life emerged. Acting.

I remember the joy of sitting with the class under a chestnut tree and reading from *A Midsummer Night's Dream* and *The Tempest*, leaping into characterizations, devouring the poetic text, eagerly looking up the more obscure meanings. Miss Thomas, the English mistress, lent subtle encouragement. It was the beginning of acceptance by my classmates too.

"How do you make it sound so real?" they'd ask.

I didn't know. All I knew was that I had found what I loved and that the difference between "things as they were and things as they were purported to be" had intrigued

Shakespeare as well. The search for truth, one man's truth or another's, and exploring how they differed was an endlessly exciting journey. One that has continued through my life.

With the summer came swimming at which I excelled due to my island background. That led to more acceptance, and, although I would always be an outsider, the put-downs became less frequent, and some of the girls made friendly overtures. I was wary and kept them at arm's length. I would not let myself be rejected again.

That summer, my parents and the Johnsons rented a mammoth house in Cowes from Lady Blanche Stanhope. It was called, appropriately, "Stanhope Lodge" and was filled chockablock with Victoriana. Every piece of furniture was skirted and antimacassared. Sentimental pictures filled every wall, including the bathroom.

Balancing my rear end on the oaken seat of the toilet, I stared at the paintings with appreciation and vowed that when I had my own house, I would have pictures on the bathroom walls too. And so I have today.

There was a billiard room curtained off from the back parlour, which I decided would make an ideal stage to direct my young relatives. But when the curtains parted to reveal my nephew Seward on the billiard table about to declaim as Puck, the howl of anguish from my father soon put an end to that.

Johnny Johnson, Ruth's husband, and Bayard won the Prince of Wales Cup race that summer, and the house was filled with yachtsmen from the American team..

Then it was back to Upper Chine, this time without Fan who was deemed to have finished her formal schooling.

Under Miss Thomas's tutelage, my reading expanded. Reams of poetry was memorized and the library made available. In later life, people have doubted that a young child could read and enjoy the entire *Forsyte Saga* for instance, but if there's nothing else to read—no comics or Bobbsey Twins—you devour whatever you can get your hands on. I didn't understand all of it, but I sure as hell enjoyed it, with their mysterious goings on and fetid family life.

At Christmas Mother, Father, Fan, and I were at Dunholme Manor in Bournemouth when a handsome English family arrived. Colonel Moore, late of the Indian Army, his wife Vera with sharp blue eyes and a sharper tongue, and their adolescent children—Jock, aged nineteen and Billee, aged twelve. The families instantly took to each other, and Jock was quite obviously smitten with Fan, much to my irritation, as I wished to monopolize her attention. We went to see Norma Shearer in *Smilin' Through* and wept copiously, skated in the local skating rink, putted on the putting green, and I tagged along, being surly to Jock. He must have been madly in love not to have popped me one.

However, there were soon other interests; I had an idea for a play. Part written, part improvised, it had something to do with pirates and derring-do. Of course, I was the hero, brave and swaggering in baggy tights and a beret. My father was cast as the evil Pirate King, which he took to with great zest, though he would never stick to the plot. I persuaded Mother and another couple, to join in. They had a daughter with long, blonde hair who was perfect casting for the heroine. We did a performance for the assembled boarders on Christmas Eve to much kind applause. Knowing the agonies of stage fright I went through as an adult, it amazes me to think of the lack of fear I had as a child. I think it says something good about my parents and their joyful approach to life.

Fancy dress balls were a big thing in the thirties, and, though costumes were homemade, they often showed a lot of imagination. Father borrowed a toy wagon, filled it with apples and strapped it to his head. He came as Shaw's newly opened play *The Apple Cart*. Jock looked suitably romantic and sinister in a black cape and hat.

"Who are you, Guy Fawkes?" I asked.

"Of course not. I'm Sandeman Port," was the wounded

reply.

"Will you shut up?" Fan hissed at me.

I grinned evilly as Jock blushed.

I think it was during the spring holidays of 1933 that I became aware of plans afoot for a return to Bermuda. My father had passed his English law exams and finished his compilation of the Bermuda laws, so his work in London was done. It seems to me that we went to Guernsey in the Channel Islands for this holiday, but I could be wrong about the date. I do remember the rough Channel crossing with Fan throwing up on her deck chair. I had to change chairs with her so she could stretch out in comfort. I assured every passerby, "I didn't do it. She did!"

Anyway, when I found that Mother, Daddy, and Fan were going and planning to leave me in England, all hell broke loose. Knowing my mother to be the weakest link, I directed the full force of my pathos on her. I pleaded, wept, promised brilliant schoolwork, and didn't let up until I prevailed, though how she persuaded Daddy to go along with it, I'll never know.

Once I knew I was going, the excitement was almost too much to bear, particularly as we were due to sail on the maiden voyage of the *Queen of Bermuda* as guests of the line. My parents were friends of Lord and Lady Furness, owners of the Furness-Withy Line, and only ten people had been selected to sail from Glasgow, where the ship had been built, to New York.

It was a magical voyage. Running round the empty decks, tasting salt in the spray, pillow-fighting with the library steward, a handsome fellow in his twenties, swimming in the great pool, and trying out all the equipment in the gym. I could have stayed on board forever, circumnavigating the globe like the Flying Dutchman.

When we arrived in New York, there was more magic. Fireboats were out to greet us, circling the steamer with sprays arcing in the air, and overhead an airplane flew, trailing a banner saying "Welcome to the Queen of Bermuda." I turned to my sister.

"Gosh, Americans are nice! They're really glad to see us."

"This is done at every maiden voyage, silly."

I was packed off to stay with my Aunt Helen in Orange, New Jersey, for the week we were to be in the States. She had a daughter, Alida, who was severely retarded, and I think it was hoped that we would form some kind of bond. I don't think I was unkind, but was not very long on patience, and the experiment didn't work. I recall being sent to a day- care centre where all the children, save me, were in various stages of retardation. We marched in circles singing "Columbia the Gem of the Ocean" over and over.

My parents and Fan went to the premiere of *King Kong* when it opened in Manhattan. Fan told me later that my father, who had had too much to drink, nodded off during the film with a big box of chocolates on his lap. King Kong gave a roar, and Daddy leapt up—chocolates flying.

"Jesus Christ! What was that?" he yelled, to the amusement of the audience and the chagrin of my mother.

Bermuda had never looked more beautiful upon our return. The water, a brilliant turquoise that hurt one's eyes after the muted colors of England, the slow clip-clop of the horses' hooves and the lazy, gentle speech of the Bermudians.

"Oh, well," they'd say. "Never mind." But it came out "Oh, vayull. Nevah mahnd." It delighted my heart.

I was enrolled in the Bermuda High School. It was not a high school as Americans understand it. It went from kindergarten through London matriculation, though most Bermudians who could afford it, sent their children abroad for at least part of their education.

The strict English curriculum was far ahead of its Bermuda counterpart, so I started off in a class with girls two years my senior. Finding the work a breeze and relishing the lackadaisical tempo of life, I soon fell behind and got into sloppy study habits, daydreaming and staring out the window at a kiskadee on an oleander branch.

Miss Emmy Gray, a spinster with a nervous habit of rolling ribbon ties up to her neck and down, taught us English and Scripture. She liked mundane poetry with a rhythmic beat, and we soon learned to oblige her with terrible Kiplingesque knockoffs. She blushed uncomfortably when "The woman with the issue of blood" was mentioned in the Bible. Some of the older girls giggled, so I knew something was up, but no one would answer my questions as to the mystery.

Mother once made a vague allusion to "I suppose you know all about um…uh…," but looked so uncomfortable that I quickly nodded.

"Oh, yes. Sure." And that was that.

It wasn't until two years later, at King George's Silver Jubilee, that Laurence had the uncomfortable task of filling me in on the facts of menstruation after my first period.

Looking back, I wonder why Fan and I didn't communicate more at this time. We no longer shared a room, and she had entered the mysterious world of adults, doing secretarial work for Daddy with a passel of young naval officers pursuing her. It seemed our paths seldom crossed.

I hung out with the Arnell girls and Lyle Mayer. I would ride Joe, my pony, over to the Middle Road, and we would head for the Agricultural Garden, where the baobab trees had tentacles, which were wonderful for swinging while screaming Tarzan yells. Blissful days were back again: sundaes at the Goody Shoppe, romping in the surf, biking through flowered lanes, neglecting homework.

Which brings me to a memory that still makes me blush.

My marks had slipped so that I was now with girls my own age and even repeated lectures couldn't make me concentrate. I swam in a warm soup of self-indulgence. Suddenly, a French test was announced. Of course I hadn't prepared for it. So I cheated.

A classmate saw the book open on my lap, reached

over and closed it, and I silently thanked God that it was she and not the teacher who had spotted my sin. I counted on the fraternity of students to keep my secret. Ha! Fat chance!

The school had a practice that in the morning prayer assembly, anyone caught cheating would have to sit on a platform at the back of the auditorium. I was aware of the puzzled look from Miss Gosling, the principal, while I sat there, whitefaced. She stopped me on the way out.

"Diana, dear," she said. "What was the matter? Couldn't you find room down front?" Sheer agony.

"I cheated, Miss Gosling."

"Oh, no." She was stunned. "I've had Ruth Dill and Fanny Dill in my school. The Dill girls don't cheat."

I had not only let down myself and the school, but the whole damn family. There was nowhere to hide my shame.

I suppose my parents must have been told of my wrongdoing, but I don't remember any mention of it. Miss Gosling's reaction was enough to keep me from ever trying to repeat my crime.

It should have been no surprise that at the end of the school year the decision was made to ship me back to boarding school in England. This time I didn't kick up a fuss. I think I knew that I deserved it, that I had absolutely zero self-discipline, and that I was getting on my father's nerves. I tried to stay out of his way as much as possible.

I loved watching him in court, though. He was impeccably distinguished in his wig and gown, monocle fixed in his eye. I learned that whenever he was about to make a particularly telling point or scathing remark to defeat the opposition, he would give a cheeky nudge to the back of his wig so that it tipped rakishly over an eyebrow. His sarcasm was lethal, and the other lawyers and MPs quite obviously stood in awe of him. I was glad to see that he scared other people too and felt a pride in his stinging wit.

One exchange related with relish throughout Bermuda took place when a member of the opposition mocked a speech he made, saying, "As far as I'm concerned, any words the Honorable T. M. Dill says go in one ear and out the other." To which Father replied, "I'm not surprised as there is nothing in between to stop them"

When told of his appointment as attorney general of Bermuda, he happened to be in London. A celebratory dinner was arranged for him at the Royal Thames Yacht Club. Dressed in white tie and tails he was on his way, striding through Piccadilly Circus, where he was propositioned by a local tart. Full of the pride of his new office, he drew himself up.

"My good woman," he said. "Do you know who it is you are addressing?"

"No, guv'nor, not a clue."

"You are addressing the crown solicitor of His Majesty's oldest self-governing colony."

"Coo, and you're addressing the 'alf crown solicitor of Piccadilly!"

The voyage back to England was on the *Orduna*, one of the "banana boats" that plied their way between South America and Southampton, with stopovers at Bermuda, La Coruña, Vigo, Santander and La Rochelle. I remember going to Santiago de Compestela and seeing the enormous saints in the cathedral. That was a stopover for lunch between La Coruna and Vigo. I collected some stones from the town square, washed and polished them, and thought I'd start a collection of stones from all over the world, but soon gave up the project.

I had become quite a movie buff during my time of freedom in Bermuda. Katharine Hepburn was one of my idols at age ten, and it's interesting to speculate how much cloning was done at that time. Fifteen years later, she was to recommend me to Philip Barry as her replacement in *Second Threshold*, saying she felt I could have been her younger sister.

She and Ginger Rogers sported a sleek pageboy hairdo, which I slavishly followed. I thought I was fairly devastating, but on my return to Upper Chine I was greeted with,

"Is that how they wear it in the colonies? Rather wild and woolly, wouldn't you say?"

And my locks were chopped off to the regulation "above the earlobes" horror.

This time Upper Chine didn't seem quite so bad. I knew what to expect and knew the basic rules. Work hard enough to get decent marks, but don't flaunt intelligence, being a "brain" was "wet." Cultivate sports—"a jolly sort of gal, good at games, y'know"—was the ideal strived for, and I was fairly agile, though inclined to daydream on the hockey or netball fields.

When I paid a return visit to the school in 1980, Miss Pasmore, the games mistress, was still there. She greeted me.

"Diana Dill. I remember you. Rotten goalie. Always dreaming about becoming an actress or something stupid like that!"

Some things never change.

I made some friends: Margaret Jackman, "Jacko" who also wanted to be an actress and had considerable talent; Sybil Jackson, "Tiddles" who had a wry, dry sense of humor; "Buckles" who was the class comedienne and who could make farting sounds with her vagina to our amazement and amusement.

We marched in crocodile order for miles along the cliff roads, returning to warm our chilblained hands on the hot tap-water pipe running along the corridor. The food was hearty and heavy. Our parents had to pay extra if they wanted us to have milk once a day. My parents had paid up and also said that I could choose one extracurricular activity: ballet, ceramics, or riding. For my acting future, I wish I had chosen ballet, instead I went for riding.

Once a week, a wizened old man would take four or five of us up to the downs, barking commands.

"I don't want to see daylight between those knees!"

"Elbows tight, hands down!"

"You jiggle around like a sack of potatoes!"

Having seen Katharine Hepburn ride side-saddle in *Mary of Scotland* and, I drove him mad. I was determined to emulate her. There was no side-saddle in his stable, so I would fall behind. When he wasn't looking, I'd take off one stirrup, sling my leg over the pommel, and take off at a full gallop.

"I'm going to report you!" he threatened. But he never did.

Our workload was fairly heavy by today's standards. We had arithmetic, algebra, geometry, Latin, French, geography, history, literature, Scripture, chemistry, and biology. Later, trigonometry and logarithms.

We rose at seven, stripped, washed at the basin in the dorm, made our beds, and dressed. Then we filed down for breakfast, our napkins hanging in a bag over our arms. A prefect inspected our nails as we entered the dining room and stood behind our chairs during prayer, thanking the Almighty for our food. It was generally gray porridge or oatmeal, but on Sundays, there was sometimes a treat—fried bread.

From eight till one, we had classes. Lunch was at one, followed by a compulsory half-hour nap. From two-thirty till four-thirty: games. Hockey and netball in the winter, tennis and cricket in the summer. This was followed by baths and a uniform change from tunics to uniform velvet dresses. Then came "prep" (homework) for two hours, dinner, lantern-slide lectures on art, or a cello concert. Sometimes we could play popular records and dance with each other.

Holidays were spent with Dr. and Mrs. Horsfall in West Acton, a suburb of London. They had three children: Frances, an adult; Emily, who was about five years older than me (and alarmingly brilliant!); and Bill, a sweet but taciturn fellow about my age whose chief interest was building Erector sets. My delight was to walk their Scottie, Mungo, in the park.

Menstruation still remained a deeply held secret. As soon as a girl began her period, she was whisked away from the junior dorms and installed in "Clevelands," the middle-school dorm. We who were left behind figured that she must have gotten "it," though exactly what "it" was was never spelled out, and when questioned, our erstwhile pals in the middle school just smiled mysteriously and were maddeningly superior.

"We're not allowed to say. You'll find out."

Around this time, I was nearly expelled. Fan had taught me a faintly bawdy song called "Bell-bottom Trousers and Coats of Navy Blue," which I in turn taught to several of the girls, and we came rollicking back from a hockey match singing it.

The next thing I knew, I was summoned to Miss Damon's study.

"I want to read you a letter that I'm sending to your parents," she said. "'As you know, we do not allow filthy language or sexual discussions in our school so I do not know if we can allow Diana to stay here. She has been teaching the girls a smutty song about "never let a sailor get an inch about your knee…"'"

"No, no, Miss Damon," I said without thinking. "It's an inch *above* your knee!"

She blinked but sealed the envelope.

I waited in trepidation for the next few weeks, but God bless my sensible and loyal mother. She wrote back to Miss Damon and sent a copy to me. The gist of it was that I came from a family that enjoyed some bawdy humor and that they had never seen anything wrong with it, so that if Miss Damon had a disagreement, it should be with them, not me.

The subject was never mentioned again.

Alternate holidays were spent with Cousin Mabel and her daughter, Enid, in Rotherfield, Sussex. Cousin Mabel was a humorless gorgon with a West Indian accent and a grim demeanor. She was probably in her sixties. Enid, with whom I shared a room, was about forty and unmarried, with a diffident, apologetic air. She always put her nightgown on over her underwear, then rustled her way to bed in the dark. In the morning, she was always the first one in the bathroom so I never knew whether she slept in her corset or not.

I was about twelve or thirteen when I developed my first serious crush. There was a working farm down the hill from Cousin Mabel's, owned by a family named Bain. Whit Bain, the eldest son, was blond and blue-eyed. A veritable Adonis in his twenties who barely noticed my existence. After mooning around about him for a time, I switched my affections to his younger brother, Chris, aged twenty-one and dark. Not as handsome, but good company. He let me assist him in chores around the farm and chatted to me as an equal. I spent all my waking hours at the Bain farm, to Cousin Mabel's disapproval, milking cows, shoveling out the pigsty, and talking with Chris about our individual futures.

His heart was set on becoming a mounted policeman in Southern Rhodesia, and he longed to escape from the farm. I told him of my determination to become an actress, and he didn't laugh. There must have been a shortage of young women around Rotherfield at that time as I don't recall either of the Bain brothers having a proper date.

When the time came for me to go back to school, Chris and I met to say good-bye in the barn.

"I hope you make it to Rhodesia," I said.

"I know you'll make it as an actress," he said. "Let's write to each other and keep track of how everything turns out."

"Good."

I stepped toward him, and he put his hand under my chin and kissed me, a long, soft, innocent kiss. My first and one I'll always remember.

I wrote to him twice from Upper Chine, but never received an answer.

Almost two years later, I was in Bermuda for the summer holidays when Fan came in waving a letter.

"It's for you," she said. "Who do you know in Southern

Rhodesia?"

For a moment, my heart stopped. Then I started to seethe, remembering the tear-sodden nights. I read his unremarkable letter through briefly, then tore it up, and dropped it in the wastebasket. Fan couldn't contain her curiosity.

"What are you doing? Aren't you going to answer it?"

"No."

I wonder if Chris is still there now that it's Zimbabwe. He had sounded disillusioned by the police force, "so much eye-wash," but loved the country, so I imagine he made it his home. I hope he found happiness, but I'm awfully glad I didn't tie my future to his.

That summer, my first time home in three years, was an epic one in the family. Events had been going on of which I was unaware. Seward Johnson, my sister Ruth's husband, had asked her for a divorce, citing as the reason his love for Fan and hers for him. Fan had denied knowledge of any such thing. Johnny said he still wanted a divorce and Ruth had consented on the condition that they wait a year before filing because of the children.

There had never been a divorce in our family, such a thing was unheard of. The fact that Fan was involved could have brought about a crisis that would tear the family apart.

But, true to form, nothing was mentioned. All unpleasantness swept under the rug.

Fan and I shared a room, which she had decorated prettily in shades of green and pink. I knew she was enormously attractive to men, and I loved to wear her hand-me-down evening dresses as they seemed imbued with her glamour. She was twenty-one, but unlike the rest of my family, she didn't drink at all. She was naturally vivacious and flirtatious and had a crowd of adoring young naval officers who would follow her around. I remember her sitting on the veranda singing Calypso ditties and strumming her guitar, which had the sailors' hat ribbons from H.M.S. ships fluttering from it. Her "scalps," we used to call them.

One evening as we were getting dressed to go out on dates, I found Fan sobbing, her head bent over her dainty dressing table, shoulders heaving. Mother stood by looking anxious. I glanced from one to the other.

"Good Lord, what is it?"

Fan looked up at me in the mirror, mascara running down her cheeks. She made several attempts before she got the words out.

"Ruth and Johnny are getting a divorce," she whispered.

"Is that true?" I asked my mother.

She nodded, never taking her eyes off Fan. I looked back at Fan. She had always been emotionally volatile, but I'd never seen her in despair like this. She seemed more deeply shocked than Mother, which seemed strange. Something was peculiar here. Secrets hung in the air like a fog. Through all the summer nothing was mentioned, and it wasn't until Ruth confided in me the following year as she left for Reno that some of it was clarified for me.

Fan and I double-dated a couple of times during the summer, though I was only fourteen. That summer I got the first inkling of what it would be like to be an adult. I wore long evening dresses and went to dances, got my first taste of feminine competition.

"You danced far too often with that Arton boy," snapped Fan. "Stay away from him. He doesn't have a good reputation."

I smiled silently, flattered to be considered competition, as I had heard her tell her friend Dorothy that she thought he was terribly, terribly attractive.

After the dances, we would ride our bikes home, long skirts looped around an arm, and sail down the hills like schooners, spinnakers flying. After our dates pedaled away, Fan and I would strip off our finery and plunge naked into the ocean in back of the house. In the summer, the phosphorescent water made silver flames that licked along our limbs, and we swam in a heady ecstasy, giggling and gossiping about the evening we had just passed.

When the time came to sail back to school, I had gained some social graces and reacquired my fashionable pageboy, feeling quite the sophisticate. The Bermuda boys, also on their way back to English school, kidded the hell out of me and treated me like a kid sister, which I found exasperating. So when a handsome Cuban came acourting, I was determined to show *them!* His name was Fernando de Palicio, Jr. I think he was the son of the president of Cuba or something, and he danced a seductive rumba. We would slink our humorless way around the floor while the Bermuda boys made rude remarks and hit each other on the back, laughing.

We would watch the sun set over the wake of the ship and gaze soulfully into each other's eyes. Conversation was at a minimum as his English was skittish and my Spanish was nil. I wasn't astute enough to catch the predatory gleam when he found out that I would have to stay overnight in Liverpool when we docked.

We docked in the evening, and there was no train to Leicester until the morning. Feeling very grown up, I checked into the Adelphi Hotel, ate a solitary dinner in the grillroom, and went to bed.

I had just closed my book and was getting ready to turn off the light when I heard a gentle rapping at the door. I held my breath.

"Leetle one?"

It could be no one but Fernando.

"What do you want?"

Now that I look back on it, not a bright question. I could hear him breathing. Heavily.

"I only want to talk to you. Please."

"Go away, Fernando."

"You are so cruel. Always so cruel. Let me in."

"No."

"I will make you happy. So happy."

"Just shut up and go away."
"Please."
"No."
"Bitch."

As I listened to his retreating footsteps, I reflected that he knew more English than I had suspected.

I was to spend the last few days of my holiday at Rolleston Hall in Leicestershire, in the heart of the hunting country. Johnny Johnson had found another pastime after yachting, and that was hunting. He yearned for the life of an English squire and acquired all the accouterments: twelve handpicked Irish hunters, an English country estate with a lake, woods, manicured terraces, folles, a full staff of servants and a private chapel where the local padre would preach to the gentry once a month, forsaking his own parishioners. Giddy stuff.

However, due to their marital difficulties, neither Ruth nor Johnny were in residence, and the children were surrounded by nurses, tutors, governesses, and a riding master, Eddie Bennett. We visited the stables together, and he was strangely diffident when I told him I wanted to ride Ruth's horse. She didn't seem lame or anything, so it didn't make sense to me until I took her out and she turned into a bucking bronco. It turned out the horses hadn't been exercised while their owners were away, and I damn near got my neck broken.

The staff of servants was forbidding. The butler informed me that as I was the nominal head of the household, now that Ruth and Johnny were absent, I must dine alone in the dining room. The Johnson children were to be fed supper separately in the nursery wing. This made little sense to me as they were only a few years younger than I, but I was too cowed by the man and the equally formidable housekeeper to protest much.

So there I would sit, at the end of an impossibly long polished table. I was served by a footman under the watchful eye and beaked nose of the august butler. The idea of school was almost a relief.

There was a subtle change after I got back to Upper Chine. A new young teacher named Florrie Dobbs had joined the staff, teaching English literature and poetry. She was about twenty-four and fresh out of Oxford. She was full of new ideas, and she challenged me and my rebellious ways.

"What is the satisfaction you get out of being late?"

"Huh?"

"Why did you decide to forget turning in that paper?"

"B-b-but I didn't *mean* to…"

"Of course you did, or you wouldn't have done it. I'm just interested to know what the reward is."

She had me buffaloed. Essays that used to earn me an easy "A" were turned back with notations scribbled on them.

"Smacks of journalese. You're capable of better work than this."

Well, I would show *her!*

And in doing so, all my behavior was affected. Slowly I was becoming part of the establishment I had so despised.

Mary Lea, my niece who was three years my junior, had joined me at the school while her parents were going through their troubles. I remember her awe when I was summoned by Miss Damon in front of the whole school and awarded a prize, though what it was for I can't remember.

"I didn't think our family ever won anything," she said.

A sad comment from a sad little girl.

After that, I was made a subprefect, part of the establishment, having to inspect girls' nails before dinner and that sort of thing.

On the day I was to receive my badge, I made my last gesture of defiance. I smoked a whole pack of cigarettes up on the downs.

There was a summer ('38 perhaps) spent in Northern Ireland at Buncrana on the banks of Lough Swilly (the Lake of Shadows in English—a far more poetic name). The countryside was stark, mysterious, primitive. From the massive stones of the Giant's Causeway in the north to the craggy hills to the south, one felt that it would be no surprise to see a dinosaur poke his head around the rocks.

I played tennis with a young Irish schoolteacher, Paddy Drummond, who complained bitterly at the new law requiring that all subjects be taught Erse (a form of Gaelic). He felt that the search for cultural identity was severely handicapping his students for life in the real world and slowing down their comprehension of subjects such as math.

One day on the tennis court, I wound up for a smashing serve and hit Paddy on the bridge of his nose, breaking his glasses, which flew out to either side. Luckily he wasn't hurt, but the look of shock on his face had me doubled up. I have always had an unfortunate habit of bursting into helpless laughter when something awful happens, sort of a nervous reflex, I suppose. I tried to apologize, gasping through my giggles, but from then on, he was decidedly cool to me, and I can't say as I blame him.

I asked my father for permission to wear the family signet ring as the curse was meant to apply only to the male members of the family. He granted permission on the condition that I use caution and return it to my mother after the vacation was over. All went well until one memorable morning when I was taking a bath in the dim light of dawn. As I soaped, the ring slipped off my finger and out of the bathtub, landing amongst the cavernous shadows of the room.

I searched desperately on my hands and knees, unable to locate it. I planned to come back later with a flashlight to continue the search. I hadn't counted on my father and his eagle eye.

When I came down to breakfast, there was an ominous silence.

I chatted on merrily about my plans for the day, but there was no response except the clatter of forks on the plates.

Finally, my father put down his fork.

"Do you have something to tell me?" he asked.

I widened my eyes in innocence.

"I don't think so, Daddy. Why?"

He opened his hand. The signet ring lay in his palm.

"When I was shaving, I saw something gleam in the corner. This has been in our family for over 200 years. I'm afraid you are too young and irresponsible to have it in your possession. That is all."

And that was all.

I would ride along the strand of the lake with an elderly gnome of an Irishman who had twinkling blue eyes and a kindly grandfatherly air. I was fond of him until one day when he described the sinking of a British battleship at the mouth of Lough Swilly back in World War I. He practically salivated as he described it.

"I came down here," he said, pointing to the beach, "and I counted those English bodies as they rolled in, one by one. And I says to myself, 'One Englishman gone…two more of them gone.' Ay, that was the day!'"

"I'm a Britisher, you know," I said, looking him in the eye.

"Ay, darlin', but you're different."

But you're different. Today, I wonder how often the Jewish men I married heard that same phrase.

During my early teens came a recognition of homosexuality. I think my first awareness came when, walking back from a tennis game one day, Laurence asked me what I thought of a mutual friend.

"He's okay," I pronounced breezily, "though a bit of a pansy."

Laurence looked as though I had struck him, and suddenly I knew.

"I don't want you ever to use that word again," he said quietly. "You know better than that."

I did indeed, and I was deeply ashamed.

Female homosexuality was something else again. The girls at Upper Chine were always getting adolescent crushes on each other, but as far as I know, none reached any overt physical congress. However, the girls would talk about two of the teachers with something akin to envy.

"They have a cottage together in the summer. They do everything together. Miss T. is so sweet, and Miss P. is so strong and so clever. They're just like husband and wife."

I listened to this and didn't comment, but I found the whole concept hard to fathom. It joined other facts to puzzle over.

There was pain as well as puzzlememt in the adolescent years.

When I was fourteen, I contemplated suicide.

I climbed out of the dormitory window at night. Undetected, I made my way through the paths and over the downs, arriving at the cliff tops a mile or so away. I sat for a long while staring at the waves below, wondering if I had the nerve to fling myself down. It turned out I didn't.

What had brought about this crisis was a loss of faith. Not in any religious sense. I had believed in the judgment and justice of the adult world, and when that was shaken, I felt that I was making my way through a marshland where solid ground could suddenly give way. I felt I could fall into an abyss.

I had been accused of stealing some ballet slippers. They were found in my locker, the nearest one to the corridor and so the most available. I pointed this out to Miss Damon as well as the fact that given the choice by my parents between ballet and riding, I had unhesitatingly opted for riding. I had started out in a calm and reasonable fashion, but in the face of her cool disbelief became more passionate in my protestations, finally shouting, my eyes filled with tears.

"Look at me! Can't you tell? Can't you tell I didn't do it? What's the matter with you?"

"Your dramatics will get you nowhere with me, Diana. Save them for the stage."

The school had been promised an unusual treat. The

movie *Romeo and Juliet* was playing in Shanklin, and for the first time, we were going to be allowed to go to a movie.

Everyone except me.

After the scene with Miss Damon, I bore my punishment stoically and elected not to speak to the young under-matron in the dormitory building with me. As I sat on the edge of my bed in the dark, I didn't know if I could contemplate life without justice or trust. I quietly unlatched the window…

Looking back from an adult vantage point, I surmise that my viewpoint was colored by visions of Miss Damon sobbing in regret over her mistake, but I don't remember it that way. Bewilderment and sadness are what I remember.

After an hour or two on the cliff top, I made my way back down to the dorm, climbed back into the window and into my bed undetected, I supposed. But later the undermatron came in bringing me a mug of hot Ovaltine.

As she put it in my hands, she said, "I believe you. I know you didn't take those slippers."

I couldn't answer her. When she left, the tears came in a torrent. I shook so hard I spilled the hot drink on my chest and sobbed even harder.

I never did find out who planted the slippers in my locker.

I was very active in the drama department. Jacko and I had good-natured rivalry going on between us as to who would get the starring roles. We came out pretty evenly. She played Viola and I played Olivia in *Twelfth Night*. She was cast as Lady Precious Stream in a play of the same name, and I was Wan Yung, prime minister of the Emperor's court. I was Rosalind, she was Celia.

We planned on going to RADA (The Royal Academy of Dramatic Art) when we finished our schooling. We would take an apartment together which we planned in detail. It was to be decorated, as I recall, in silver and black. Ugh! Very "au courant" and art deco.

One summer was spent at Ladyplace at Hurley-on-

Thames with the Johnson family. Our next door neighbor was Boris Karloff. Nancy Carroll and her daughter Pat Kirkland lived at The Old Bell Inn down the road from us. Pat and the Johnson kids and I turned the monk's refectory into a theatre. The summer passed too quickly. Years later I was going to Sandy Meisner's professional class on Twenty-third Street in New York. As I hurried through the lobby, I was hailed by a well-dressed woman.

"Diana Douglas?"

I stopped and turned.

"Yes?"

"Didn't you used to be Diana Dill?"

"Thats right."

"Fink!"

"I beg your pardon?"

"I said 'fink.' You stood me up!"

I considered whether the woman was insane as I edged away.

"I think you must have the wrong person."

"Didn't you used to live at Ladyplace in Hurley-on Thames?"

"Why yes, I did. And you are…"

"Pat Kirkland."

"Oh, my God…after all this time. How are you?"

"I'm okay now, but I sure was mad at you then."

"What did I do?"

"You said that instead of going back to boarding school, we should ride our bikes to London and become actresses. I believed you and waited at the end of the lane with my bike till two in the morning. You never showed up!"

I looked at her aghast. I didn't remember a thing about the incident. Nevertheless, that meeting renewed a friendship, which has continued to this day. It wasn't until a couple of years ago that she and my niece, Mary Lea, agreed that it was Mary Lea, not I, who was the culprit. Pat and her husband, Don Bevan have been my close friends ever since.

Through 1937, '38 and '39, more and more Jewish

refugee children arrived at Upper Chine as their parents fled the Nazis. They would listen to the radio, tears running down their cheeks, as yet another country was invaded. I sympathized, but could in no way empathize as England was still secure. After Munich, we were all issued gas masks and taught to identify the smells of different poison gases. Mustard gas, I recall, smelled like geraniums.

In August of 1938, Fan and Jock were married at a little church at Burnham-on-Crouch in Essex. Billee, Jock's sister, and I were bridesmaids. Poor Jock suffered from a dreadful stammer that was exacerbated by nerves. We worried about his getting through the ceremony. Our fears were justified.

The Church of England ceremony has a passage that goes: "With my spirit I thee cherish, with my body I thee worship and with all my worldly goods I thee endow." Now, Jock had a particular problem with "Ws" and "Hs" and we waited in trepidation as he approached his Waterloo.

Sure enough, he got out "With my spirit I thee cherish" and then "with my body I thee w-w-w-w-w," sounding like an old Ford engine revving up.

After a few seconds I heard my father's exasperated whisper. "With his body he thee what's for Christ's sake?"
That did it. I shook so hard with repressed laughter that blossoms kept falling out of my bridesmaids' bouquet.

Later, at the reception at a London hotel, the congratulatory telegrams were being read out by a rather pompous footman. At Jock's bachelor party the evening before, he and his friends were discussing the newly released film *Lost Horizon* and speculating on the meaning of the enchanted valley of Shangri-La. They had decided that it was everyone's personal Eden, their vision of eternal happiness. One of his best friends, who was unable to attend, sent a telegram:

"I hope you find your Shangri-La."
All well and good, except the confused footman read out, "I hope you find her…Shangri La?" to the shock of some and

hilarity of others.

In the spring of '39, Jacko and I took the Blue Train to St. Raphael on the French Riviera where my parents were staying. We biked through hills, sunned on the beaches, and flirted with the French boys. On one of our bike trips, we met a professor from Heidelberg who remarked that it was sad that our countries would be at war in September. We looked at one another, startled, remembering Chamberlain's "Peace in Our Time." The prefessor's prediction turned out to be right on the nose. I've often wondered who he was and how he knew.

Just before this time, Ruth had taken a flat on Rue Spontini in Paris and was seeking to rebuild her life after the divorce. She was studying painting at La Grande Chaumiere and taking French lessons from a handsome young Russian archduke, Nicholas, one of the displaced and impoverished Romanov clan. He took me to an Easter service at the Russian Orthodox church in Paris, and I shall never forget the magic moment when the elderly priest came to the top of the stairs, dressed in golden robes and carrying a lighted taper.

"Christ has risen!" he proclaimed, lighting the first candle in the crowd. Whereupon, like the stars coming out at night, lighted candles spread through the congregation while everyone embraced his neighbor joyfully, repeating "Christ is risen!"

It was the first time I had experienced any kind of religious ecstasy since renouncing my faith shortly after confirmation.

That had come about because of our local priest, Dr. Orpen. He was an intense man with a slightly fanatic look in his eye, and he prepared the girls of Upper Chine for confirmation with an avid interest in their sins. He gave us a little red book in which we were to note down every possible sin committed for as far back as we could remember. It was a soul-wrenching experience. I remember meticulously noting down and reliving every shameful moment, then having him read it back to me with comments.

After that we were told to go up into the downs and burn the book. I suppose this was to symbolize forgiveness of sin, but it did nothing of the sort for me. I felt personally violated, and I sensed a creepy enjoyment that Dr. Orpen got from his work.

Shortly after we were confirmed by the bishop of Portsmouth, Dr. Orpen was defrocked and dismissed from the priesthood for seducing choirboys. I felt a sense of great relief that I no longer had to strive to make contact with God.

In Paris, horse-meat steaks were prescribed for Ruth's children to counteract anemia. They were tasty until I found out what they were, then I promptly threw up. I let Mary Lea into the secret by neighing as I came out of the kitchen. Eventually all the children rebelled, and a few more horses in Paris were safe.

In Paris, too, came my introduction to opera, which I was to cherish later in my life, but Wagner's *The Ring* was hardly the ideal fare for a scatterbrained teenager. The Rhine maidens were fat and were heaved up and down on wires. This sent me into fits of helpless giggles, and it wasn't until my early twenties, when I was introduced to music like *Rosenkavalier*, *Boheme*, *Carmen*, and *Butterfly,* that my interest began to take hold.

I was tall and looked older than my age. Ruth would lend me evening dresses in which I would sweep down the staircase of the opera house on Nicholas's arm, feeling frightfully grand. One evening I decided to go for a walk in the Bois de Boulogne. Having lived in the country in England, I had no fear about walking by myself at night, but luckily Ruth elected to join me.

On our way we passed a cadet from St. Cloud, the French military academy. He was wearing the distinctive slate-blue cloak with the red lining, and the effect was rather stunning. I nudged Ruth.

"Look!" I said. "Isn't that gorgeous?"

"Stop staring," she replied. "He thinks you're talking about him."

"Don't be silly."

We continued on our way to the bois and once there, wandered to the plaza that had the floodlit statues of Debussy and Saint-Saens. Ruth was at one end of the plaza and I at the other, gazing at Debussy when I heard footsteps behind me.

Suddenly a shadow loomed over Debussy. As I turned, a hand reached out, ripping the front of my blouse down to the navel. It was the cadet, his face pale and eyes glittering. In my shock, all I could think of was that the blouse had cost me three-weeks' allowance at the Galeries Lafayette, and I hauled off and swung my pocketbook at his head, cursing loudly.

Ruth, at the other end of the plaza, heard me, but couldn't figure out what had happened. All she could see was a man backing up while I clobbered him with my bag and swore. She ran up, laughing hysterically, and the man ran off into the woods.

For weeks afterwards, I would drag my mattress into her room and sleep on the floor, and later, on the Blue Train with Jacko, I warned her to be very, very careful around Frenchmen, as they were prone to misinterpret one's motives. I'm glad I didn't take that walk alone.

In the spring of '39, I became conscious that a confrontation with my father was in the offing. Our final exams would be taken at the end of the summer term, and he had made mention that he wanted me to go to Girton, a women's college at Cambridge, and study for a law degree. I protested that I had no interest in law and was determined to become an actress, but he scoffed at that idea. So I did the unthinkable. I went to Miss Damon, saying that I wanted another year at school if I passed my finals. I figured that I would concentrate on the few subjects I enjoyed—history, art, drama—while I gathered my courage together to defy my father.

To my surprise, Miss Damon agreed. She felt that at sixteen, I was a bit immature for university life anyway.

"However," she said, "it will all depend, of course, on the international situation. No doubt if there is a war, your parents will want to take you back across the Atlantic."

So I sat for the Cambridge School Certificate, which that year had been expanded so that it stressed general knowledge and current events. Lucky for me, or I would never have passed.

When I got back to the dorm, I found a note on my pillow. It was from a Danish girl, Birgit Friderichson. I didn't know her very well, but had found her pleasant.

"Dear Diana," it said, "I like you very much and I know my family would too. I'd like you to come and visit us in Denmark this summer. Please say yes. Birgit"

I was surprised and delighted and called my parents right away for permission, which they readily gave.

That last summer before the war is remembered in a golden haze. Actually, Shakespeare kept running through my mind at the time as I watched the beautiful, tanned young people playing on the beach:

"Golden boys and girls all must/
Like chimney-sweepers come to dust."

Birgit's father was a surgeon and her mother a top movie star in Danish cinema. Their apartment in Copenhagen was exquisite, and their beach house at Hornbaek rustic and cozy.

"Cozy" was a favorite word of her mother's.

"Don't shave your legs," she said to me. "It does not look so cozy."

She broke an ankle shortly after we arrived at the beach house, but wanted to attend a movie of hers that was opening at the local cinema. So we wheeled her down the street in a wheelbarrow, while she bowed to her fans in a most queenly fashion. I was totally smitten with her glamour.

The house was filled with young people, snacking on smorrebrod and drinking beer, and a handsome young Dane, Harald Hansen, swore he would love me forever.

There was a freedom and lack of hypocrisy in sexual matters among the Danes that was very attractive, but I sensed that I was not ready for any actual experience. As the couples paired off into the piney woods, I would walk down the beach with Harald, holding hands and occasionally exchanging a chaste kiss.

By that time, we all knew that war was in the offing and the days of summer were precious. I played the ostrich, as I could not read the Danish papers and didn't respond to my parents' worried requests that I return to England.

"Everything's fine," I told them. "Just another crisis. Don't worry."

The next call was from Copenhagen.

"We thought we'd like to see something of Denmark," my mother said. I knew my days were numbered. When the train left for the ferry back to Harwich, Harald ran alongside, holding up a large bouquet of roses as we both wept copiously. I never saw him again.

We were at Burnham-on-Crouch the day that war was declared, having gotten the last ferry out of Denmark. Fan had just discovered she was pregnant, and she burst into tears.

"You have to take me home with you," she sobbed to mother, "because I'm having a baby!"

My mother reacted like a stalwart Roman matron of old.

"You belong here with your husband," she said. "Do you think you're the only woman who's pregnant?" Fan dried her tears and later told me how much she learned to appreciate mother's wisdom. The war years were unbelievably tough, but it cemented their young marriage.

However, I was another matter. From my own perspective, I was torn between the desire to stay on in the country that now had become a second home to me and the excitement of seeing the New York's World Fair of '39, which I had been reading about in the papers.

With the self-centeredness of youth, I was miffed that the war had upset my plans for RADA and being presented at court. My parents left me no choice.

" You can't stay here. You're coming home."

Chapter 4
AMERICA

Passage was booked on the *Athenia*.

We stayed at the Ivanhoe Hotel in Bloomsbury while we awaited the sailing date.

Antiaircraft blimps had gone up over the city, sandbags were being piled up against buildings, and everywhere you heard the sound of marching feet, as the young, khaki-clad brigades marched by whistling "The Beer Barrel Polka," which became the most melancholy tune in the world to me.

Two days before we were due to sail, we got word that the *Athenia* had been overbooked and we were to be switched to the new *Mauritania* sailing from Southampton in two weeks. The headlines a week later announced that the *Athenia* had been torpedoed by a U-boat with a large loss of life, the first civilian casualty of the war.

My father folded the paper and sipped his tea. I looked back and forth to my parents over the breakfast table, but there was no comment. My mother reached over and patted my hand. Nothing was said. The tragedy might never have happened.

When we got off the boat train in Southampton, the city was all blacked out. We stumbled our way up the gangplank in the dark. Then we went to look for our cabins, booked in first class on "A" deck. They were nowhere to be found. On inquiry, we were told that we were on the old *Aquitania*, as the authorities didn't want to expose the new *Mauritania* to the U-boats. Furthermore, another shipload had been dumped on the *Aquitania,* so there was an acute shortage of cabins.

Being one of the first on board, we were able to obtain cabins, but they were well below the water line on "F" deck. We took these gratefully, as the alternative was to sleep on deck. However, the second night out, I made the discovery that the watertight doors locked above "D" deck, so that if a torpedo hit, those above would have a chance to survive. I decided to sleep on deck. My parents, however, opted to stay below.

At night everyone on board gathered in the saloon, singing popular songs and national anthems. I remember my surprise at my mother knowing all the words to "The Star-Spangled Banner" I had truly forgotten that she had been born an American.

During the day, Daddy marched around the deck, spyglasses in hand, searching the horizon for U-boats. In his habitual yachting cap, people mistook him for an official of the crew and were forever asking advice, which he would give, unhestitatingly.

The ship sailed in a zigzag pattern across the Atlantic, which was meant to make it harder for submarines to zero in on us. On a hot day in late September, we made it into New York harbor, a summer haze hanging over the city and the Statue of Liberty.

I remember sitting on our luggage on the sidewalk outside of the Hotel Pennsylvania, sweltering in a Harris tweed suit and watching the New Yorkers pass by while my father called Ruth in New Brunswick, New Jersey, to tell her that we were in the country. The stylishness of the passers-by fascinated me; all the girls and women seemed to be wearing frivolous shoes as opposed to the "sensible" footwear usually seen in Europe.

Everyone seemed to be walking and talking at an accelerated pace. It was my first exposure to the souped-up energy of New York.

After the hot and sticky train ride, it was a relief to get to Merriewold, Ruth's house in New Brunswick.

She and Johnny had had it built back in 1926, and it had

won the architect's prize for that year. It was modeled on a French chateau with towers and a courtyard. The roof had been imported from the Cotswolds in England and soft beige stone of the walls had been quarried in Pennsylvania. There were formal rose gardens and a clay tennis court.

I was put in one of the tower rooms, which I loved. It had arrowlike slits for windows, framed in Virginia creeper, and was totally octagonal. It was the perfect place to retreat and plan my future.

As Mother and Daddy started making plans to move on to Bermuda, I knew the time had come to make my stand. Walking with Mother down by the rose garden, I put forward my plea.

My father had always scoffed at American law schools as being vastly inferior to those in England, so I knew that half my battle was won. Now I just had to get their permission to go to a drama school in this country rather than accompanying them back to the island.

"We'll see," said Mother. "We'll see."

And I knew I was on my way.

It was decided I would apply to the American Academy of Dramatic Arts in New York ("to get the damn foolishness out of your system," said my father) and, if accepted, would live at Merriewold and commute into the city by train.

Mother accompanied me in for the interview. I'm embarrassed now when I think of it.

The American Academy was, at that time, situated in Carnegie Hall, a marvelous old Victorian edifice with the concert hall below and the upstairs stories a jumble of studios, twisting corridors, and different levels.

Emil Diestel and Charles Jehlinger headed the academy with Mr. Diestel in charge of the interviews for entering students and Mr. Jehlinger in charge of the senior class. It was a two-year course with around three hundred students in the junior class, which was winnowed down to eighty who became seniors after the examination plays.

The walls of the halls were filled with photos of distinguished alumnae that I studied while waiting for my interview. Spencer Tracy, Edward G. Robinson, and Rosalind Russell among them. I felt that I had come to the right place.

Mother accompanied me in to Mr. Diestel's office. He got up from behind his desk.

He was a balding man with a hawklike nose and piercing eyes behind steel-rimmed spectacles. We chatted about peripheral matters; the war, the state of the theatre in England and the U.S.

I was conscious of his observing me closely, but in a kindly manner. Finally he leaned back in his chair and said to my mother, "I think we can schedule an appointment for an audition in a week or so."

"Why not now?" popped out of me.

"Now?"

"Yes, why not? Wouldn't that save time?"

"Well, certainly, but…"

"Yes?"

"Uh…do you have something prepared?"

"What would you like to hear?"

"Do you…what do you have?"

"Well…I can do *As You Like It*"

"Playing which part?"

"All three: Rosalind, Celia, and Orlando."

His eyes bugged a little, but he said nothing.

"Or," I went on, "there's Macbeth. I can do Macbeth, Lady Macbeth and…"

"No, no, no," he said hastily, waving his hands. *As You Like It* will be fine."

So I leapt to my feet, and, with my mother smiling encouragement, launched into a rendition of a scene, the memory of which makes me cringe. I played Celia with a high voice, Rosalind in the middle register, and Orlando with a sexy growl. I flung myself with happy abandon around the office, having a whale of a time while Mr. Diestel looked on in startled disbelief.

I finished up with a flourish and beamed at him.

"Well?"

It took him a moment to find his voice. He cleared his throat, shook his head in bewilderment, and took a deep breath.

"Accepted," he muttered weakly. "Accepted."

I think he was afraid I would launch into Macbeth if he hesitated.

As we rode the train back to New Brunswick, I was in seventh heaven. At last I was taking a step into what was going to be my life's work. I was sixteen.

****

On the first day of school, I got off the train at Penn Station and got on the Seventh Avenue bus to go uptown to Carnegie Hall. Unfamiliar with American money, I fumbled around in my bag, finally coming up with a quarter which looked much like a nickel to me.

"Nah, nah, nah," said the driver. "What's the matter with you?"

"Oh, dear, I'm frightfully sorry!" I exclaimed in my English accent.

He peered at me to see if I was putting him on.

"Frightfully sorry, are we?" he said in deadly imitation. "Well, ain't that too bad, duchess."

People in the forward seats laughed, and I blushed scarlet.

There is definitely something off-putting to a lot of people about an English accent. It must sound condescending or something. On the other hand, some people can't get enough of it.

That is what I found at the academy.

"Talk some more," the students would say. "It's so cute!" That was enough to shut me up for good.

Looking back now, I realize that I was much too young and had too many adjustments to make to get the full value out of the academy training. The culture shock was one thing. After my English schooling, reticence, self-deprecating humor, and modesty were valued, and "being full of oneself" definitely was not. I found my schoolmates' need to be "on" and noisy self-dramatization very alarming. I dreaded having the spotlight turned on me.

Also, most of them, in fact all of them, were older. Some having graduated from college and others having had some professional experience. Everyone seemed ready to impart the most intimate secrets of their life and expected the same from me, and they all seemed to possess the most daunting self-confidence.

I recall passing my junior year almost totally mute in class except when I was overcome with girlish giggling fits at some outlandish exercise. Aristide D'Angelo threw me out of speech class because I could not contain my mirth, eating an apple and declaiming Shakespeare at the same time.

I made friends with some of the girls, but dating was limited as I always had to catch the afternoon train out to New Brunswick. I do recall sitting next to a blond young man toward the end of our junior year while Mr. D'Angelo summoned the whole school to watch a student do one of his exercises.

The student's name was Paul Wilson, and he was a good friend of the man sitting next to me, Kirk Douglas. Mr. D'Angelo recited a poem...

> A wise old owl sat on an oak
> The more he saw the less he spoke
> The less he spoke the more he heard
> I wish I could be like that wise old bird

...while Paul hypnotized himself into a facsimile of an owl.

Then Mr. D'Angelo spoke to him in hushed terms.

"How old are you, Owl?"

Paul ruffled his feathers. "Very, very old," he hooted.

I started to crack up, biting my lip. The rest of the audience sat in reverent silence. Then I became aware that Kirk was having a hard time mastering giggles too. We looked at each other then quickly away before we would both explode in shameful laughter.

Kirk reached over and wrote in my notebook, "How many owl parts do you suppose there are on Broadway?"

And that did it. My shoulders shook, and the tears ran down my cheeks, while Mr. D'Angelo glowered at me.

That's all I remember of Kirk (or "Doug," as I called him, his name was being newly acquired) in the junior year, though I was conscious that he was always with one pretty girl or another.

My steady date at the time was Dick Van Middlesworth who lived in New Brunswick when he wasn't attending Yale. His parents were friends of Ruth's, and everyone approved of our going together. He was sweet and steady and a bit square and would take me to football games and proms, bringing a gardenia corsage to start the evening and end it with a chaste kiss at the front door. However he did drop a bit in my estimation over an incident that happened after a visit to Bermuda.

At the end of the junior year, I went back to Bermuda for a month. When the time came to return, I went to the American consul to see if any special visa was needed on my passport for reentry to the U.S. and was assured that there was not.

But when the boat docked in New York, they wouldn't let me off. Immigration authorities were summoned. They put me in handcuffs and took me to Ellis Island. As I walked down the gangplank with the authorities on either side, I spotted Dick in the crowd on the dock. I raised manacled hands to call to him, but he turned white and fled. He said later that he was in a hurry to make phone calls to help me, but there was no record of them, so who is to know?

Ellis Island was a truly scary experience. It was vastly overcrowded, due to European refugees fleeing the Nazis. Many families had been there for months, others had been going back and forth between Lisbon and New York, with no country willing to accept them. There was one Ping-Pong table for recreation, and close to a hundred people stood in line waiting for it and for a chance to alleviate the boredom and fear.

I was told that I would be allowed two phone calls before going before the judge. I was badly shaken, and I asked the reason for my detention. I was told that I needed someone to vouch for me that I was a student and that I had means of support, so that I would not be a drain on the wartime economy.

My first call was to Ruth.

"She's out playing golf," Ira the cook announced. "She won't be back till this evening."

My heart sank. Who to call next? Her lawyer? What if he were also out playing golf? I could be here for months. I called the academy.

"Mr. Diestel," I pleaded. "Could you please send somebody down to Ellis Island? I need them to vouch for me that my tuition has been paid and that I won't be a public charge."

"Good Lord, child," he said, "how extraodinary. We've never had something like this happen before. I don't know who I could send."

I started to weep.

"Please...please..."

"Don't cry, child. Don't cry...I'll find someone...or I'll come myself."

And so he did.

Like an angel from Heaven, in his derby hat, galoshes, and furled umbrella, he appeared on Ellis Island. We stood up before the judge.

"This young woman attends your school?"

"That's right," Mr. Diestel nodded enthusiastically. "Talented child. We've asked her back for her senior year. Lovely family. Her mother's charming..."

"Her tuition is paid?"

"But of course. She lives with her sister, Mrs. Johnson. You know, of Johnson and Johnson. Band-Aids. the toothbrushes..."

The judge looked much as Mr. Diestel had when I deluged him with Shakespeare.

"Okay. Okay. You can take her out of here."

Mr. Diestel and I rode back on the ferry together, chatting like old chums.

"Extraodinary," he kept muttering. "You certainly don't look like a spy!"

So ended my junior year.

Doug and I initially got together during a production of *Bachelor Born* by Ian Hay. Doug was playing the lead, an old schoolmaster in the "Mr. Chips" tradition, and I was the ingenue. Doug, who had had nothing but adulation from the teachers during the previous term, had gotten a little bit lazy and decided to rest on his laurels. His characterization was definitely on the cliché side as he doddered and quavered his way around the stage.

Mr. Jehlinger zoomed in like a shark to the kill.

"Mr. Douglas," he said, "I don't know why you're wasting our time and your time attending this school. You are obviously not interested in learning anything. Don't care enough to even do your homework. You might as well leave, for you'll never be an artist, son. I'm sure you'll find work as a cheap stock actor, but you'll never be an artist."

Doug turned white, and I saw the confidence drain out of the cocky young man. He stammered and made excuses, he pleaded and tried charm, but Mr. Jehlinger was unimpressed. Sitting in the wings, watching his humiliation was almost more than I could bear, even though I knew him only slightly, and I burst into tears.

As he left the stage, Doug stopped in front of me.

"Would you come and have a cup of coffee with me?" he asked. "Please?"

I nodded, blowing my nose, and we ascended to the Carnegie Coffee Shop.

Doug sat in stunned silence, staring into his coffee cup for several minutes. Then he spoke.

"I don't know what to do. I don't know what in hell to

do. If I can't act, if I'm really no good as an actor, it's all for nothing. My sisters all sacrificed so I could go to college. I worked my ass off, wrestled professionally, anything to get here. Got a scholarship. Thought I had it made, was on my way…and…now…"

He shook his head.

I watched him, chewing on my apple pie. He turned.

"What do you think?" he asked.

I took a deep breath.

"Look, you're talented. That's a given. You know it, and Mr. Jehlinger knows it. He wants you to do the work."

"But after what he said…"

"I think he'll work with you if he sees you're willing." He thought it over.

"God, but it's going to be hard to go back down there. I don't know if I can take any more."

But he did.

And in putting his ego aside and exposing his vulnerability made enormous strides as an actor. When Mr. Jehlinger saw that he was open, he carefully and painstakingly showed him how to build a character from the inside out, drawing some clues from the text, some from imagination, and the result was a lovely, sensitive, truthful portrayal of age, by a twenty-four year old.

We started dating after that.

As the start of the senior year approached, I had asked my parents for permission to live in New York, and they agreed, as long as it was a supervised and disciplined arrangement. So began my stint at the Three Arts Club, an establishment run for young women in the arts with strict curfew hours and nominal fees.

It became easier to get back and forth to school and easier to form after-class relationships. I began going out with guys in my class, Doug among them. He was working at Schrafft's on Broadway and Eighty-fifth to earn extra money, making it convenient for him to drop down to the Three Arts Club. We would walk over to Riverside Drive, sit on the stone wall, and talk about everything under the sun.

Having come from a fairly privileged background, I found Doug's stories of his slum childhood and his struggle to survive endlessly fascinating. He, on the other hand, was intrigued and amused by the attitudes of my family. "Miss Everything-is-lovely Dill" he'd call me.

We'd discuss books, John Dos Passos's *U.S.A.* was a big favorite. Poetry, plays, and politics. Coming from a conservative family, I knew little of trade unionism, and what I did know was negative. So he filled me in on a lot of information on that subject.

There was a strong physical attraction between us, but he didn't have the best reputation as far as women were concerned, and I didn't want to be part of the mob. After a few breathless encounters, I knew that my resistance was wearing down, and I started dating less-threatening figures. Faithful old Dick Van and another Van, Bill Van Sleet, a handsome, sleek, polite fellow student who had a delicious sense of humor.

Doug was angry, even though he had been dating other people.

"How can you go out with him?" he demanded. "Don't you know he's queer?"

"Nonsense," I said haughtily. "Just because he's a gentleman and doesn't try to rape me in the doorway of the Three Arts Club, like someone I could mention, doesn't mean he's homosexual."

But then, alas for me, he was.

So we careened our way through the senior year. I got my own tongue-lashing from Mr. Jehlinger for not adequately rehearsing a scene where I had to clear a table and the resulting shambles brought down his wrath upon me. I don't think I did any particularly interesting work during my senior year, though once Mr. Jehlinger congratulated me for having made him "see the body" after I had presumably found a corpse offstage.

However, during our final plays at the Empire Theatre,

I was the only one of the students approached by a talent scout—a representative of Warner Brothers, who offered me a stock contract. I was stunned and flattered at being singled out and was inclined to leap at the offer. Doug tried to talk me out of it and wrote me a lengthy letter, urging me to "stick it out with the rest of us" and not give in to "the tinsel of Hollywood," where I would surely become as "vacuous as the rest of them out there." The letter irritated me and made me more determined than ever to accept the offer.

We fought, then made up passionately, then fought again. Emotions were at a fever pitch. He had aroused my sexuality as no one else had, but I was wary of his dominance, his take-charge attitude.

So, I did the unthinkable. I went to bed with Dick Van.

We booked a room at the Lincoln Hotel the night before I was to leave for Hollywood. Both of us virgins and highly unskilled, it was not the bliss that I had imagined. In fact, it was damned painful, but, as I had originated the idea, I didn't feel that I should call a halt in the middle of it, and Dick's enthusiasm knew no bounds, once released.

The next day, Ruth and I left for California. Part of the terms my parents laid down for accepting the contract offer was that Ruth accompany me. We took the Twentieth Century to Chicago, then changed to the Super Chief for the rest of the journey. I seem to remember that she brought a woman friend along. One who was embarrassingly star struck and who approached Oliver Hardy for his autograph on the way out, pointing me out to him as a potential star. I could have died of shame, but he was kind and gracious and wished me luck.

Chapter 5
Hollywood

We were met at the L.A. station by a man who said he was a Warner Brothers representative named Johnny Meyer. He was a balding, slightly florid man with an air of contagious enthusiasm. He pumped our hands up and down while he declaimed on the beauties of California and Warner Brothers in particular. He drove us to the Hollywood Roosevelt Hotel and said that he would be back in the afternoon to pick us up. True to his word, he was there on time.

"Are we going to the studio?" I asked.

"What's your hurry, kid? You want to relax a little. Take in the sights. You got a bathing suit? We're going to the Beverly Hills Hotel."

I glanced at Ruth. She shrugged. If that was the way the natives of Hollywood played it...I swam the length of the pool at a fast crawl, then surfaced to see Johnny's face beaming down at me.

"Kid," he said, "there's someone I want you to meet."

I looked beyond him and saw an incredibly handsome man, dressed in white flannel slacks, a silk shirt, and an ascot...he flashed a dazzling smile at me.

"Hi!" he said. "Welcome to Hollywood. I'm Errol Flynn."

I damn near drowned. He was the most beautiful man I had ever seen.

"How do you do," I burbled in my best boarding-school manner.

He laughed delightedly.

"A limey!" he said. "Johnny, you didn't tell me that this lovely child was a limey."

I saw Ruth get up from a poolside chair.

"Mr. Flynn," I said. "I'd like you to meet my sister, Ruth."

His smile never wavered as he rose to shake hands with her.

"How lovely that you came to California. Will you be staying here for some time?"

"Just till I get Diana settled."

"Well, I must show you both something of our town. How about meeting me for lunch tomorrow at the Brown Derby?"

Ruth and I glanced at each other.

"Um…" I said, "I think I should report in to the studio, or something."

He laughed again.

"Don't worry," he said. "They know you're here. They'll be in touch with you when there's something they want you to do. So why don't you both have lunch with me and we can discuss your future?"

Ruth smiled graciously.

"Thank you," she said. "I think that would be lovely."

When we got back to the hotel, I gushed, "Isn't he the most beautiful man you ever saw? And so nice, too!"

"Easy now," she said. "I think I heard somewhere that he's married."

"Oh, really! I wouldn't think of him *that* way!"

Ruth said nothing, but threw me a cynical look. There was a knock on the door. When I opened it, I was greeted with an enormous bouquet of roses.

"It must be from the studio," I murmured as I took out the card.

"As your name is Dill, you won't mind if I call you Pickle? Looking forward to our lunch tomorrow. Errol"

I blushed bright red and avoided Ruth's eyes.

"I think I'd better call the studio after all, to let them know that I'm here."

"I think that's a good idea."said Ruth, dryly.

I was put through to various departments who all

seemed bewildered as to why I was calling, then finally ended up with the studio drama coach, Sophie Rosenstein, who said that I could attend one of her classes if I wanted to the following week.

"There!" I said to Ruth, who continued to eye me with some calculation.

Lunch was spectacular. Lobster crepes, as I recall, and some exotic salad. Surrounded by all the caricatures of the greats of filmdom and sitting next to one of the most popular, who seemed interested in everything I had to say. Dealing with autograph seekers with polite decorum, but immediately turning his attention back to me. Life seemed blissful indeed.

In the next few weeks, Ruth tried to get me settled in the Studio Club, over my strenuous objections. I felt that I'd had enough of all-women's clubs and wanted my own apartment, and Ruth was trying to fulfill her duties to my parents that my chastity be preserved. Little did she know.

The matter was settled to my satisfaction when it turned out that the Studio Club had no more openings and I set up housekeeping in a bachelor apartment with a pull-down Murphy bed and some rather hideous furniture. However, I bought some plants and cooking utensils and surveyed my kingdom with satisfaction.

It was one block from the Red Car Line that ran over Cahuenga Pass to Burbank and the Warner Brothers Studios, so was ideal for what I hoped would be my daily commute.

I showed up eagerly for Sophie Rosenstein's class, but was disappointed in the caliber of the work I saw there, most of the young actresses seemed more interested in posing rather than acting, and Sophie confided in me that the majority were beauty-contest winners or models and she had an uphill job to get logical readings out of them. One of them was Peggy Diggins, a beautiful model who had been in the junior year at the academy and had had quite a romance with Doug before I dated him. She was one of the

Navy Blues Sextet who showed up en masse at bond rallies in skimpy shorts and naval caps.

I was told to report for studio-still pictures and after the obligatory sultry poses in evening gowns, donned shorts, bathingsuits and straw hats for the "cute" cheesecake shots. I went along with all of it, waiting for the marvelous roles that I felt they had in store for me.

One day Sophie smiled mysteriously and told me that I was to report to Wardrobe for fittings. I galloped across the lot and was met by the costume designer holding a bonnet and an 1870s dress.

"I understand you were signed without a screen test," she said. "Well, now you're going to get one, and it's for a specific role, you lucky girl."

"What is it? What is it?"

"It's for Errol Flynn's younger sister in a western that is starting shooting next month. It's called *They Died with Their Boots On*. Raoul Walsh's directing the test, and Mr. Flynn is going to do the scene with you."

"Wow! When can I get the script?"

I rode back in the Red Car with the script under my arm, and my spirits soared. I locked myself in the apartment for the whole weekend, subsisting on avocado sandwiches while I read and reread the script. The part was not big or pivotal, but it had a couple of nice scenes that I felt I could do something with. Ruth was still with me, but she tactfully went out sightseeing so I could concentrate.

The day of my test, my mouth was dry with fright. I sat in the makeup chair being pancaked and curled, muttering my lines and a few prayers.

We ran through the scene once in front of the camera while Raoul Walsh watched, unsmiling. He had a black eyepatch and looked very sinister.

"The kid knows what she's doing," he said tersely. "Let's shoot it."

And we did. Three pages, one take. Then on to the closeups. On one of my closeups, Errol muffed a line, apologized, then whispered to me, "Little more to your left. The light's better." Dear man. I shot him a look of gratitude. When we finished, he gave me a large hug.

"Well, Pickle dear, you can really *act!* One take! One take Pickle!"

"Isn't that usual?"

"Well, bless your heart, I should say not!"

Over lunch we talked of many things, and one of the things he discovered was my love for horses.

"Wonderful!" he said. "I've got four horses at my ranch up on Mulholland, and they need exercising. I've got to go to San Francisco on a publicity junket, and you could do me a great favor by going up there and exercising them. You can use the station wagon from the farm."

It sounded like a great idea to me. It didn't to Ruth when I related it to her.

"Are you crazy? I saw that car when we had lunch. It has 'Mulholland Farm' in big letters on the side. A great reputation you'd have, riding all over town in Errol Flynn's car!"

I argued in vain with her. She was unbudgeable. So with regret, I called Errol and told him that I couldn't take him up on his offer, the horses would have to remain unexercised.

Shortly after that Ruth left, cautioning me to watch my health, watch out for predatory males, write my parents regularly, etc. I didn't tell her of my night with Dick or my throat-clutching fear that I might be pregnant.

Whether I waited for the Red Car, went to the movies, or woke up at night, the sense of dread was waiting. I took boiling hot baths, ran up and down stairs, and when Errol called again and said he'd drive me to his farm to ride one of the horses, I responded with an alacrity which must have had him very confused. I had read somewhere that riding might bring on one's period.

Later, we sat on the grass overlooking the Valley, chewing on blades of grass while he pointed out where the house was going to go. I decided to test Ruth's supposition.

"And does Mrs. Flynn like it up here too?"

He was silent for a moment.

"Mrs. Flynn? There is no Mrs. Flynn."

"But I..."

"I married a woman named Lili Damita. She prefers to be known that way. She's an actress. We're separated."

"Oh."

"And since you're curious about her, you'll probably find out she's pregnant. I have serious doubts that the child is mine."

I was getting more information than I'd bargained for and was confused and embarrassed.

"Look at those tiny kangaroos!" I said, getting up and heading down to the corral. "Aren't they dear!"

"Wallabies, " he said shortly. "Come on, I'll drive you home."

He kissed me lightly on the lips as I left the car, and I didn't hear from him again for two weeks. Then he called.

"Pickle." He said. "I have something to tell you."

"What is it?"

"No. It has to be in person. I'll pick you up in half an hour."

We drove to the farm, but sat in the car.

"I'm afraid I have bad news," he said. "The part of my sister has been written out of the script. Not your fault. Your test was fine. They just decided that it didn't further the story."

I gripped my hand tight over my belly, trying to contain my anguish, but the tears poured down my cheeks.

"Dear girl," he put an arm around me, and I sobbed on his shoulder. "Don't take it so hard. There'll be other parts."

"It's not that. It's not only that, it's..."

"What?"

And then the whole story came pouring out—my night with Dick, my fear that I was pregnant, my horror of my family finding out, the end of my acting aspirations.

"My poor, poor Pickle," he said. "Your first time. A one-night stand and getting knocked up. What rotten luck."

I was grateful for his lack of condemnation. He seemed almost amused.

"To think," he said, "that I was certain you were a virgin. How about the chappie responsible? Does he know?"

"Oh, no," I said. "I don't want him to. He'd feel he had to marry me."

"And you don't want to?"

"No."

"Right. Then we have to figure out how to get you out of this mess." And he did.

It was no kitchen-table abortionist he sent me to, but a Beverly Hills doctor who packed me with some corrosive material to induce a miscarriage. I was warned that it would be painful, and it was.

As the pains started, I paced the length of my small apartment back and forth, chanting whatever songs I could think of. I remember idiotically singing "The Farmer in the Dell" getting a little hysterical when I came to "The cheese stands alone. The cheese stands alone." Finally the small embryo slipped into the toilet, and my sobs were a combination of relief and grief. I looked at my reflection in the mirror and saw blue circles under eyes that were sad and reflective and had lost the cocky optimism of youth. I knew that I had passed some invisible barrier into adulthood. I didn't know whether the tears I shed were those of loss or relief.

I went back to Sophie's classes and tried to concentrate on the scenes, but there was very little challenge and I was bored. When I went to the front office to ask to be assigned something to do, I was told, "Stop complaining. You're getting paid, aren't you?" I asked to be allowed to do a play, but was told that it was unacceptable as long as I was under contract. I remember that time as one of the more frustrating in my life.

I made some friends among the other contractees and would play tennis or go bowling with them. I didn't see much of Errol at that time, as he was busy shooting *They*

Died with Their Boots On. We had lunch once, and I thanked him for his help.

"You were a true friend," I told him, "and I'm deeply grateful. You really were like a brother to me. Kind and protective."

He laughed, embarrassed.

"Don't. You'll spoil my reputation as a rat."

"A rat, is it? Okay, you're my 'Brother Rat.'"

And Brother Rat is what I called him from that day onward.

A few months later, I came back from a bowling date to find Errol sitting in the lobby of my apartment house, holding two bottles of champagne and definitely the worse for wear.

"Pickle, darling, I'm a father!" he beamed. "You must help me celebrate!"

He was very, very drunk.

A passerby stopped in the lobby and gawked as Errol popped the cork off one of the champagne bottles.

"Brother Rat, you can't stay here," I whispered furiously.

"Where else can I go? Gotta celebrate."

"Oh, God. Well, come on upstairs."

I helped him weave his way up and into my apartment, where he sat on the couch, gave me a sweet smile and passed out.

I watched him for a few minutes. He had the same innocent look that I'd seen on my brother's friends, and it was infinitely touching. I took off his shoes, brushed my teeth, and went to bed.

Just before dawn, he came into my bed. We made love. It was good. It was very good.

The next morning was relaxed as we sipped coffee.

"The boy's mine," he said. "No questions about it. Little bugger looks just like me. Got a whanger this long."

"Are you…?"

"Going back to Lili? Not a prayer, Pickle, not a chance. Over and done with."

The next four months are a remembered kaleidoscope. Tennis at the Westside Club, weekends sailing to Catalina on the *Sirocco*, luaus at the Isthmus on the island, mostly in the company of his friends, Bud and Gwynne Ernst.

Two incidents just popped into my mind regarding the Westside Tennis Club, both dealing with my lack of knowledge of American slang.

Brother Rat suggested he "put me up" at the Westside, meaning, he explained later, he wanted to suggest me for membership. In England "put me up" meant install me and pay for my rent, and I was highly insulted. In my chagrin and anger, I didn't ask for a clarification, but just hauled off and whacked him across the jaw, temporarily dislocating it. "Jesus Christ!" he said, holding his jaw. "What did I say?"

When I realized my mistake, I was appalled, but as usual my inopportune laughter took over, and he must have thought he was dealing with a crazy woman. It's a mystery that he continued to stick around.

Later one afternoon, waiting for him on a court at the Westside, I was amusing myself hitting balls against the backboard when I spotted him up on the balcony with a raft of other members.

"Brother Rat," I called. "Come on down. I'm ready to knock up."

Even I could hear the shrieks of laughter as he ran down the stairs, redfaced.

"Pickle, hush! You don't know what you're saying."

He then explained that rallying before the game had quite a different meaning in Americanese.

Gwynne was the niece of Mary Pickford, and I would often swim with her up at Pickfair. One afternoon, when we were in the pool, I looked up to see, as in a mirage, two figures dressed in flowing chiffon, shaded by parasols, drifting across the lawn. It was Mary Pickford and her friend Lillian Gish, and I was awestruck at this duo of filmdom history materializing before my eyes.

Unfortunately when her Aunt Mary was around,

Gwynne, normally a self-possessed twenty-eight year old, regressed to nursery-school behavior. Her voice became little and piping, and she almost wagged her tail in her eagerness to please.

"And who is your little friend, Gwynnie, dear?"

"This is Diana Dill, Aunt Mary, and she's from Bermuda."

"Really. How fascinating," drawled Aunt Mary, sounding decidedly unfascinated "My new line of cosmetics has just come in. Would you and your little friend like to come and play with them?"

I look at Gwynne, bewildered. But she rose to the occasion.

"Oh, yes, Aunt Mary," she piped. "That would be so much fun!"

She gave me a nudge.

"Oh. Yes, sure. Thank you."

Aunt Mary gave a nod, and the two apparitions drifted back across the lawn.

We ended the afternoon in Aunt Mary's dressing room, smearing perfumed unguents on our faces and collapsing with laughter.

The war seemed very far away at that time. Letters from Fan were few and far between. We read *Time* Magazine and knitted for "Bundles for Britain." We made a record with Ida Lupino for Robert Coote, who had just joined the Canadian Air Force.

I remember Errol remarking when Hitler marched into Russia that it was "the beginning of the end. This time he's bitten off more than he can chew."

It took another four years before that prediction came true.

It was a sybaritic time. We drank too much. I remember his introducing me to a lethal drink called Missionary's Downfall at Don the Beachcomber's. It tasted like a delicious concoction of fruit juices. I downed them in quick succession then marched out of the restaurant, maintaining that I felt perfectly fine, and walked smack into a lamppost.

There was never any talk of any kind of commitment, though there was an easy affection. He talked of writing a book and described it to me, but admitted that he didn't have the self-discipline to follow it through. We sailed, swam, danced, snorkeled, and made love in a hedonistic Eden. I stopped showing up at Sophie's classes as my tennis game improved. I was being willingly "Californicated."

It all came to an abrupt end one night at Chasen's.

It was a fairly large party, and I was seated away from Errol, at the other end of the table. As usual, wine flowed copiously, and Errol put away more than his share. A very young, buxom blonde seated herself next to him. Soon they were deeply engrossed with each other. He shot me a challenging look, and then he buried his face in her bosom. I got up and left the restaurant, deeply offended.

I never called, and he never called. I was hurt and angry. I worried about running into him at the studio, but that was soon solved for me. The studio failed to pick up the option on my contract.

Now I was in a financial bind. I hadn't saved much of my Warner's salary, and I had to find a cheaper place to live. I read that they were auditioning at the Pasadena Playhouse for *The Philadelphia Story*, so I went out there, read, and got the lead—Tracy Lord, the part Katharine Hepburn had played on Broadway.

I acquitted myself fairly well, though my approach was a bit shallow as I look back on it from a more sophisticated vantage point. However, *Daily Variety* praised my performance to the skies and advised Warner Brothers. that they had made a mistake in letting me go. At the next performance, a lot of the Warner's brass were in the audience, but, as I heard nothing, I guess they decided they hadn't made a mistake after all.

After the run, I got a job modeling at Saks Fifth Avenue and moved into the Studio Club, which was all my salary would allow. Actually I found it rather nice to be among a bunch of like-minded girls, more sophisticated than my cohorts at the Three Arts Club. They were very liberal about lending clothes for auditions and full of gossip about who was sleeping with whom and who to watch out for. I kept my counsel to myself as to Mr. Flynn.

For a meager sum, we had our room and two meals a day; breakfast and dinner. That wasn't enough for my ravenous nineteen-year-old appetite, so I'd fill up on gigantic submarine sandwiches and never gained a pound.

I did a small part in *Keeper of the Flame* at M.G.M. and was fascinated by the sizzling chemistry between Hepburn and Tracy, evident to everyone on the set. I was encouraged by George Cukor's kindness to me and his faith in my future, but my living was made in modeling, runway and photographic. I amassed quite a portfolio.

I dated a variety of guys: Norman Brooks, to whom I briefly became engaged; Steve Barclay, who recited reams of poetry; and, a couple of times, Huntington Hartford. I had no idea of the latter's wealth and when he took me to the Mocambo, an expensive nightclub, I was careful to order the cheapest things on the menu. I thought the poor boy was just showing off.

Norman Brooks was a charming, funny young man who played a good game of tennis and had aspirations of becoming a writer. His best friend was an Englishman, Dick Woodruff, and the two of them kept up a running patter that was brittle and witty and sounded like something out of Noel Coward.

The three of us ran around together, and somehow Norman and I drifted into an affair. We would spend evenings with his sister, Phyllis Brooks, an actress, in her Westwood apartment playing "Indications," a sort of charade game with Hoagy Carmichael and his wife, Ruth, as well as Johnny and Connie Maschio, Lee Bowman, and other assorted thespians.

My career was at a standstill. Aside from *Keeper of the Flame,* all I did in film was a show-girl part in an undistinguished "B" movie about Nils Thor Granlund. I wore a few strategically placed sequins and strutted about with an enormous feathered headdress. I had nightmares about the film being released in Bermuda, my father seeing it and never allowing me off the island again.

One day, sprawled behind a set on the sound stage, I was reading *War and Peace* and fell asleep. The flash of a camera bulb woke me up, and I scrambled to my feet. The still photographer was convulsed with laughter.

"If this don't beat all! A gorgeous dish in a few feathers reading Tolstoy. I'll get some mileage out of this one."

I begged him not to publish it and asked for the negative. He refused. For weeks I scanned the papers and magazines, but it never surfaced. I think perhaps he honored my request, though he was puzzled by it. With young actresses all over Hollywood jostling for publicity, he must have thought I was a strange one, indeed. He didn't know my father.

Norman Brooks had his initial air-force training at March Field near Riverside, and he asked me to deliver him back to the base one weekend. Phyllis was in New York, so I could use her car, he said, both of us ignoring the fact that I had no driver's license.

I was picked up on the way back. Beside my not having a license, there was no registration in Phyllis's car. I narrowly escaped being thrown in the poky, but a sympathetic judge surmised from my accent that I'd just arrived from Britain and couldn't be expected to know the rules. One time when it served me well.

When Norman left to join the air force, he suggested I move in with his mother Daisy, who had an apartment on South Bedford Drive in Beverly Hills. I was living there when Pearl Harbor was bombed.

For a week or so after, there was a sort of controlled hysteria that permeated L.A. Rumors of Japanese planes being shot down over the city, of submarine landings at Santa Barbara, of the many Japanese gardeners forming a fifth column. Air-raid wardens patrolled the streets at night, giving stern warnings if a crack of light was showing.

After a month or so, I found living with Daisy oppressive. She was a very curious woman, wanting to know my every thought. For my part I wasn't at all sure that I wanted to be engaged to Norman, but she was pushing for a wedding and even sent pictures of Norman and Norman's father to my family in Bermuda, to my mother's puzzlement.

When the New Year dawned, I felt it was time to call an end to my Hollywood sojourn, I was going nowhere. I packed my bags and took the train back to New Jersey.

Chapter 6

NEW YORK

My sister's husband, Philip Crockett, greeted me with jeers for my failure in the film capital. Ruth was kind, as always, but suggested the time had come for me to be a dutiful daughter and join my parents in Bermuda. The idea filled me with panic. I felt that if I went back, I would never get off the island again and would be doomed to a safe, conservative, comfortable life.

"But, Ruth," I protested, "you don't understand. I have to work."

"Well, dear, it's not necessary," she said. "But if you feel you *must* work, I'm sure we can get you a nice little job down at the bank in New Brunswick. I'll speak to the manager."

Desperate, I took the next train into New York, checked in at the Barbizon Hotel for Women, and started making the rounds of the modeling agencies with my portfolio.

For several weeks, nothing happened. I investigated joining the armed services, but the WACs wouldn't have me because I was still British. I thought of going to Washington to see if I could join the British WRENs, but my funds were running too low to take a chance. Just as it looked as though I'd be locked out of my room at the Barbizon, the Powers Agency said they would represent me, and I suddenly started to get modeling jobs.

With my trademark Powers black hatbox, I would dash from studio to studio in Manhattan, sometimes going on location for "shoots" in the country. One was a pose in front of the Minute Man statue in Westport, a place that was to be my home in the years to come. I remember freezing in a gazebo high above the Hudson River, garbed as a June bride while a photographer's assistant scraped away the snow.

Some of my acting experience became useful in creating lively shots, and I was the pet of a few photographers. However, in spite of the money I was making, I felt a deep dissatisfaction with my life. I decided to sign up for training as a nurse's aide.

Bellevue was my first assignment, emptying bedpans three nights a week. The contrast with my daily life couldn't have been more pronounced. The poorest of the poor lay there in large wards or in the corridors, while the overworked staff tried to keep up with the flow of humanity.

The smell was dreadful. Suppurating wounds, urine, Lysol, decay. Skeletal alcoholics plucking at my skirt, seeking some kind of human contact, recognition. Some men exposing themselves. An old woman, barely conscious in the utility room, flickering an eye at one of my jokes.

The next day, an orderly casually flipped a sheet over her face.

"Don't do that! She won't be able to breathe."

"Honey, she hasn't been breathing for two hours."

There was a gold wedding ring on the hand sticking out from under the sheet. Someone had loved her. Who knew she was gone? The tide of death and decay became overwhelming, and I asked for a change of assignment to a maternity hospital. It seemed a hopeless battle at Bellevue. Although I knew someone had to wage it, I felt I wasn't strong or tough enough to cope. I longed for some infusion of new life.

I was transferred to St. Anne's Maternity Hospital on Lexington Avenue, just a few blocks up from the Barbizon. Even though young, unwed mothers were scared and screaming their way through labor, the place pulsed with life. Some kept their babies, and some were placed in the orphanage at St. Anne's. I worked in the nursery, handling batches of squalling infants, feeling happy and useful in my starched blue uniform.

One evening, as I walked up Lexington Avenue, I saw a crowd of people standing in the hospital block. As I passed by, a man grabbed my arm.

"You've gotta do something!"

"What?"

"You're a nurse, aren't you?"

"Just a nurse's aide. Why?"

He stood aside and pointed to a man collapsed on the sidewalk.

"He's not drunk, I don't know what's wrong with him."

"Well, take him into the hospital," I said.

"I tried to, but they said they won't take him."

"What do you mean? That's ridiculous."

"Okay, lady. You try."

The receptionist in the hospital was adamant.

"This is a maternity hospital," she said primly. "It's not for men."

"It's a hospital, isn't it? There are doctors here, aren't there? They've had medical training, haven't they?"

"There's no need to talk to me that way."

"Oh, for God's sake!"

I raced upstairs and found Miss Chung, the Chinese head nurse, and poured out my story to her. She moved fast to get help to the poor man, who it turned out was suffering from insulin shock. From then on, I was her pet.

"Have you ever thought of a career in nursing?" she asked.

I shook my head.

"Well, think about it. I'm going to arrange for you to assist at a delivery. I think you'll find it very exciting."

"No, that's all right."

"You'll see. You'll find it very interesting."

It was summer. The delivery room was stifling. I stared at the legs and feet in the stirrups, trying to fight off dizziness. The legs had long, black hairs, and the toenails were yellow and thick. I vowed to shave my legs and have a pedicure before I had a baby.

The girl moaned and grunted in deep, animal sounds. She gripped my hand in a bone-breaking vise as she looked up with pleading eyes, the hair matted across her forehead.

"Here it comes! Get down here—you'll find this interesting," shouted the doctor.

I gulped and made my way to the end of the table.

The baby slithered out in a rush of blood and mucus. The doctor scooped it up and placed it in my arms, the umbilical cord still dangling from its navel.

"Look, here's the placenta," he said, turning the bloody mass over for my edification. "Now you'll watch me do the episiotomy."

The room was beginning to spin.

"Can I just get the baby cleaned up?" I whispered.

"Okay, go ahead."

Somehow I made my way to the nursery. Somehow swabbed the small body down with oil, put a pad over the umbilicus, diapered the tiny rump. Then, dumping him unceremoniously in a crib, I headed for the rest room, but fainted dead away in the corridor before I got there.

The sharp sting of ammonia in my nostrils brought me to, and I focused on the doctor, squatting in front of me.

"How old are you, kid?" he asked.

"Nineteen."

"Your first delivery assist?"

I nodded.

"Don't worry. After about three or four, you get used to it."

I smiled, weakly...

Later, I asked Miss Chung if I could please stay on the nursery detail. Solely. She was disappointed in me, but acquiesced.

It was around this time, or perhaps a little later that I posed for what was to be the cover picture on *Life* magazine.

Lisa Fonsigrives, a top model who had worked with me on a *Vogue* layout, and I were to meet the photographer

Horst out at the Brooklyn Botanical Gardens for a spring fashions issue. I was sure that if any of the shots were used, it would be those of Lisa. She was an exquisite Nordic beauty and the highest-paid model in the business. But, to my surprise, the May 3 issue featured me on the cover, looking rather sulky under a silk parasol.

Immediately I acquired a minor celebrity status, my modeling fees went up, and I heard from all sorts of people who hadn't contacted me in years. Among these was my old classmate from the academy, Kirk Douglas, who wrote from the Notre Dame midshipman school where he was training to be a radar officer on a sub chaser. He wrote that his roommate didn't believe him when he said he knew me, so would I please verify the fact? And how about having lunch next time he came through New York?

Sure, I wrote back, as long as it didn't fall on a day when I had to be at the hospital. I clung to my duties at the hospital as a raft of sanity and self-esteem. I didn't hold modeling in high regard, and my confidence in myself as an actress had been badly undermined by the Hollywood year.

Of course the first time he called was on a hospital day, so we didn't make contact. I was slightly regretful, but didn't think too much about it. I was dating various fellows: Norman when he came to town, although that was cooling down; a very nice, serious man, Dick Goddard, fourteen years my senior; a dashing officer serving with the Free French, Georges Gudefin; and a couple of photographers.

When next Doug wrote, he said that he would be coming to town on a Saturday when he *knew* I'd be free. Would I please meet him at his midtown hotel at around noon? Please?

I sat in the lobby, little suspecting that my life was to be completely turned around.

He shot out of the elevator in a burst of energy and enthusiasm. My first thought was, "He's shorter than I remembered"; my second "Good God, what a life force!"

We had lunch somewhere, I've forgotten where, talking

nonstop all the time. He announced that he had tickets for *Kiss and Tell*, a popular comedy directed by George Abbott, the father of another of our classmates, Judy Abbott.

At the matinee, he said he had made reservations for dinner at the Penthouse Club, a very expensive restaurant overlooking Central Park. I was a bit worried as to how he could manage it on an ensign's salary, but his joy was so contagious, I kept my counsel.

While we drank champagne and looked down on the lights of the park, he announced that he had been telling everyone since the academy that I was the girl he was going to marry.

I gulped, getting a bit giddy with the pace of his wooing. He was undeniably attractive, more so than in our student days, but there was an obsessiveness that worried me.

"Let's get married!" he said. "As soon as possible!"

"Why so fast?"

"I can't wait to get you in bed!"

"But, darling Doug, you don't have to marry me to get me in bed."

He looked at me in silence.

"Did you think I was still a virgin? Well, I'm not. I won't tell you who they were, but there were not a lot. If you want to spend the rest of your leave with me, great. Let's go back to your room."

With that he gulped.

"Great," he said.

For the next two weeks, we crammed in a lifetime of experiences. Sexually we were omnivorous, had to keep touching in or out of bed. As we'd walk down the street, his favorite song was "They'll Never Believe Me," which he'd bellow at the top of his lungs. "That of this whole wide world you've chosen me!"

We went to museums, ice-skating, the theatre, movies—all in a glow. Knowing that time was precious, that soon he would be joining his ship, a sub-chaser, and heading off to a war zone.

One day we went riding in Central Park.

As we strode into the stable, "Give me a good piece of horseflesh," said my doughty suitor. An enormous, snorting steed was brought out.

"Sure you can handle it?" asked the groom.

"Sure."

I led the way to the reservoir on my well-behaved mare. Then, as we reached the turn, "If there are no mounted cops around, we can let 'em out for a gallop," I said over my shoulder, then dug my heels in and took off.

In a few minutes, I heard a woman scream, then Doug's horse came around the bend, riderless. I grabbed for its reins, and retraced the bridle path, terrified at what I might find.

Doug stood in the middle of the path, dusting himself off and cursing.

"What happened?"

"What do you think happened? I noticed you went for the goddamned horse before you came to see what had happened to me."

I bit my lip, feeling the nervous giggles beginning to rise.

"I figured you'd stay put," I said.

"Fuck you."

That did it. I started laughing as I helped boost him back in the saddle. I howled helplessly as his horse kept turning in circles and he cursed the poor beast. Finally there was nothing left to do but change horses, as his mount knew it had got the better of him.

His final humiliation came when we returned to the stables, and he was bawled out for riding a ladies' horse. He took a deep breath to retort, then caught my eye, and started to laugh. We staggered home, breathless with laughter, going over every moment, collapsing into fresh paroxysms of giggles, happily, helplessly in love.

At the end of the two weeks, he left for New Orleans, and I boarded the train for a modeling assignment in

Arizona. Doug had lectured me about wasting my time and talent on modeling when I should have been growing as an actor, and his single-minded drive gave me fresh impetus and stiffened my backbone against rejection. I was determined to make the rounds again as an actress when I returned from the modeling assignment.

Once in Arizona, we wrote daily, interspersed by phone calls. I had confided to Ruth our plans to marry, and she begged me to wait until after the war, promising a big and beautiful wedding if only we'd postpone it. I checked with Doug.

Doug and I talked it over and decided we didn't want to wait, knowing that he was likely to be sent to the South Pacific any day. Suddenly there was a further reason for hurry when I missed my period.

I was ecstatic, knowing that this was the man I wanted to be the father of my children. Doug seemed happy, too, and started making plans for a Jewish ceremony as well as an Anglican one. We agreed to bring up the child, or children, outside of any formal religion; if there were boys, they would be circumcised, though not necessarily by a rabbi. Neither of us would have to join the other's faith. We were confident that our love would see us through any prejudices our families might have and that our children would have the best of both worlds.

The night before I left Arizona for New Orleans, my fellow models gave me a humdinger of a going-away party and a beautiful negligee, making me very contrite about the snide things I'd written Doug about their airheadedness. We all got very drunk and sentimental, vowing eternal friendship.

Texas seemed to go on forever outside the train windows.

I had written to my parents on the way out to Arizona, saying that Doug and I had met again and that I really liked him a lot. I thought that I should introduce the subject of marriage in a subsequent letter, knowing that it took Daddy time to get used to an idea. Now I was on my way to making it a *fait accompli* and I composed and tore up a dozen letters to them as the train chugged its way to New Orleans.

Doug met me at the station and drove me back to an apartment he had rented in the attic of the Pontalba Building, a lovely old Louisiana landmark. He explained as we went along his plans for the naval wedding to be held in two days. Francis Robinson was a man he'd known when he was with the Cornell-McClintock office, before enlisting. He was to be best man while Angela Gregory, a New Orleans sculptor, was to be my maid of honor.

The Jewish ceremony would take place later, after I had been interviewed by a rabbi and after Doug's family had been notified.

The apartment was enchanting and quaint. Doug was thrilled that I was pleased with it. Being a converted attic, the windows were at floor level, so we'd lie on our bellies, looking out across Jackson Square to the St. Louis cathedral to tell time since we had no clock in the apartment.

The morning of the wedding, after a night of some vigorous sex, I woke with familiar cramps, and the sheets were covered with blood. Either I had miscarried or just skipped a period. Well, we didn't have to worry about our families counting months anymore.

As we rode the ferry across the Mississippi to the Algiers Naval Station where the ceremony was to take place, we were both silent. I was conscious of Doug watching me closely.

"It's not too late to back out if you've got doubts," he said.

"And the same goes for you."

"I know."

We studied each other for a moment, then burst out laughing, and threw our arms around one another.

"Hell, no!" we said in unison.

Francis Robinson met us at the door to the chapel, and I took to him immediately. He was a courtly Southern gentleman with a great appreciation of music and later the assistant manager of the Metropolitan Opera for many years. He introduced me to Angela Gregory, a sweet, gentle woman who later gave us our reception in her studio, which she had banked with flowers and candles.

I was so grateful to Doug for his sensitivity in all the plans he had made and for bringing these two dear people into my life. What could have been a hasty, callous wartime wedding became something quite magical.

We were due to have about three weeks in New Orleans before Doug's ship was commissioned and sent to sea. He had to report daily to the naval base for radar instruction. I surveyed my territory and wondered how one went about being a housewife.

Chapter 7
MARRIAGE

The apartment was lined with bookshelves holding more than a thousand books. I decided that a worthwhile project would be to dust them all and set to it as soon as Doug had left the apartment.

When he returned that evening, I was still at it, surrounded by books, not having eaten, fanatically dusting and stacking.

He tilted his cap and scratched his head. "What do you think you're doing?"

I burst into wild tears. "What does it look like I'm doing, you horse's ass? I'm trying to get the place all shipshape and tidy like your sister's. And I can't get it done. I can't...I can't..."

Some explanation about the sisters is needed. There were six of them. Doug was the only boy. All of them prided themselves on being meticulous housekeepers. If they were displeased with the job the laundry had done on their husband's shirts, they would immediately wash and iron them again. Doug had told me this with some relish, also the fact that their kitchen floors were so clean you could eat off them.

"And they probably do," I muttered uncharitably.

Doug looked at me with some misgiving, but kindly helped me get the books back on the shelves.

A day or so later, it was time to have the Jewish ceremony. One of Doug's sisters, Marian, and her husband were due to come over from his army camp in Mississippi on the afternoon of the ceremony. They arrived in the morning just as we were getting up. Marian was a bit of a card and feigned shock at finding me there, but couldn't keep it up for long. She confessed they'd seen news of the first wedding in the local paper.

I found the Jewish service very meaningful, and the rabbi's dissertation over the symbolism of the rings and the crushing of the glass moving and thought provoking.

I returned to my duties as an inept housewife, occasionally going over to Algiers Naval Station with Doug.

One afternoon we were walking down the quay when I saw a familiar figure approaching in navy blues. The last time I had seen him, he was in civvies, so I had a moment of panic that I would not remember his name. His face lit up, and he came toward me with outstretched hands. Suddenly, his name came to me.

"Dick Goddard!" I said. "I'd like you to meet my husband…uh…uh…"

I went blank.

Both of them stared at me.

Finally, Doug said, "The name is Douglas, dear."

"Of course…oh…um…ah…"

"And the first name is Kirk."

I wanted to sink through the cement. Goddard looked from one to the other with an amused grin, obviously thinking this was a one-night stand.

"Nice to see you again." He waved jauntily, and was gone.

To this day, I can't remember what Doug and I said to one another after that. It's buried deep in my subconscious.

The day the ship was commissioned is vivid in my memory, however. The day was bright and clear. A chaplain blessed the ship. A brass band played. Doug, as the officer of the deck, ran up and down the length of the ship exhorting the crew while the skipper gazed dreamily at the horizon. He was a displaced college professor who had been to sea only once before; the rest of the crew were totally green save for one noncommissioned officer. It was 1944, and the nation was grabbing whomever it could get, then training them and shipping them out fast.

The crew ran helter-skelter, shoving life rings and bumpers over the side as the ship bumped against the dock and adjoining vessels. The band played valiantly, on and Doug kept shouting, "Let's go, men!" as the sub chaser ploughed around like a bull in a china shop.

Finally, with a great churning of propellers, she backed out of her berth, only to sink a small boat moored to the rear, luckily uninhabited. That did it. Standing next to the skipper's wife, I howled with laughter. She gave me a frosty glance and, as I remember, never spoke to me again.

The ship weaved its way down the Mississippi for its shakedown cruise to Miami. I prayed that it would make it. We had planned to meet in Miami to spend the week together while the ship was having her final outfitting for the South Pacific. Time was very precious, and we didn't want to miss a minute of it.

On the train ride down to Florida, I remember being appalled by the "Whites only" drinking fountains and washrooms and getting into a vehement argument with a Southern man over the practice. He seemed surprised that we didn't have the same custom in Bermuda. His attitude caused me to rethink some of the prejudices from my childhood and the paternalistic attitude of the white families there. We didn't think of ourselves as racist, but we were not as altruistic as we thought we were, I decided. We were actually pretty damn smug.

This time I found the apartment as I arrived first. It did not have the charm of the Pontalba, but was small, serviceable, and right on Miami Beach. It was inhabited by a bunch of other young service couples. Doug joined me, staggering at first like a drunk. The voyage through the gulf had been rough, and his balance was off. He all but fell into my arms.

The week we had planned turned into two, then three, then a month as the P.C. managed to bump into a Russian cruiser and foul up her steering mechanism as well as some more minor catastrophes whenever she left dock.

However, not knowing when the shipping-out orders would come, we could make no long-term plans, no laundry could be sent out, so I developed my own way of dealing with his oil-soaked khakis. I would dump them all in the bathtub, pour in a lot of soap, then march up and down on them for an hour or so while I read *Time* magazine. They were spotless, and so were my feet.

Other things did not work so well. Again, with my bone-headed housekeeping, I decided that the kitchen would look much better if I emptied all the condiments, soaps, and powders into little glass jars and lined them up above the stove.

All worked fine until one memorable evening when I decided to make some pasta and sprinkled it liberally with what I thought was grated Parmesan and what turned out to be soap powder. It says something about the quality of my cooking that, when I asked Doug how the dish tasted as I sat down, he replied with bubbles floating from his mouth, "Not up to your usual standard!"

No wonder he suggested that after he left I take some kind of domestic-science course.

Playing at the local cinema was a comedy about a child-wife, Claudia. Dorothy McGuire was the fresh and charming ingenue. As we left the theatre, Doug remarked glumly, "Claudia may be fun to see on the screen, but just try being married to her!"

Our days when he was off-duty were spent frolicking on the beach, the evenings socializing with the other young officers and their wives, and the nights in lovemaking. I bought and decorated a tiny Christmas tree, we threw streamers and toasted one another on New Year's Eve, but underneath there was a desperation, a consciousness that it all could end any day now. That we might never see each other again.

One night I awakened with a touch on my cheek. Doug was sitting on the side of the bed, cupping my face in his palm.

He was gazing at me in the dim light. "You have such a tiny face," he said. "Such a tiny face." We held one another for a long, long time.

In the second week of January, he shipped out.

I took the train back up the coast to New Jersey, once more to avail myself of Ruth's kindness and hospitality. I had promised Doug that I would go to Schenectady at the first opportunity to meet his mother and sisters, but I had to get a job. I figured that I could learn to cook from Ira, Ruth's cook, and that the other domestic graces would follow. I wanted to build up a nest egg for Doug's eventual return and the baby that I suspected was growing in me since its conception on Christmas Day. I had used a diaphragm, but somehow I knew that conception had taken place.

I read in the local paper that E. R. Squibb was hiring trainees, so I applied. They were involved in manufacturing medicines for the war effort, and it seemed like an apt opening for me. I felt modeling was out of the question, as I was a navy wife with a husband overseas.

I had no college degree or background in science, so I was surprised and delighted to be hired to work in the lab testing the brand-new, hush-hush drug, penicillin.

I made my preparations to meet my new in-laws with some trepidation.

It was freezing cold in Schenectady that last week in January. Drifts had frozen solid in high walls along the sidewalk as I made my way, shivering, down the street in search of the address of the Simons, Doug's eldest sister and her husband.

Bryna, Doug's mother, was living with her. The rest of the sisters were coming there to meet me. It was the lower half of a frame house with a wide front porch. I stood there several minutes summoning up my courage before I rang the buzzer.

A large woman with a jaw like Doug's opened the door. "Hi," she said. "I'm Ida. This is my twin, Fritzie. This is Kay,

Ruthie, Betty, and Marion."

"Hi."

"And of course, Mom…"

I turned and saw a tiny, bent woman beaming behind her rimless glasses. She held out her arms, and we embraced. I felt immediately comfortable with her, though I wasn't so sure about the sisters, the size and number of them was a bit overwhelming. They brought out some blackberry wine, and, though it was only eleven in the morning, I thought it must be a Jewish custom and knocked back a few glasses with them.

Mom went into the kitchen as the sisters plied me with questions about Doug, the weddings, his ship and shipmates, and the duties he faced. This last brought about all their angst and fears for his safety, which they discussed in detail, wringing their hands and lowering their voices.

It hit too close to home for me. I couldn't speak of danger as it was too painful to contemplate. I just sat, silent and white-knuckled, until Bryna poked her head around the door. Seeing my distressed face, she beckoned me into the kitchen.

"There," she handed me a dish towel, "You can dry."

Then…

"Don't pay any attention to them. He's going to be fine. He's going to be fine."

She was the first one I told that a baby was on the way. She held a hand over my stomach like a benediction.

I went back to take up my duties at Squibbs. We wore badges to give us special clearance to work in the penicillin labs, and we could be searched at any time as the miracle drug had not been released for civilian use yet.

We tested it against various bacteria, sucking the latter up gingerly in our pipettes. The smell of rabbit's blood was overwhelming and triggered many bouts of morning sickness. Each night, I would go back to Ruth's cottage in New Brunswick and write yet another letter to Doug. The mail came in fits and starts. Long missives from Panama. Then a crocodile purse, a tablecloth, and napkins from Manzanillo, Mexico.

Ruth had given up the big house and moved into what used to be the gardener's cottage on the estate. Her husband, Phil Crockett, was home on leave from the navy and was not at all happy with my presence there. I did my best to keep out of his way. Ruth had decided to get her degree from the local college, so she was busy with classes during the day and homework at night.

After the package from Manzanillo, there was no word at all for more than a month. I would lie awake at night imagining the worst. Ira would coax me to eat, but I threw up continually and kept losing weight. Ruth was getting quite concerned.

Then, at the end of March, there was a phone call.

Doug was in the naval hospital at San Diego. There had been an accident on the ship, and he was hurt, but not seriously. The absent-minded skipper, upon being told that it looked like an enemy sub on the radar, meant to say "drop the depth-charge marker," but instead had said "drop the depth charge." It had blown their own vessel sideways out of the water!

Doug had been thrown against the torpedo racks and had some internal injuries that were being checked on.

For the first two weeks of his stay in the hospital, he expected to be reassigned to another ship at any moment, but as time dragged on with no immediate plans forthcoming, we decided to take a chance. I quit my job and boarded the train for the West Coast.

Upon my arrival in San Diego, Doug was told that he could live off base, just reporting to the hospital once a day for psychiatric counseling. He appeared to be suffering from psychosomatic symptoms caused by stress. We then had what amounted to an extended honeymoon sponsored by the navy.

Days were spent on the beach at Coronado and nights at the officers' club. We played tennis on the court at the hospital, still expecting him to get his orders to report to another ship momentarily, so he was visibly shaken when he came home one afternoon and said that he was going to be given a medical discharge.

Psychiatry still being in a relatively infant state as far as the general public was concerned, there was still a certain stigma about the labels that were given when diagnosed. Though anxious to get back to his true profession and grateful not to be going to the South Pacific, he worried and swore me to secrecy.

Meanwhile, my pregnancy was proceeding well, checked out by the navy doctors. I was going along in my usual blithe way when I got a rocket of a letter from Ruth, bawling the hell out of me for not keeping her and the rest of the family informed as to my health and whereabouts. "You don't treat people who love you in a cavalier fashion like this!" she wrote. I realized that in my passionate absorption in my new marriage, I had been immature and thoughtless with my family.

My mother had been terrific when she got the cable that Doug and I were married, long before she got my letter, written on the train. Though she took her time breaking the news to my father, she had immediately shot back an answering cable to me: "We are happy if you are."

I learned later that she had taken more than three weeks to break the news to Daddy, doing it in bits and pieces in her usual tactful fashion. First, she had intimated that I had met a very nice young naval officer and that I seemed to have a romantic interest in him. Knowing that Daddy would assume that he was a career officer, the intimation made him perfectly eligible in his eyes.

Later, she let slip that we seemed to have become engaged and that he had something to do with the theatre in civilian life, probably production or something. When he was in a particularly mellow mood, she let him have the truth—that I was married to a Jewish actor.

My father had been known to make some anti-Semitic

remarks and regarded actors as low on the scale of human intelligence, quite probably homosexual to boot, so it must have required quite a bit of tact for her to handle this.

Doug was given his medical discharge, and we traveled east on the train, sharing an upper berth. This was quite a feat given the size of my expanding belly.

We arrived back at Ruth's to find that Phil had departed, posted to England. A garden party was in full swing. All Ruth's friends were there and made quite a fuss over Doug, who looked pretty devastating in his navy whites. After everyone left, Ruth sat us down and suggested that we move into the nursery wing of the big house, which had been empty for a couple of years.

Doug and I agreed immediately. It gave us a breathing space while we awaited the birth of the baby. We found an old-fashioned icebox and located a place where we could buy blocks of ice. We then got a two-burner hot plate and a mattress and moved in.

The nursery wing was at the far end of a corridor on the second floor in Merriewold. When Doug started work in the theatre, I would walk up from the gardener's cottage at night with a flashlight, making my way up the spiral staircase and through the dark halls. Doug said that he was surprised that I was unafraid, but having spent some of my childhood there, I could find my way about in the dark, and didn't find it frightening.

Much later, I was told that some soldiers from Camp Kilmer had broken in downstairs one night and vandalized the contents of the drawing room. They stuck a knife into a portrait of me that was hanging there. I was relieved that I didn't know about them, and even more relieved that they didn't know about me.

Early in June 1944, D-Day was upon us, and all America was glued to the radio. The end of the war was in sight at last, but it would be a time before the young men came home.

Doug's early medical discharge turned out to be a

bonus for him. He and Richard Widmark were about the only juveniles available that summer, and Doug went to work immediately in *Kiss and Tell* replacing Widmark who opened in a new play, *Trio*. Eventually, Doug became his replacement in that as well.

Judy Abbott let us stay in her Park Avenue apartment while we searched for one of our own. The summer of '44 was an unusually hot one, and I found the heat unbearable toward the end of my pregnancy. Her air-conditioned apartment and its freezer stacked with eight ice trays was a godsend.

We found a charming walk-up in Greenwich Village with a bedroom balcony overlooking an internal garden, a tiny room for the baby next to it, and a good-sized living room with a fireplace. Ruth said we could take some lovely antiques from the big house to furnish it. I returned contentedly to New Brunswick to await the birth.

My obstetrician was due to go on a vacation, so he tried to induce labor early in September with massive doses of castor oil. I went off to the hospital suffering from heavy contractions, which gradually stopped. I lurched home again to sit around for another three weeks.

Meanwhile, my parents arrived from Bermuda. I was a bit apprehensive as to how Doug and my father would get along, both being strongly opinionated and outspoken. They circled each other warily and formed a sort of grudging respect. Mother was clearly enchanted by my young husband.

We got word that Bryna had a slight heart attack, and Doug made plans to go up to Schenectady after the show on Sunday to make sure she was all right. I couldn't travel as I was due to give birth imminently, but my father offered to accompany him on the journey. Doug refused, thanking him, but later came to me convulsed with laughter over the picture of my British, autocratic parent and his illiterate Russian one. Bryna recovered and was to live another fourteen years.

On the night of September 24, the true labor began, and Doug delivered me to St. Peter's Hospital in New Brunswick. Miss Filiatro, a French-Canadian private nurse who had seen Ruth through all her pregnancies, was delegated to check on me and coach me through the first weeks of child rearing.

When labor started in earnest after midnight, I enquired about painkillers, but was informed that my doctor had neglected to order them before he left on vacation. A Catholic hospital did not dispense them as a matter of course.

I felt trapped and furious, proceeding to curse noisily the absent doctor, the hospital, the country, and anyone around.

A sweet-faced young nursing nun put her head around the door. "Please, Mrs. Douglas, scream if you must, but don't curse that way," she gestured to a crucifix on the wall, "in front of our Lord."

"What does He know about it? He never had a baby!"

Pain had made me unkind, and the gentle soul crossed herself and ducked out of the room.

It was a beautiful, clear fall day. The leaves outside the window were just beginning to turn. In between the wracking pains, I watched the birds hopping between the twigs and thought about what a perfect day it was to be born.

Various interns and doctors would stroll in and peer under the sheet.

"Beautiful," they'd say. "Coming along nicely."

I'd mutter dire threats and references to their parentage.

A little before ten, Miss Filiatro put in an appearance. "They tell me you've created quite a stir," she said, an amused twinkle in her eye. "It looks as though it's about time you went upstairs."

Upstairs being the delivery room, I was elated.

"Looks like we'll have to use high forceps. Better give her a whiff of ether," the doctor said.

"Well, about *time*," I gasped, reaching for the cone.

The journey back to my room was hazy. The next thing I clearly remember is Miss Filiatro placing a blue bundle beside me. Wet, white-blond hair stood up in a peak at one end.

I unrolled the blanket, looked at the tiny hands, a miniature replica of my own, the feet with their long, prehensile toes, the dark golden lashes on the porcelain skin and felt a surge of love unlike anything I had ever known.

"Hello, Michael," I said. Michael had entered this world at 10:30 A.M.

We had agreed on the name Michael Kirk Douglas. Later Doug said that he would never have called a child after himself, as it was not a Jewish custom to name one after someone still living. I don't recall any dispute over the matter.

Regarding our different customs, though, we did tell Bryna that Michael had been circumcised by a rabbi, even though it was done in the hospital. Mother had brought a long, embroidered christening robe from Bermuda that had been used in the family for generations. I had to gently tell her that we were not having the baby christened.

"But what do they do in Kirk's religion?" she asked. "They must do *something*."

"Well, they have the baby circumcised. It's called a bris."

She paled.

"Good Lord," she said faintly. "Good Lord."

Doug made it back to the hospital between the matinee and evening shows of *Kiss and Tell*. He hadn't slept since dropping me off at the hospital the night before and looked tired and harried.

"Christ," he said as he stepped in the door. "What a day I've had!"

I reached for the heavy water jug and contemplated throwing it at him, but was prevented by the arrival of my parents.

My mother cooed over the baby, and my father popped

his monocle in an effort to amuse the sleeping infant. For the week I was in the hospital, my father went through the same routine. He would walk the four miles to the hospital, bend over his newest grandson, and pop his monocle. "Oy, oy, oy," he would say, wagging a forefinger in the baby's stomach. "Oy, oy, oy, oy, oy."

He must have had a reaction from some other babies, but Michael just stared at him solemnly. All through his babyhood, Michael never smiled or laughed much. People would waggle their ears, make ridiculous faces or rude noises, and occasionally would be rewarded by a ravishing grin, but mostly he contemplated the world with a serious and reflective mien. Joel, arriving a little more than two years later, found the world around him endlessly amusing and chuckled happily at any antics. He made a great audience.

One evening, when Doug was at the theatre, my father arrived at the dinner table somewhat the worse for wear with several drinks under his belt. Alcohol always brought out sarcasm in him. Fixing me with a red and baleful eye, he started to declaim on his theme for the evening: "Actors are the parasites of society."

I tried to gather my thoughts together for a rebuttal, but in the throes of postpartum depression, I could only gasp. Nothing came out until I finally leapt to my feet shouting, "You mean old bastard, why don't you go to hell?" and fled the room.

Mother and Ruth raced after me, both of them saying, "Be careful! Don't get upset! You'll sour your milk!"

It struck me funny, and soon the three of us were laughing helplessly. The women in my family all shared the same sense of humor and were endlessly supportive.

However, looking back, I think our marital troubles may have had their seeds during this time. It became more evident after we moved into our apartment in New York

Cushioned by my family's love and concern, as well as material goods, I was insensitive to the many anxieties besetting Doug as a young father trying to make his way in the most insecure of professions. Also, the two of us came at life from totally different viewpoints. He once said to me at a later time, "You're basically happy unless something comes along that makes you unhappy. I'm basically unhappy with moments of happiness."

And it was true.

His deep, dark Russian depressions and sudden rages had me confused. He was readily employed, going from *Kiss and Tell* into *Trio*, then into *The Wind Is Ninety* for which he got excellent notices.

"Nothing short of superb...," the caption said under his picture in the paper. When I rushed in excitedly to show it to him, he frowned. "What do they mean 'nothing short of'?"

I laughed, but he wasn't kidding. To me, he had everything that made life worthwhile: work in a profession that he loved and a loving wife and child. Still he was restless and unhappy.

It took me many years to realize that there was nothing I could do to change this.

Of course, all was not doom and gloom. We still laughed and loved as we had before, and his wild somewhat manic sense of humor continued to entrance me. I cued him through his scenes. We gave parties for our friends, walked Michael in his pram in the park. Yet our differences became more frequent and more acute.

I began to get a bit restless myself and decided to take a short-story course at N.Y.U. I was preparing to leave one evening with my friend, Barbara Van Sleet, when Doug came in with a telegram in his hand.

"Bad news from Bermuda," he said. "Your father has died."

We stared at each other for a moment. I blinked. Then I turned and picked up my books.

"What are you doing?"

"I'm going to class," I said. "I don't know what else to do."

It wasn't until weeks later that he came upon me sitting in Michael's room, holding a baby shirt with T.M.D. 1876 embroidered on it, howling like an animal as I rocked back and forth.

"Daddy's dead," I sobbed. "And now I'll never know... never know..."

"What?"

"I don't know."

But I did. I desperately wanted to know that he loved and approved of the adult I had become.

A few months before we had locked horns in a discussion of the Sacco-Vanzetti case, the first time I had dared to disagree with him, over a legal matter no less.

"But surely," I maintained, "all the evidence pointed to their innocence."

"No matter," he had rejoined. "By their example, they were inciting against the established order. Inciting to riot is a crime."

I sat back and stared at him.

"Ooohh, boy," I breathed. "There are some things we'll never see eye to eye on."

"You can count on it." His monocle flashed, and he gave me a slight smile. I had been let off lightly.

Life went on through the summer. I played Mariana in an Equity Library show of *Measure for Measure*. Doug did a successful audition for a new musical, *On the Town*, written by a brilliant pair, Adolph Green and Betty Comden and a score by Leonard Bernstein. All of them were under thirty, and the world was their oyster. They were very enthusiastic about the casting of Doug in the romantic role of Gaby. Then, as rehearsals were about to start, disaster struck.

Doug lost his voice completely. Not a croak nor a whisper came out of him. Tension had always manifested itself in his clenched jaw muscles and tightened neck cords. He always had had vocal problems, but never like this.

He saw a throat specialist who prescribed total rest of the whole area, no mouthing words or trying to whisper until the inflammation of the vocal cords was gone. He could not predict how long that would be.

The tension around the apartment was palpable. Doug would write long and furious messages on shelf paper that he'd tear off by the ream, while I would reply vocally, also furious.

Michael would sit on the floor, eyeing us both anxiously, the phone ringing with yet another inquiry from the producers of *On the Town*. Rehearsals were postponed twice, but finally they could wait no longer, and another actor was cast in the part. A week later, I heard Doug singing in the shower. "Gaby's comin', Gaby's comin' to town." His voice was back. The doctor could find no sign of inflammation in his cords. Strange the connection of body and the mind.

Doug called his agent, but was told that they were satisfied with the replacement. He grumbled about it, but I could sense the relief he felt.

Soon, he was approached about doing *Heaven Can Wait*, a play that had been made into a successful movie called *Here Comes Mr. Jordan*. Before rehearsals started, he had to learn to play the trumpet. He started practicing at home.

I decided it was a good time to take Michael to visit my mother in Bermuda.

The trumpet was not the only reason. Doug had been making passes at a girlfriend and a teenage relative. Angry and hurt, I was at a loss as to what to do. I could not admit to my family or anyone that there were problems in my marriage, having been brought up to avoid "scenes" at all cost. I gave Doug a chilly ultimatum.

Later, he told me he had envisioned that I would react competitively, shout, scream, and throw things, then fall weeping into his arms. He said he felt very unloved by my reaction. How our cultural patterns contribute to misunderstanding!

The end of the war. V-E Day and V-J Day. The dropping of the atom bomb. Cartoons in the paper of a buck-toothed Japanese holding his belly. "I got atomic ache!"

John Raitt waving his shirt out the window of his dressing room in the theatre where he was playing in *Carousel* while the crowds went mad in Times Square. The end of gas rationing. The end of food rationing. Being able to buy shoes again. It was almost too much to contemplate after five years.

The windows of the plane were still blacked out when Michael and I flew to Bermuda. He had his own American passport, and I still had a British one, so upon our arrival on the island, we had to wait until everyone else had been cleared through immigration before they allowed my tiny American citizen to accompany me.

Newbold Place seemed very quiet, lacking my father's robust presence. However, the atmosphere was more relaxed. I realized how we all had tensely watched his moods and adjusted our behavior accordingly. Mother's grief was very private, mostly revealed by a certain vagueness and absentmindedness. She did confide in me that Father had been a magnificent lover, up to and including the night of his death. As children often are when confronted by the sex lives of their parents, I was ridiculously embarrassed.

We celebrated Michael's first birthday with all the family in attendance. Although there were no peers of his age, a slew of ten-year-old cousins made a fuss over him, and he gave them one of his rare, beaming smiles through layers of cake icing.

Lord Burghley, who had been a classmate of Bayard's at Cambridge, was now Bermuda's governor, and I was invited to dinner at Government House. Seated next to me at the long dining table was his A.D.C., a lean pink young man with a blond mustache, Sir Peter Gibbs.

We made inconsequential chitchat while the soup was served, and somehow the conversation turned to family crests and mottoes. Peter confided in his hesitant way that his family crest was a thistle surrounded by thorns, and he reeled off a Latin phrase that was the family motto.

"My Latin's not that good," I smiled. "Would you translate?"

"Oh," he stammered, "the translation is something like 'we may look very pretty, but watch out for our prick.'"

The soup spewed off my spoon, and I collapsed in laughter to the mystification of the rest of the table and the chagrin of Peter.

"Oh, I say," he whispered, blushing furiously. "I didn't mean *that!*"

"I know, I know," but I couldn't stop laughing and soon he was giggling too. For the rest of the evening, through the chamber-music concert, we would catch each other's eye and were off again.

A few days later, he called and asked if I would like to go riding with him. As a married woman, I should have said no, as my relatives were quick to point out. Partly to show them that I couldn't be dictated to and partly out of boredom, I said yes. We spent a pleasant few weeks in each other's company. There was definitely an attraction between us, but I had no intention of breaking my marriage vows and kept our relationship on a joking and platonic level.

Meanwhile, many things had been happening to Doug. The play for which he'd been preparing (the first production of a young man named David Merrick) had started rehearsal without full backing. The promised backing was not forthcoming, and it had to be canceled after a week, leaving everyone involved unemployed. However, Hal Wallis, a Hollywood producer, had seen Doug in *The Wind Is Ninety*. After making tentative overtures over the months, he had come up with a firm offer of a part in a film, *The Strange Love of Martha Ivers*.

So Doug wrote me that he was on his way to Hollywood, was closing the New York apartment, and would contact me on his arrival. A week or so later, he called saying that he now had a Hollywood agent, Famous Artists, who wanted to sign me as well, having seen a still photo of me. They would pay for my transportation to California. He suggested I bring my mother along and that she could help with the baby.

Mother liked the idea. She'd always enjoyed traveling with my father, had friends in Santa Barbara, and felt it would provide a focus, a feeling of usefulness to help her deal with her grief. Together we packed up belongings from the New York apartment, loaded up with disposable diapers for Michael, and boarded the train for the journey to the West Coast.

Chapter 8
HOLLYWOOD REDUX

Doug had given me the name of his personal agent at Famous Artists, Milt Grossman, and told me to contact him upon our arrival. There was a studio strike pending, and he was not sure where he would be. So in the cavernous Union Station, with Mother holding a howling Michael, I dropped nickels into a pay phone and called Famous Artists. Milt Grossman, I was told, was on vacation and could not be reached. I identified myself as Doug's wife, but the receptionist seemed not to have heard of him. Mother watched me, looking more and more worried. I tried to stay calm, but felt I was entering a nightmare.

Next, I tried Hal Wallis Productions, which Information told me was located at Paramount Studios. Someone, thank God, had heard of Doug, but I was informed he was in the middle of shooting and could not be contacted. Furthermore, due to the strike, he and other actors who had agreed to work were locked in the studio day and night until the strike was settled. I wondered about this, knowing of his strong pro-union beliefs. I found out later that the Screen Actor's Guild had taken no stand and had counseled the actors that they could work or not as they chose. It being his first movie, he had elected to work.

I asked if anyone at the studio knew where we were to go, where to spend the night. No idea. Mother was looking pale, and Michael was screaming his head off. My voice shaking a bit now, I asked if by any chance they had Milt Grossman's private number. Normally, I was told, they would not give out anyone's number, but as these were special circumstances (I did sound desperate), they would make an exception.

I thanked them fervently and prayed, as I dropped one more nickel into the slot, that Milt Grossman had not departed for Europe. A woman answered.

"This is his wife, Esther," she said. "What seems to be the matter?"

Tired and choking back sobs, I identified myself.

"Oh, for heaven's sake," she said. "We wondered when you were going to get here. Grab a taxi and come on up." She gave me an address, and, euphoric with relief, we taxied to an apartment house off the Sunset Strip.

Esther greeted us at the door, blonded, slender, and with shining black eyes that blinked a few more times at the sight of our bedraggled little band.

"I didn't know..." she began. Then, at the sight of Michael, "Who's this adorable one?"

"My son, Michael. And my mother."

"Aha," she said. "We have a bit of a problem. But come on in."

We filed after her into the living room of an attractive, but small apartment. "Milt isn't here," she explained. "Kirk is locked in at the studio. The apartment he got for you was meant to have been ready last week, but they haven't moved out yet."

I felt my mother's eyes on me as I did a mental calculation of how much cash we had with us for a hotel. Esther read my mind. "We don't have a lot of room, but if you don't mind the couch, or some pillows on the floor..."

I could have cried with relief.

"It'll only be overnight," I vowed. "I'll figure out something by tomorrow, I promise."

The dear Grossmans put us up for three days while I worked out the details with our would-be landlords. Their departure had been held up because their promised apartment in New York had fallen through, so I suggested we do a swap. I could tell from a cursory glance around their duplex that our tastes were not similar in terms of decor, but it had the right number of rooms for us—three bedrooms and a bath—and was near a park which was ideal for walking the baby.

As for ours, they were a middle-aged couple with no children, so our one-bedroom walk-up in the Village should suffice. We exchanged keys, and they were off.

We moved in, and I removed the hordes of breakable knickknacks from tabletops and bookcases and set Michael's crib up in the room next to ours, then Mother and I scoured the neighborhood for groceries. Doug called, saying that a limo was going to pick him up after dark if he could sneak out of the studio. He'd be able to stay until shortly before dawn when he would sneak back in. He made it shortly before ten, and Mother discreetly busied herself with sewing in the living room while we repaired to the bedroom with indecent haste.

Later that night, Doug filled me in on what had been happening at the studio. The strike was close to being settled so there would be no disruption in shooting. The part that he was originally meant to play had been given to Van Heflin. Doug had been assigned the part of Barbara Stanwyck's weakling husband, a rather interesting bit of off-casting given his powerful presence.

He told me of an amusing incident of actor's one-upsmanship involving Heflin. For a final take in a confrontation scene, Doug decided to grab Heflin by the knot in his tie while he denounced him. After the take, Heflin asked for just one more, and the director agreed. When Doug made his move, Heflin looked at him calmly, looked down at Doug's fist on his tie, then back up and smiled, removing all menace from Doug. A lovely, old professional's trick.

Within a few weeks, Morty Gutterman, one of the agents at Famous Artists, had set me up for a screen test at M.G.M. that resulted in a contract. Not with Metro, but with Fox. It offered yearly options and a damn good salary that made it likely I would be put to use. I decided that now was the time to make my legal name, Diana Douglas, my professional name as well. I had it changed on my Equity and SAG cards. No more "pickle" jokes.

Mother had settled into a comfortable routine, taking Michael to the park, writing letters, and assiduously reading the trade papers in an effort to learn something of the strange business we young folk were into.

However, I was conscious of a quiet struggle going on between Doug and Mother. In his culture, grandmothers (or *babushkas*) were relegated to baby care and the kitchen and did not mix with the younger generation. My mother had never learned to cook and enjoyed the social life as well as her Scotch or martini before dinner.

"She expects to be included when we have our parties, doesn't she?" he whispered.

"But of course she does," I whispered back. "What's wrong with that?"

He shook his head in bewilderment.

"Not the way I was brought up. I don't get it…"

As Doug was finishing up *Martha Ivers*, I was testing for *My Darling Clementine* over at Fox. It was an elaborate test directed by John Ford involving horses, wagons, and a full Western set. Mr. Ford indicated that he was very pleased with the test and said that he would see me at the start of principal photography. All that was required was the say-so of Darryl Zanuck, who was out of the country. I would be playing the title role of Clementine, a schoolmarmy type who displays unexpected fire and gets into a fistfight with the character played by Linda Darnell.

As I started costume fittings, Doug finished his film and immediately began calling the agents.

"What's next for me?"

"Hey, you only finished last week. We're looking around."

"Well, if you don't have something good lined up for me by next week, I'm going back to New York."

The agents were flabbergasted. They'd never had a young actor display such independence. I was amused and enjoyed Doug's feistiness as I listened to the conversations.

I waited with anticipation to see Mohammed move the mountain.

"But you can't do that!" they protested.

"Watch me."

And, by golly, he managed to get himself a part in Sam and Bella Spewack's new play *Woman Bites Dog*, which was about to go into rehearsal in New York.

However, I'd previously discovered while driving Mother back from Santa Barbara after visiting her friends that she really wanted to be home for Christmas. I knew that she had tried very hard to fit in, but that the whole culture of Hollywood was totally alien to her. She was puzzled that I could adapt to it. I felt that in some obscure way I had failed her.

When the time came for her to leave in December, it was next to impossible to get train reservations. She was determined to be on her way, so a seat was found for her on a converted army plane. It was a bucket seat that I feared would be most uncomfortable, but she said she'd be fine. Although she had never traveled on her own before, she packed a flask of Scotch, bid us a cheery farewell, and was off.

When Doug left early in the year, it was just Michael and me. He was an unusually companionable little kid, and I schlepped him around with me everywhere, even to wardrobe fittings at the studio. He would sit quietly, observing all the goings-on with his usual solemnity. While Doug was with us, we had made some good friends, principally Mickey and Walter Seltzer. They had a small daughter, Michael, who was about a year older than my Michael, so we saw quite a lot of each other.

I was told at Fox that while I waited for Mr. Zanuck's okay, I could attend the Actor's Lab with some other contractees. I was very excited about that, as some of the remnants of the Group Theatre were teaching and directing there, including Stanislavski-trained George Schdanoff. They were due to start rehearsals of a play, *The Twig Is Bent* directed by Roman Bohnen. I was tentatively cast as Jane Wyatt's younger sister depending on the schedule of *My Darling Clementine.*

When Darryl Zanuck returned, I had my answer soon enough. The producer of *Clementine*, Sam Engel, called me into his office to say that in spite of his and John Ford's pleas, I was not to be cast in the part. Mr. Zanuck was firm on the subject. His reason was that my front teeth were slightly crooked.

"My God!" I said. "I'll get to a dentist right away. They can make caps or something, can't they?"

"Don't waste your time or your money, dear," he said. "If it wasn't your teeth, he'd find something else to object to. He met somebody while he was away and promised her the part, and that's that."

There was a silence while he studied me. I stood up.

"Well," I said. "If that's that..."

"We'll just have to find something else for you."

"Mmmm." I turned to go.

"Wait a minute. You in a hurry?"

"Sort of. My baby is with a sitter."

"Oh, that's right. Your husband's out of town. Back east doing a play, isn't he?"

"That's right."

"You must be lonely."

"Well, sure."

"Very, very lonely."

"Well, it's not *that* bad. I've got friends and my baby, and I keep busy at the Actor's Lab..."

"You see, I'm concerned about you. Very concerned."

"Gee, Mr. Engel, that's awfully nice of you. But I'll be fine, really. But thanks anyway."

He looked nonplussed as I waved my way out of the office. I sound naïve to the point of dimwittedness, but it wasn't until several months later that I realized that a pass had been made and that there was indeed a casting couch in the offing. However, building a career on my back never figured in my scheme of things.

Meanwhile, Doug was touring with the play and, as is the tendency when traveling on the road, became somewhat involved with a young actress in the company. I had a sinking feeling when my call was transferred to her room because he was "helping her with her lines," but I wasn't about to get into a confrontation long distance. His excuses were so many and varied that he obviously didn't want the marriage threatened. So I swallowed my fears and plunged into rehearsals at the lab.

Beside Jane Wyatt, the attendees consisted of Jocelyn Brando, sister of the as-yet-unknown Marlon, Jean Wallace (married to Franchot Tone), Susan Blanchard (who later married Henry Fonda), and a whole bevy of enthusiastic young actresses thrilled to be working with serious craftsmen. I don't recall any of the competitiveness that was usual at the studios. Roman worked us hard, and I recall that Jocelyn was particularly effective as a mentally disturbed teenager.

Suddenly, a week or so before opening, the project was abandoned. As I remember it had something to do with rights that hadn't been cleared. We were all disconsolate, but went back to our exercises and scene work.

I recollect getting into a discussion with George Schdanoff while working on the balcony scene from *Romeo and Juliet.* He suggested that I find the "psychological gesture" for Juliet. I offered that it was a reaching out to envelop. He agreed and said that I should perform this gesture several times before beginning the scene.

To me, that felt like putting the cart before the horse. The idea comes first, and the gesture follows. He insisted that it was a useful tool. Pouting a bit, I went along, reaching out to empty air as I waited offstage. I wish I could say it brought me a newfound revelation, but I just felt faintly like a horse's ass. However, the general atmosphere was stimulating and professional with a warmth, camaraderie, and a willingness to experiment.

I gathered from my conversations with Doug that the young actress he was so concerned about had been fired, which made him sad, but that he was staying with the show even though he felt the rewrites were not improving it. The next thing I heard, the show had closed, and he was on his way back to the West Coast. I felt some trepidation.

Life had been easier and calmer while he was away. Although I missed the heady excitement during times that were good, I didn't miss the criticism and temper flareups when they weren't. Still I felt it was up to me to make the marriage work and to do what I could to make it so.

On the day he was due back, I arranged for Michael to stay overnight with friends. I rented a room at the Beverly Wilshire Hotel, bought a fetching white negligee, and ordered champagne to be chilled in the room. Then I drove out to Burbank to pick him up at the airport.

Almost immediately, we got into a fight. Something ridiculous about which was the best route to take. The bitter bickering lasted until we got to the hotel. We were both tired, nervous, and intolerant of one another. It looked like the evening was going to end in disaster. Fortunately champagne, music, and proximity eventually won out. After a night of fierce lovemaking, we fell asleep in each other's arms and woke to laugh about it.

We decided to buy a house. Doug had saved up enough from *Martha Ivers* for a down payment, and I was making steady money at Fox. It seemed a logical thing to do, as well as a symbolic totem for a solid marriage.

We found a ramshackle, but charming house off Laurel Canyon with a two-story living room and a little rustic guest house. Rough stone terraces surrounded it. It had a Swiss feeling about it, as though it had just slid down from the Matterhorn. We moved in during early summer of 1946 and began one of the happiest times of our marriage. Doug and his buddies set about repairing the terraces and building a patio out back.

A Rube Goldberg contraption was rigged up to get the

cement up the hill to the back. A rope was tied to a wheelbarrow containing the cement and snaked through a pulley tied to the front bumper of my car. My duty was to slowly and smoothly back the car down the driveway to aid the man shoving the wheelbarrow. It all went well until one day when my foot slipped off the pedal and the wheelbarrow and shover (I think it was Paul Caruso) went flying in the air, the cement sloshing all over. We had to hose him down quickly before he turned into a garden statue.

We hired a housekeeper to help care for Michael when I was at the studio. We got a dog from Tony and Catherine Quinn, a beautiful German shepherd bitch who we named Banshee, after a dog I'd had as a child. We planted flowers and tomatoes. Doug was signed to do another movie with Hal Wallis called *I Walk Alone*. It co-starred Burt Lancaster, another young Wallis contractee, who with his wife Norma, became our friends.

We entertained quite a lot. We threw informal parties with other young folk in "the business." "The Game" was a form of charades we especially favored. We drank wine and tried to outdo one another in joke telling. It was a golden time. On top of it all, I found out that I was pregnant again.

It wasn't the most opportune time to have a baby, as Fox had started me doing screen tests for *Forever Amber*. Doug said it was up to me whether I wanted to terminate the pregnancy or not. I thought long and hard about it, but I felt in my heart that if I didn't have this child, I would never have another. I didn't want Michael to be an only child, both for his sake and for mine. Even though the marriage was rocky, I felt it was the right thing to do.

Dear Mary Corso in the wardrobe department at Fox was the first to suspect my condition as she tried to fit me into a cinch-waisted period costume. She checked my measurements of a month before.

"Either you're eating like a horse, or…oh, my God, that's it! You're pregnant!"

I nodded.

"Well, don't tell those bastards in the front office. They'll drop you like a hot potato, and Kirk's not on salary yet, is he?"

I shook my head.

"Okay, honey, it'll be our secret for a few months. I'll just keep building those frills higher and higher so no one will know. You can get away with it."

It was probably not the most honorable thing to do, concealing my condition from my employers, but we persuaded ourselves that as long as I was able to appear on film, I was fulfilling my contract.

However, in my seventh month, I was summoned to the front office. I wore my sailor's pea jacket which had become the staple of my wardrobe, and the steely eyes of the executives were fastened on my middle.

"We have heard a rumor that you are expecting a baby."

I allowed that that was so.

"And when is this baby expected?"

I waved a hand airily. "Oh, later in the winter."

It was now November.

"Let's put it this way. If we were to cast you in a part in two or three weeks and the picture was to run another month or so, would you be able to complete it?"

I hung my head and admitted I couldn't.

"Okay. You're off salary as of now. Your contract is due to come up in March. It will not be renewed."

That was the end of my illustrious career at Fox. I never thought to set foot on the lot again, but two years later Joe Mankiewicz cast me as Luther Adler's wife in *House of Strangers*, and I was back again temporarily.

During this time two incidents came up which further undermined my marriage.

I received a package from Bermuda containing Peter Gibbs's regimental ribbons and pips. The accompanying letter said he was leaving the island, but remembered his time with me as the happiest that he had known. He had intended these mementos for his wife, but had no intention of marrying anyone as I was unavailable. He wanted me to have them.

I opened the package, then sat in shocked silence.

Doug reached over and took the objects and the letter. "It must have been quite an affair."

"There was no affair."

"You mean to tell me you didn't sleep with him?"

"No, I didn't."

"Why not?"

"Why not? Because I'm married to you. I'm your wife."

"But you thought about it. You must have thought about it."

"Yes, I thought about it."

"Then you should have done it. It would have been the honest thing to do."

I stared at him.

"What's the matter?"

"I don't understand you," I said finally. "I don't understand you at all."

He stood up. "That's obvious," he said. And left.

Banshee sat with me as I stared out the window puzzled, sad, and filled with foreboding.

A week or so later, Doug announced that the actress he had been seeing while in the play was visiting Los Angeles with her parents, and he wanted us all to have dinner together at Don the Beachcomber's.

"Well," I reasoned to myself, "it was all in your imagination. He wouldn't have wanted us to meet, particularly with her parents there, if there had been a romance between them." So I put on my most chic maternity clothes and sallied forth. It was perhaps the worst evening ever.

Doug and the young woman gazed at each other with glowing eyes, hands and knees brushing together "accidentally" while her parents and I made stilted, polite conversation. I longed to turn over the table and hurl the coconut drinks at his head, but due to my English upbringing, loathe to make a scene, I soldiered on.

I sometimes wonder how the evening ended for the actress and her parents. I know it ended in bitter fury for the two of us.

Aside from Michael, the house, and career talk, we did not have a lot in common. We had different expectations of marriage.

According to my upbringing, married couples were best friends as well as lovers, participating in sports together, sharing interests in the arts, etc. Doug's dictated that the sexes were more divided in their duties and interests. He found it strange that I expected to go fishing with the fellows and participate in political discussions. He wanted a perfectly run house and an attractive hostess for the dinner parties we were giving with increasing frequency as his career gained momentum. He also wanted a partner who did not express opinions quite so readily.

The night of my twenty-fourth birthday was celebrated at our friends, the Seltzers. I was very pregnant, but the expected birth was two or three weeks away. They had laid out a groaning board replete with lobster and champagne. We toasted our friendship and the coming baby until close to two in the morning.

At around four, a familiar mule kick in the back awakened me. "I think this is it."

"Indigestion. It's that lobster and champagne," Doug mumbled and went back to sleep.

I lay in the dark, awaiting the next contraction and trying to get a rough timing on them. Finally, I went into the bathroom, checking the pains on my watch. They were about six minutes apart.

I shook Doug awake. As we drove downtown to Cedars of Lebanon Hospital, they suddenly increased in frequency.

"Don't worry about the stoplights, just keep going," I muttered and resumed whistling.

"Why do you keep whistling 'All the nice girls love a sailor'?" asked Doug.

"Just keep going."

As we pulled up to the front of Cedars, I opened the door.

"Wait till I find a parking space."

"No time." I went galumphing up the steps and tore over to the admissions desk. Panting, I said, "I'm having a baby. I need to get upstairs right away."

The nurse surveyed my pigtails and scrubbed face. "Now, now child. There's no need to get excited. You've plenty of time. First babies always take longer. Let's just take down the information…"

"Goddammit, it's my second baby, and I'm going to have it here on the floor if…" And with that my water broke. It was five-thirty.

At a quarter to six, Joel Andrew Douglas made his appearance. They had tried to delay his birth by holding my legs together while they splashed Mercurochrome and wielded a hasty razor, calling for the doctor, but he was not to be deterred.

Doug had found a parking space and had just settled down in the waiting room with the morning paper when a nurse poked her head around the door.

"Mr. Douglas?" Doug looked up.

"Don't tell me she's had the caudal analgesia already?"

The nurse smiled. "You are the father of a baby boy.

Doug said he damn near fainted. "*That's* why you kept whistling that tune over and over," he said to me later.

At six I called Mickey Seltzer. "Hey, guess what?" There was silence on the other end, then Mickey cleared her throat. "What?" she said sleepily.

"Guess who just arrived?"

Another silence. Then: "My God, you couldn't have! We just said good night to you on the doorstep!"

After five days in the hospital, I returned home.

We thought we had prepared Michael for the arrival of the baby, but sibling rivalry reared its head immediately. The first time he saw me holding the baby, tears welled in his eyes, and his face flushed. "No, Mommy! No, Mommy!"

Quickly, I handed the baby to the nurse and picked him up, hugging him. "It's okay, Mikey, it's okay. That's your little brother, and you can help me take care of him."

He shook his head vehemently at the idea. It took a few months before he stopped glaring at Joel, but as the baby began to crawl, he took an interest in his efforts and finally became quite protective of the little guy.

Later, when Joel was a toddler, I had them both down on the beach at Santa Monica. Michael was building sand castles by my side, but Joel seemed fascinated by the waves and kept heading toward the shore. After stopping him a few times, I decided to see how far he would go before the noise of the waves stopped him. I knew I could move fast if he was in danger.

Michael looked up from his labors and tore down the beach, grabbing Joel in his arms.

"You *watch* that baby!" he shouted at me.

"Michael, it's all right..."

"No, it's not! You *watch* that baby."

He always was a responsible kid.

Doug and I became more immersed in the party life of the movie colony. Two incidents stood out in our busy social life.

The first was a party at Armand Deutche and his wife, Benay Venuta's house, a black-tie affair. This was an *A* party as they used to call them then. (I think the term originated with Atwater Kent, who actually has his A, B, and C lists.) I had always thought of myself as able to cope socially and was not intimidated even though I knew hardly anyone there. I moved around the room, introducing myself, as our hostess disappeared, as did Doug, through the French doors with a beautiful blonde married to Cornel Wilde.

I was met with the most astonishing rudeness I had ever encountered. Cold, fishy stares; people turning away. I actually heard an exchange:

"Who *is* she?"

"Probably some starlet."

I was suddenly acutely aware of my off-the-rack Macy's evening dress and how it stood out amid all the designer numbers. Then I spotted a familiar face, Van Heflin's wife Frances was sitting at the bar by herself. She waved me over.

"This, kid, is called a French seventy-five," she said, raising her glass. "Have one. It'll do you good. Have two, it'll do you better."

After a couple of them, I figured I'd better pull myself together. I headed for the buffet table. Solemnly, I marched out to the swimming pool, balancing my plate. I sat at a table for two by myself, trying to ignore the merry laughter from the tables around me. Frances elected to stay at the bar. I always liked her. She was an outspoken redhead with a penchant for calling a spade a spade. She had little use for the hypocrisy of the movie world. Alas, she was a two-fisted drinker, and I knew that I couldn't keep up with her without falling on my face.

As I sat forking up my food, a man approached from an adjoining table. I looked up. He was a pleasant-looking, middle-aged man wearing glasses and a kindly grin.

"May I join you?"

I gulped. My recent wallflower status made me suspicious of a normal, friendly gesture.

"Please do," I quavered.

"Benny!" came the voices from the next table. "Benny, darling, what are you doing? Come back here."

The man shook his head and waved them away as he sat down. I realized then that my table companion was Benny Goodman. We smiled at each other. He cleared his throat.

"Warm weather we've been having lately," he offered.

I nodded vigorously.

"But it certainly was cold before." I replied. Oh, God, where had all my social graces gone?

"You're new out here?"

I nodded.

132 In The Wings

"You'll find it's not such a bad place, once you get used to it."

"Benny, Benny dear," came the chorus from the other table.

I got up.

"Thank you for your company. Now I have to find my friend who's inside. Bye."

"Good luck, kid," he said.

A kind gentleman as well as a great musician.

The other party that comes to mind was one hosted by Leonard Spiegelgass, a screenwriter of great elegance. Noel Coward was the guest of honor. Although he had been entertained by my family in Bermuda, it was during my days at the academy. I had never met him and was anxious to do so. I had quizzed my mother when I'd heard that he had been at Newbold Place, but she couldn't seem to remember him. She suggested I ask my father.

"Daddy, was Noel Coward really here?"

Father scratched his head.

"Coward...Coward...Yes, there was a sublieutenant Coward here for a cocktail party. That's right."

"Well, what was he like?"

"I dunno. Seemed a bit of a bounder to me." Sometimes I could have killed my family.

Doug and I dressed for the Spiegelgas party with anticipation and excitement. The evening was a success. At the end of it, eight or ten people clustered around the piano demanding songs. Noel complied, doodling his way through "Mad About the Boy."

"Any others?" he asked.

"How about 'Don't Say Good-bye'?" I asked.

He looked up, astonished. "You can't know that song. That was from a musical of that only ran a week in London back in 1933."

"I know. I was there."

"You weren't! Do you remember the lyrics?"

I nodded.

"Then would you get up on the piano and sing them with me?"

Feeling like the all-time belle of the ball, I hoisted myself up onto the piano and harmonized with the master, remembering every word:

"Don't say good-bye...
Somehow it's wrong..."

It was the first time I'd seen Doug look impressed.

"You're amazing," said Mr. Coward. "You must have been a toddler when that came out."

"I was ten," I replied. "But I loved the musical, I remember every song."

"It was one of my favorites too. I was heartbroken when it didn't go. Let's do the whole score."

And we did. It may have bored the hell out of the rest of the party, but we had a whale of a time.

Before Joel was born, we decided that the house would be too small for both boys. A live-in nanny would be needed if I was to go back to work, so we fixed up the little guest cottage, which was on the property.

I had spent the last months of my pregnancy painting fanciful figures from the nursery rhymes on the walls where the boys would be. The nanny would have the large adjoining room, and there was a little kitchen and bathroom. An intercom attached it to the main house.

We hired a distinguished-looking Bostonian, Mrs. Bonillas, who came highly recommended and seemed to enjoy being around children. Her father had been the ambassador to Mexico. She had married a Mexican and was now widowed with a son, living somewhere in L.A.

She seemed like the answer to our prayers domestically, enabling us to concentrate on our careers. It wasn't until many months later that I discovered gin bottles hidden all over the cottage. It explained her diffident aloofness and the strong odor of peppermint that surrounded her.

In the fall of 1947, Michael started nursery school, and I went to work over at Columbia in *Sign of the Ram*.

134 In The Wings

Dame May Whitty was in the cast, a delightful old English character actress who served tea in her dressing room every afternoon. Also Alexander Knox who, with his wife Doris, became good friends of mine.

Susan Peters was the star. She had suffered a terrible accident and was confined to a wheelchair. On her honeymoon, she and her new husband had gone hunting. Climbing over a fence, he had stumbled and his gun discharged a bullet that pierced her spine, making her a paraplegic for life.

This same husband, Richard Quine, was now directing the film that was to be her return to acting. She was beautiful, painfully thin, and the shooting schedule had to be juggled around her rest periods.

I had the ingenue lead, an interesting part and not the usual sweet little thing. In the script, I was engaged to her stepson, a romance she was determined to break up for nondescript reasons with definite sexual overtones.

We had one marvelously confrontational scene with all the stops pulled out, and afterwards the crew broke into applause and the makeup man confided in me that they were taking bets that I would be nominated in the supporting category come Oscar time. I tried not to take it seriously, but it was lovely to hear. The scene was later cut in a way that focused on Susan's lovely face while I emoted in a long shot or off camera. It was my first clue as to how cinema is first and last the director's medium.

I finished the film feeling I had done good work and that I was beginning to learn something of the technique of movie acting. Benno Schneider, who had been the test director at Fox, gave me a good tip about not projecting.

"Trust the camera," he had said. "If your thoughts are correct, truthful, and clear the camera will go right into your eyes and pick them up."

For some time, Doug had been urging me to become an American citizen. I had not been particularly enthusiastic about the idea. I didn't really feel American, but practically speaking, it made sense particularly in terms of traveling. Both my children were citizens, and I was living and paying taxes in this country.

I applied for papers and dutifully studied American history—of which I'd been woefully ignorant. Finally the day dawned when I was due to be sworn in.

I am ashamed to say that I woke with a hangover that morning. Doug and I had been partying until the wee hours the night before. I groaned at the idea of the journey to downtown L.A. closeted with others in a courtroom, but I grumbled my way there. I was seated next to an elderly man, well into his nineties.

I looked around at all the faces, glowing in anticipation, the man next to me, trembling with excitement, and I began to realize what a gift citizenship can be.

When we were finally sworn in, the old man embraced me.

"Congratulations! We've made it!" He made me ashamed, and I had a hard time not weeping.

Early in 1948, I did a small film produced by Frank Seltzer (brother of Walter Seltzer) called *Let's Live Again*. Meanwhile fascinating things began happening with Doug's career.

He turned down the second lead in an M.G.M. movie, much to the consternation of agents who felt they were building his career slowly and carefully. He then agreed to do a film by a young producer named Stanley Kramer.

Stanley had only produced one movie before, a comedy which had done so-so business, but he was working on a script with Carl Foreman that had him very excited. It was called *Champion*.

They met regularly at our house as they worked on the script, involving Doug in it at every level. I kept them well supplied with sandwiches and drinks, intrigued by the creativity and enthusiasm that seemed to bounce off the walls.

I think everyone involved was under thirty.

When they started shooting, Doug asked that I not visit

the set as it would make him self-conscious. I agreed not to do so, although I was disappointed at having to miss the results of all the conferences I'd witnessed. Later I learned that this was the start of his romance with Marilyn Maxwell, a leading lady in the film.

When shooting was over, we took the children and Mrs. Bonillas to Bermuda for a visit with my family. My mother hadn't seen Michael since he was a toddler and had never met Joel, who instantly won her heart with his happy laughter.

Ostensibly, we were there for a happy family vacation, but we were both aware of undertones that precluded it. We both engaged in stupid flirtations at parties, each looking for a reaction from the other. We were testy and short with each other in private, our one meeting ground now seemed to be the children, to whom we were both devoted.

If my family sensed there was something amiss, they said nothing.

On our return to L.A., I was asked to do *The Hasty Heart* at the Lobero Theatre in Santa Barbara. Roddy McDowall played Lachie and Tom Brown played Yank. I, of course, was playing Sister. I jumped at the thought of working on stage again. Mrs. Bonillas seemed to have the children well in hand, and Doug was not working at the moment so I left for Santa Barbara with a high heart.

It was a good working experience. Rogers Brackett was a competent director. Roddy was touching in the role of Lachie, and Tom Brown was a very good Yank when he was off the bottle. Unfortunately, he was known to tipple before a performance. On one memorable night, he forgot the entire roster of the books of the Old Testament that Yank was proud to have memorized. After making up a few unintelligible names, he said "Aw, hell, you know the rest," leaving the cast and audience totally bewildered.

When I returned, Doug's career had shifted into high gear. With the imminent release of *Champion*, he had hired a publicity agent, Warren Cowan of the newly formed firm

Rogers and Cowan. Warren was around the house continually calling Doug "Champ" and buttering him up no end. Doug's ego, never a small one, swelled visibly under the stroking, and I viewed the developments with a caustic eye. Doug accused me of being jealous of his career.

"I'm not jealous. I'm the loyal opposition."

"What do you mean?"

"I'm on your side. I'm loyal. But someone's got to tell you when you're full of shit."

It was not appreciated.

Things deteriorated during the fall. Doug's absences became more frequent, and I started working at an acting class run by Batami Schneider, Benno's wife, in the evenings. I spent the days playing with the children.

By January, it was clear that a separation was in the offing, but I still could not bring myself to face it. Joe Mankiewicz had cast me in *House of Strangers* with the proviso that I bleach my dark hair blonde. It was a story point, she being the only WASP in an Italian family headed by Edward G. Robinson.

So off I would traipse to the makeup department at Fox daily to have the color stripped out of my hair and then replaced with lighter and lighter shades.

"Mommy," said Michael when I got out of the car, "You have magic hair. It changes color every day."

In the makeup chair, I was also privy to the gossip going around the studios, a lot of it having to do with Doug and his inamoratas

He said later he realized the marriage was over when he came home and found me kicking his shirts viciously into the closet, swearing a blue streak. As I said previously, the separation announcement was worked out with the ever-present Warren.

Doug moved out, and I went to work

On the day the announcement hit the papers, Joe Mankiewicz closed the set to reporters, much to my relief.

Everyone on the set was being extra kind and gentle,

but not mentioning anything about the news. However, Luther Adler, who was playing my husband, kept eyeing me with a speculative air.

"Come for lunch," he said, tucking his arm through mine as we headed for the commissary.

Then, as we sat down, "How old are you, kid?"

"Twenty-six."

"Twenty-six. I'm in my forties. I can't remember what it feels like to be twenty-six. You must be in a lot of pain. Huh?"

My defenses shot up.

"It's not the best of times."

"Don't give me that stiff upper-lip British shit. You're losing your husband. You've got two small children. You must be hurting like hell."

I tried to stop the tears from welling up in my eyes.

"Let it go. Use it. You're an actor, use all the pain, all the emotion. Walk down lonely streets, look into lighted windows at happy families. And use it. Use it. It's actor's gold."

It was wonderfully astringent after all the careful cosseting. I laughed through my tears.

"You son of a bitch, that's the best advice that's been given me to date. Thank you."

Mr. Robinson said my shoulders looked tense and that he would be delighted to massage them for me, which he did between shots. Joe said later that it was lucky that I was not privy to the lascivious gleam in his eye while he performed that function.

Blissfully unconscious, I involved him in a discussion about the American Academy, which I learned he had attended. It hit a nerve.

"That sadistic son of a bitch Jehlinger?" he exploded. "I couldn't take his riding me anymore, and I picked up a table off the stage and threw it at his head. Wish I'd killed the bastard."

"Oh, so *you* were the one!"

It was part of the lore of the American Academy that a

nameless student had once thrown a table at Jelly from the stage, who was knocked down, but never once missed a beat of his critique and went right on talking while the student fled the stage and the academy. I was glad to find out the story was true.

I went home to a quiet and empty house.

I thought about moving the children down to the main house to be with me, but they seemed to be thriving under Mrs. Bonillas's supervision. It seemed wrong to disrupt their lives while I was in such a shaky emotional state.

Unfortunately with a separation, people often feel they have to take sides. A lot of my erstwhile friends disappeared. Notable exceptions were the Seltzers and the Knoxes, who were warm and supportive.

The first dinner party I went to after the separation was at the Knoxes.

"Don't bring a date," chirped Doris when she called. "We have a date set up for you."

My imagination ran riot. Cary Grant, I thought, he's single now. Yippee!

When I arrived at their house, Alex ushered me into their Victorian bar. My date was sitting on a bar stool with his back to me.

"Diana," said Alex, "I'd like you to meet Barry Fitzgerald."

The little Irishman was probably in his sixties, not quite what I had in mind, but I have rarely had a more pleasant or more amusing evening. He was one of the great raconteurs of all time. I forgot my troubles and laughed my head off.

The fan magazines of the time, some of which resembled today's tabloids, managed to get my unlisted number and made my life hell until I got it changed. One call in the middle of the night: "We want an exclusive on *your* version of the split-up."

"There is no *my* version."

"He's running around with a different girl every night. How does that make you feel?"

"Please get off the phone."
"Don't you want to get back at him?"
"I'm hanging up."
And I did.
The phone rang again.

"Mrs. Douglas," the voice said, "I understand you're an actress. I just want you to know that since you've been so uncooperative, none of our publications will ever give you an ounce of publicity. You will never be mentioned no matter how successful you become."

"Fine by me."

And I slammed down the receiver.

It was a bewildering time. Men, some of them buddies of Doug's, some married, some single, started calling me up. I was a soon-to-be-divorcee and fair game. I turned most of them down, but drifted into an affair with a young actor in Batami's class. His adoration soothed my badly bruised ego and met my physical appetites, but I was emotionally drained and had little to give him in return.

As has often happened in my life, work saved me.

I was asked to do *Major Barbara* at the Circle Theatre, a small theatre-in-the-round located in Hollywood. It had earned a certain prestige doing interesting productions and attracting some local "names." It was supported by the likes of Charlie Chaplin, Katharine Hepburn, and Constance Collier.

Jerry Epstein was the producer, and a young Englishman, Terry Kilburn, was the director. Alex Geary played Undershaft and Ron Randell, Cusins.

I had never played Shaw before and found him challenging and brilliant. However, the third act gave us all trouble. In it, Shaw gets off all his political beliefs by putting them in the mouths of the three principal characters seemingly without reference to what has gone on before.

Different directors were brought in during rehearsal to have a crack at it, to no avail. One of them came up with a cockamamie idea of having the play open with Barbara giving a "Come to Jesus" speech, written by him, of course. Constance Collier put a stop to that when she saw it.

"Diana is very persuasive, and, sure as shooting, one night you will have some drunk in the audience decide he needs to be saved. With the theatre in the round, your play goes out the window."

On opening night after the performance, there was always a discussion. Charlie Chaplin and Oona were there, as was Robert Morley, who played Undershaft in the film of *Major Barbara.*

"How," we asked, "was the third act dealt with in the movie?"

"Well," said Mr. Morley, "Gabriel Pascal, who directed the film, was flummoxed by it, so he called G. B. S. down in Ayot St. Lawrence and asked him what he should do about it. According to him, Shaw said 'I haven't read it since 1912. Let me take another look at it and call you back.' He called back. 'The third act is unplayable. Do whatever you want with it.'"

We all felt better.

Luther came to a performance and hid his face with his hand, peering through his fingers.

"Good Lord, was I so bad that you couldn't bear to look?"

"My dear girl, I have never been to a theatre in the round before. I thought it would distract you to see me so I was trying to hide."

"Well, don't do it anymore!"

Many years later I ran into someone else who was there opening night.

In 1993 I was in Majorca visiting Michael and Diandra (his wife) when Michael told me he was arranging a luncheon because Norman Lear was on the island and wanted to see me again.

"I've great admiration for the man," I said. "But he must have me confused with someone else. We've never met."

"Well I dunno, he seems to know you all right." Indeed,

when he arrived, he came across the terrace with outstretched hands.

"At last!" he said. Then, "No, we've never actually met, but without your knowing it, you played a part in my coming to California."

He told us that as a very young man, he had driven across country with baby and wife on the promise of a job in L.A. They had both taken an instant dislike to the city and figured that they would probably return to the East Coast on completion of the job.

His first night in Hollywood, after getting settled in a motel, Norman decided to stroll around the neighborhood. He happened to pass a small theatre where a man was sweeping the sidewalk.

Upon inquiring, he was told that *Major Barbara* was opening that night. It was sold out save for a single ticket.

"That night changed my whole attitude about Hollywood. If a Shaw production of this caliber is possible, this place ain't all bad. Culture is alive and well here."

And he and his family remained in California.

Charlie Chaplin had not done a film since *Monsieur Verdoux* and was itching to perform. He entertained us for over an hour with priceless stories, performing each character to perfection. Oona sat knitting, casting a maternal eye on him and smiling a gentle, Madonna-like smile.

Finally, she said, "That's it, Charlie. Time to go."

"Just one more story," he pleaded. "Just one more."

"All right, then. But only one."

It was strange to think that he was her senior by more than forty years.

The next week, a large engraved invitation arrived inviting me and my children to Michael Chaplin's birthday party. I was surprised at the invitation as our children didn't know each other, but Jerry Epstein urged me to go. So I dressed the boys in their white flannel shorts and striped blazers and drove up to the Chaplin estate.

Oona was gracious and charming and remembered that

we had met as teenagers in Bermuda when she was down there with her father. While talking to her, I spied Joel going like a bat out of hell for the swimming pool and sped after him.

Too late. He plunged into the water and came up sputtering. I was busily hauling him out, with my butt in the air, when I heard a whirring sound behind me. There was Charlie Chaplin taking a home movie of the rescue.

I smiled and walked away, but wherever I turned, Mr. Chaplin seemed to have that camera aimed at me.

"You're a dancer, aren't you?" he asked.

"No, I'm not."

"But you have danced. You move like a dancer."

"No, I have never danced."

"Never even studied ballet?"

"'Fraid not. Why do you ask?"

He smiled enigmatically.

Later, Constance Collier told me that he had thought me a likely candidate for the lead in *Limelight*.

If he had confided in me, I would have raced to the nearest ballet class.

Poor little Michael had an accident during the run of the play. Driving by Hollywood High School with Michael in the front seat, we passed some students rough-housing. One pushed the other directly in front of my car, and I swerved quickly, hitting a car in the fast lane. Mike went right into the windshield and dropped to the floor, quickly covered by packages from the backseat.

He had a nasty gash on his chin, and I drove quickly to the emergency room at a Hollywood hospital. He was frightened and sobbing, but they would not let me stay with him while they stitched him up, despite my protestations that I would stay calm and not faint. Stupid of them and heartbreaking for Michael and me.

There wasn't time to take him home and still get to the theatre, so I schlepped him down to the Circle, his head wrapped like a mummy, talking between his teeth.

"I can't open my mouth at all," he told the lighting man in the booth, where he had been deposited.

"Not even to slip a candy in?"

Michael considered.

"Well, maybe I could open it just that much."

He sat quietly watching the whole performance of *Major Barbara* even though it was hardly fare for a four year old.

I often had dinner with Constance Collier around this time. She was a wonderful, vigorous old actress who had acted with Henry Irving and Beerbohm-Tree and had co-authored the play *Peter Ibbetson*. She was a great raconteur and full of marvelous theatre stories. I could listen to her for hours.

One evening, she said, "Something very interesting may be coming up for you."

"Stop being mysterious, Constance. What?"

"Kate was at the performance the other night."

"Kate? Kate who?"

"Kate Hepburn, of course. She wants to recommend you for a part."

"Katharine Hepburn wants to recommend *me* for a part?"

"It's Philip Barry's new play, *Second Threshold*. The script was given to her, but she feels that she is too old for the part and wants to recommend you to Mr. Barry. She said she felt as though you were her younger sister."

I was so damn flattered I could barely breathe.

"You'd have to go to New York to meet Mr. Barry and possibly read for him. I suppose you wouldn't have any objection?"

"Um...no...no..."

But my mind was racing...what to do with the children? I had recently had to fire Mrs. Bonillas whose secret drinking problem had been revealed.

A day or so later, when Doug came over to visit the boys, I confided in him.

"For once," he said, "have the guts to be totally selfish. Go for it. I'll move back here and watch the boys."

I could have hugged him, and probably did.

I flew back to New York and booked into the Meurice Hotel where Ron and Terry were already ensconced (rehearsing a new *Candida* production), a lovely old place on Fifty-eighth Street with the ambiance of a London club.

The pace and diversity of New York hit me like a charge of adrenaline. I loved walking down Sixth Avenue, seeing a ragged bum rubbing shoulders with a mink-clad matron. People of every race and color, fast and purposeful.

I prepared for my interview and went over to see Philip Barry in his Park Avenue apartment.

"Kate tells me you're quite something," he greeted me. "I'd hate to have to ask you to read."

"No, I'd be delighted to."

"Sure you don't mind?"

It went well.

"As far as I'm concerned, you're it. Delly has the final say, though."

"Delly?"

"Alfred de Liagre, the producer. He won't be back from Europe until next month, but I'm sure he'll agree with me."

I almost skipped back to the hotel, and Ron and Terry and I had a celebratory dinner. Then I called home to talk to Doug and the boys. A strange woman answered the phone and said that Kirk was out. I asked to speak to Michael.

"That was Auntie Irene. She's living here now."

I had heard that Doug was seeing Irene Wrightsman, but thought it a bit much that she was living in the house.

A decision had to be made.

Chapter 9
DIVORCE

I consulted with a lawyer I'd heard about through friends. His name was Arnold Krakower, and he was married to the author Kathleen Winsor. I was not sure whether I wanted a legal separation or a divorce, but I knew I needed some legal position to stop being on the reactive end to Doug's shenanigans.

After talking with Arnold, giving the general history of the marriage, it became clear to me that divorce was the only answer. I decided I'd better face up to it and make a clean break.

But it was painful, like a small death. A part of me loved him still, loved the gutsy youngster who had fought his way out of the slums of Amsterdam, New York. I loved the cocky, young actor who was brought to heel by Jehlinger, the wildly romantic young man singing, "They'll Never Believe Me" as we walked the streets of New York. I even loved the infuriating clown who followed me around a party at the Cowans' on his knees declaring, "Anyone can see I'm not worthy of you!" after he had stood me up for a liaison with Miss Maxwell.

That time I had left him a note. "I have gone to the Cowans' and you can go to hell." His secret weapon was that no matter how hurt or angry I was, he could almost always find a way to make me laugh, as he eventually did at the Cowans' party.

A day or so after my meeting with Arnold Krakower, my mother flew into New York on her way back from England. She was getting to be quite the international traveler now, and it was great to see her gaining in confidence. I met her at Idlewild and spotted her right away by the cheery red feather in her hat as she bounced down the runway.

When we got back to the suite at the Meurice, the phone was ringing. It was Doug, wondering when I was coming back. I was cool, which always seemed to act like an aphrodisiac to him, and he told me that Irene had moved out and that he and the children were looking forward to my being there for Thanksgiving, which we would all spend together. This time I would not be the yo-yo on the end his string. I told him that I would think about it, but right now I had just picked up my mother.

"Ma D. is there?" he said delightedly. "Put her on."

Mother's face glowed as she chatted with him, laughing merrily at his sallies while my spirits sank lower.

"That dear boy," she said as she hung up, still laughing.

I took a deep breath.

"Mummy," I said, "I have something to tell you. I'm going to divorce that dear boy."

Mother looked at me blankly for a moment, in total shock. Then she wet her lips, shaking her head.

"Tell you what," she said, "I think you'd better mix us a drink."

"Oh Lord, I'm sorry. I don't have anything here."

"Well, you'd better run down to the chemists or wherever they sell the stuff in this country and get us some gin and vermouth."

I complied quickly, wanting to give her a chance to absorb the news.

When I came back, she had changed out of her travel clothes and bathed.

"Well," she said as she took her first sip of the martini, "I gather this is not a sudden decision."

"Oh God, no." I prepared to launch into a litany of Doug's transgressions, but she waved it away.

"Darling," she said, "no one really knows what goes on inside a marriage except the two people involved. Sometimes even they have a skewed viewpoint. I've always had faith in your judgment, and if you've thought it over and decided it's the right thing to do, then it's the right thing to do."

I could have cried with relief, because divorce was not taken lightly in my family. To this day in our enormous clan, I think there have only been three.

It was hard for her, for she was fond of Doug. Until she died, a photo of him hung in the study at Newbold Place.

When I flew back to L.A., the house was banked with flowers for my homecoming. Doug had decided on a reconciliation, the boys were joyous.

After putting them to bed, I told him about my decision to divorce. He was taken aback, but asked me to wait before making a move until I had talked to the psychiatrist he had started seeing in the past few months. He said it was for the boys' sake and asked if we could continue to live in the same house as the affair with Irene was over.

I felt the tentacles of manipulation once again, but knew that some inner boundary had been crossed that could never be regained. I agreed to see his doctor. I was angry that Irene had seen fit to redecorate our entire house, but agreed that temporarily we would both stay there, in separate rooms.

I liked his doctor immediately. He was no-nonsense, honest, and clear about my options.

"Kirk is a restless and unhappy man," he said. "No matter what you do or don't do, he will be a restless and unhappy man. The infidelity is just a part of it. It's up to you to decide what you can put up with and what you can't."

I could have kissed him. I realized that I had felt it my duty to make Doug happy, and when I couldn't, I felt like an utter failure.

That night Doug and I had our first truly honest discussion.

"I can't take constant infidelity," I said. "It shatters me as a woman. And I really don't think you are capable of being monogamous, are you?"

He took a long time in answering.

"No," he said finally. "You're right. I'm not."

I loved him then because he freed me. The way was clear for divorce.

"Well," he said, "first you'll have to get a good lawyer."

"I already have one. Someone I met in New York."

"Probably some schmuck. I'll have him investigated."

"No, really, I'm quite satisfied with him."

The next day he eyed me with a quizzical look.

"Listen, Little Miss Red Riding Hood, how come you got yourself the number one divorce lawyer in New York?"

I burst out laughing.

"No kidding? Arnold's really that good?"

"You mean you didn't know it?"

I shook my head.

"Only you," he said wonderingly. "Your Mr. Krakower represented Kathleen Winsor when she got her divorce from Artie Shaw and got her a whale of a settlement. Then he went ahead and married her."

"Wow."

Doug asked me to delay filing for the divorce until the first of the year, due to some tax advantages for him. I complied, but said that a lot would depend on when rehearsals would start for *Second Threshold*.

One morning I picked up the paper. "Philip Barry, noted playwright, dies," was the headline. I wrote a note of condolence to Mrs. Barry and after a week or so another note to Arnold de Liagre asking if I was still being considered for the part.

His secretary called me back. Mr. de Liagre had cast the part...Margaret Philips was playing it.

That, coupled with the tension of living again in the same house with Doug, left me stressed and depressed, and I told Doug that I was going to drive down to Mexico to walk the beach, read, and think.

"You can't drive down there alone," he said. "I won't allow it."

"Allow it? Oh, come on!"

"It's not safe," he said pointing to an article in the morning paper about bandits ambushing some tourists.

I then suggested that I drive down with a friend of ours who was openly homosexual. Doug agreed, joking that he knew I'd be safe in *every* way with this gallant gentleman.

What I didn't tell him on my return was that the gallant gentleman suddenly decided to change his orientation one moonlit night in Ensenada, much to my surprise and ultimate satisfaction. The rest of the time I walked the beach and read Schopenhauer, which only depressed me further.

January rolled around and with it my twenty-seventh birthday and my due date in court. We rehearsed the testimony so that it should be as innocuous as possible, but "mental cruelty" being the grounds. Warren Cowan's wife, Ronnie, was coached as a witness, relishing her moment on the stand.

Prior to the actual date, Arnold and Doug's lawyer got into a fistfight in the law office, to our shock. Doug and I were being very civilized. He felt that the children and I should have everything we needed, and I protested that Doug had worked so hard for his success that we shouldn't stick it to him just as he was starting to enjoy the fruits of it. Both lawyers were frustrated by our attitude, compounded by the fact that Doug's lawyer had represented Artie Shaw in that divorce case and had been seething ever since. Someone said something amiss and in a minute they were trading blows over the table, while Doug and I looked on amazed.

On the morning of the court date, Doug meticulously checked out my wardrobe (television cameras would be there when I left the courthouse), and in the evening, we sat drinking beer and critiquing the performance together. It sounds cold-blooded. It was perhaps the only way as actors we could get through an excruciating time.

Ruth called to say that she had seen it on the news in the east, then said, "Do you remember dear old Frank

Patton?"

"Frank Patton? A friend of Father's. I met him once or twice. Why?"

"He died."

"Oh, that's too bad, but he was very old, wasn't he?"

"Yes. Do you want his apartment?"

"What?"

"His apartment. Apartments are very hard to get in New York right now, and his is on Central Park West and Eighty-fifth Street. Two bedrooms and a maid's room."

I started to laugh.

"You ghoul!" I said. "God bless you. You bet I'll take it!"

I had fallen in love with New York again on my recent visit. The budding television industry was coming to flower there with "live" dramatic shows, and, best of all, I would be separating myself from Hollywood and all its bitter memories.

I had been granted sole custody of the children with liberal visitation rights for their father. It must have been very painful for Doug when the decision was made to move them to the East Coast, but he raised no objections, and we flew back in early February.

Chapter 10
NEW YORK REDUX

The apartment was perfect for our needs, and while it was being painted, we stayed at the Meurice while I researched the school situation. Michael had just turned six and was ready for kindergarten and checking with Leila Hadley, a woman I had met when last in New York, decided on Allen Stevenson, a fairly conservative school with a good academic rating. Unfortunately, it was on the East Side, which meant delivering him by taxi every morning, but its reputation made it worth it.

As we moved into the apartment, I felt my spirits rise. How many people, I asked myself, are given the liberty of a totally fresh start at the age of twenty-seven? I had enough to live on, though not in luxury, even if I didn't work. I had good health, and so did my children.

Michael, however, had been showing signs of deep anger since the divorce and from being a compatible, tractable child, had suddenly become very stubborn and rebellious. He challenged me at every turn. I took him to a child psychologist who observed him in play therapy and then lectured me gently.

"This is not a deeply disturbed child at all. He has suffered a loss and blames you for it. Ease up on the discipline and give him loads of love till he feels secure."

"Ease up on the discipline? Are you sure? I really don't believe in permissive parenting."

"I'm sure. My bet is that you're getting a bit rigid with your responsibilities as an only parent. He'll ask for rules again as he gets more secure."

I had my suspicions, but, by golly, she was right, and as I became more gentle, so did he and our confrontations eventually all but ceased. Joel was seemingly blithe and mischievous, but his sunny demeanor hid a lot of sensitivity and pain that would not surface till later.

I put him into a morning nursery program that was nearby while Mike went to Allen Stevenson, hired a housekeeper (or as she preferred to call herself, a governess) named Mrs. Doubrava. She had been an opera singer and Miss Prague of 1913. We got a dog named Sam, who would stand in the window seat and point at Central Park. We all settled ourselves in.

Leila Hadley had left town, and I realized that I knew nobody in the city. I would take the children out to Ruth's place in New Brunswick every now and again, but her husband Phil was always gruff and unpleasant, and the kids were quite cowed, by him so we didn't do it often.

I acquired an agent and soon started to work regularly on the television shows, but the evenings were long and lonely. Romance was the furthest thing from my mind. I would have liked to have someone to go to the movies with, someone to pal around with.

Unexpectedly one day I ran into some members of the Circle Theatre. They were in New York trying their luck, as I was. Pat Englund, Herb Sargent, Marilyn Clark and her husband who had the unlikely name of Daniel Hollywood, as well as George Englund, Pat's brother and his girlfriend, Cloris Leachman. We would meet in the park, swap stories, and play word games.

The park figured largely in our lives. I would take the children there after school to play on the swings. On Saturdays, we would rent horses, and the kids and I would ride round the reservoir until Sam got to know every hillock and good peeing place. In the summer, we'd play tennis on the courts up at Ninetieth Street.

It was a great time for theatre. *Streetcar Named Desire* was playing, as was *Death of a Salesman*. I had remembered

Arthur Kennedy (or Johnny, as we called him) coming to our house in California, saying that he had been sent the script of a play with the wacky title *Death of a Salesman* and he was thinking of accepting it. Now I saw him on stage as Biff, and I couldn't believe the nakedness of his performance. It was so deeply personal that somehow you felt that you shouldn't be watching. Johnny really had greatness in him, and I'll never know why he didn't become a major star.

I got a call from the Theatre Guild saying that Katharine Hepburn was going to do Rosalind in *As You Like It* and had recommended me for the part of Celia. Would I please come down to the guild offices and read with her for Armina Marshall and Lawrence Langner? This lady was turning out to be my fairy godmother, and I got myself down there posthaste.

She greeted me warmly, and the reading went well, but I could see that Mr. Langner looked uncomfortable.

"Kate," he said finally, "in the play Celia is referred to as 'the little one,' and Diana is a good two inches taller than you."

Hepburn frowned, then her face cleared.

"Never mind," she said. "I can wear cork soles, and Diana can *think* small."

It cut no ice. Cloris Leachman got the part, and, I must say, was charming in it. Years later I was living in Westport when the guild called and asked if I would be willing to tour with Miss Hepburn, playing Celia. I had to give my regrets. Two kids in school and a new marriage had changed my priorities.

It amused me that the guild did not consider me too tall for the provinces, only New York. I suspect Miss Hepburn had gone up to bat for me once again, bless her.

 It is always a juggling act being a wife, mother, and actress with continual choices to be made. I might have been more successful as a mother or as an actress or even as a wife had I been more single-minded and opted for one or the other, but I doubt that my life would have been as rich, or as much fun. Understanding sons and husband helped too, God knows.

Barbara Van Sleet, the sister of my academy boyfriend Bill Van Sleet, had become a friend of mine as my pool of acquaintances widened. She said that she was going to be married to a man in advertising named Win Levine and would I please be her matron of honor. I accepted with pleasure. Herb Sargent and I had started dating, and the four of us spent some companionable weekends in the country, sometimes with the children, sometimes without. I was beginning to make a life for myself in New York.

One day Ruth dropped by with an actress friend of hers, Eleanor Phelps, who had just been through a messy divorce with a Dane, Hafdan Hebo. She was telling me that he had taken their child back to Denmark against the orders of the court and had refused to bring her back to the U.S., so Eleanor had sworn out a warrant against him. On his return, he was thrown in jail.

A few days later, Michael asked if he could wait for the school bus on the corner "like the big boys," instead of being shepherded over in a cab. I agreed, but warned him against getting into any car with a stranger.

Michael sighed and gave me a pitying look.

"Really, Mom! If a guy asked me to get in the car with him, you know what I'd say?"

"What?"

"I'd tell him that a very good friend of mine, Mr. Hebo, is now in jail for doing that very same thing, so he'd better watch his step."

I smiled at the vision of a potential child molester being confronted by the sangfroid of my six year old.

Both boys were extremely active and, as they got older, got into shoving matches that sometimes developed into fisticuffs. Joel gave as good as he got. Though smaller, he was sturdily built and strong, whereas Michael was a string bean and wiry.

One morning I woke from a sound sleep to hear them both shouting and crashing around in their room. I leapt up and rushed to the door to stop the fight.

I must have moved too quickly from a prone position, for the next thing I knew I was flat on the floor, slowly regaining consciousness, my two little angels squatted by my side, discussing the phenomenon.

"Wow!" said one. "Did ya see that? Flat on her face. Didn't even put her hands out to save herself."

"Yeah," agreed the other. "Just like she was shot in the gut with a forty-five."

"Yeah."

They both loved western movies, and when I bought them a "Puncho" clown (a life-size, weighted, inflatable doll that righted itself every time you knocked it down) to try and persuade them to hit that instead of each other, they promptly held a kangaroo court and sentenced it to death by hanging on Boot Hill.

I was around the corner in the living room when I heard them discussing his fate.

"He's going to have to be strung up, isn't he, Johnson?" said Michael.

"Thath right,'cos he'th been bad, huh, Johnson?" lisped Joel.

(For some obscure reason, both their names were Johnson.)

"It's justice. Right?"

"Thath right."

"No mercy."

"Nope."

"Shall I string 'im up?"

"Okay. String 'im up."

A moment, then an anguished cry from Joel.

"Wait!"

"What is it?"

"I forgot to kith 'im good-bye!"

In November of 1950, I went to Portsmouth, New

Hampshire, to be in a Louis De Rochemont film called *A Whistle at Eaton Falls*, directed by Robert Siodmak. Lloyd Bridges was the star, and I played his wife. Also in the cast were Dorothy Gish (of the silent film Gish sisters), Carleton Carpenter, Anne Francis, Ernest Borgnine, Murray Hamilton, and James Westmore.

It was a gritty cinéma vérité film about union workers in a small New England town and their disputes with management. De Rochemont and Siodmak preferred to use actual houses rather than build sets for a more realistic look, a postwar trend that had started with Rossellini and was being adapted by certain American filmmakers.

We were all housed in a local hotel where the makeup was done. There were no trailers, dressing rooms, or makeup wagons. It had its advantages in that we all got to know one another intimately, and that kind of familiarity and ease showed up on the screen.

On the other hand, I recall having a hell of a time trying to find a private place to prepare before an emotional scene in which I was told of the death of the Westmore character. I have never been able to cry on cue and have to connect with some disturbing memory when there isn't the logical build that a playwright provides. (Something I've always found difficult about film acting is the need for instant availability of emotion.) I remember climbing over several chairs, settling myself in a corner by a china cabinet, and visualizing the deaths of loved ones until I was a quivering mass of emotional jelly ready to be set off by a word. And then the word came…"Lunch!"

What I did manage to eat came up again immediately. We can only fool the body so much; it doesn't know that we are only poor, ridiculous actors.

Because of the location shooting, there were many days we were housebound because of inclement weather. We all became Monopoly experts, playing long and vicious games and bowling duckpins at the one local bowling alley.

Each night I would chat with my boys in New York and

get all their news of school. Mrs. Doubrava assured me that they were thriving without me and that things were proceeding calmly.

Nineteen fifty sped by with Michael's birthday party in September, an early snowfall that brought sledding in the park, and Christmas with expensive toys from Doug. An exquisite German train set and a miniature Indian tribe.

Meanwhile, I was working quite regularly, doing leads on Studio One, Kraft Theatre, etc. I monitored the boys' television-viewing habits fairly strictly, no crime shows allowed. I instructed Mrs. Doubrava that these orders were to be followed in my absence. One time, however, I came home after acting in a particularly grisly show in which I was murdered to find Michael sitting in front of the set, alone and sobbing.

"Darling! What is it?"

He turned and his face lit up as he sprang across the room into my arms.

"You're alive!" he shouted.

"But of course I'm alive, you silly goose. What's the matter with you?"

"I thought...I thought..." he hiccuped through his sobs.

I confronted Mrs. Doubrava and bawled the hell out of her for permitting him to watch it.

A note on Mrs. Doubrava. She was large and jolly and the children seemed fond of her. In fact a year or so later, when Joel was in the hospital with pneumonia, the one person he asked for other than me was Mrs. Doubrava. So it was with great shock that I learned, after the boys grew up, that she had been abusive, twisting their arms if they didn't obey, in a way that left no bruises.

"But why didn't you tell me?" I asked them then.

"We didn't think any grownup would believe us."

I felt sad and guilty for not being more aware, but then I remembered Fan's and my conspiracy over Captain Wareham, and realized that at times all adults are seen to be in the enemy camp.

For my birthday in January, Herb gifted me with a beautiful especially bound biography of Shaw, with a plaque on the flyleaf saying, "For Diana, a fan of G. B. S. from H. S., a fan of Diana's."

He was a sweet and thoughtful man, but strangely inarticulate. I liked him, but there was no way I could fall in love with him, which I made clear. He chose not to believe me. He liked the children, and they liked him, which was a plus so he stayed around.

Early in 1951, I acted in a film called *Storm Over Tibet*, shot entirely on the lot of General Service Studio in Hollywood, with location footage shot in Tibet.

Back in the 1930s, a Swiss expedition was sent to Everest to shoot a documentary. They got some fantastic footage, some of which was shot in lamaseries. Some was of Sherpa tribesmen doing their wild dances, and some terrifying shots of avalanches. With the outbreak of W.W. II, the reels were stored in a Swiss bank and forgotten.

Ivan Tors was a Hungarian writer-producer and an old friend of mine. He'd heard of their existence and decided to write a contemporary screenplay with Norman Corwin, using the extraordinary location shots.

His co-producer was Lazlo Benedek and the director Andrew (Bundy) Solt, both fellow Hungarians. They managed to find the woman who had been featured in many of the shots. As luck would have it, she had barely aged and was living in Los Angeles. The son of the head of the expedition was teaching at U.C.L.A., the spitting image of his father. These two could bridge the stories.

Rex Reason and I were starred. He played the role of a flyer haunted by the death of his buddy in the Himalayas, and I playing the buddy's widow with whom he falls in love. It was not a great film, but it was amazing that it could be done at all. The location shots are still astounding. Looking at it with a critical eye today, I feel I did a credible job, despite working with the very vain Rex Reason. He was inordinately fond of his profile, so it became difficult to get any eye contact with him.

I flew back to New York after shooting was over, and Doug called to ask if the boys could spend their summer holidays with him. They both seemed amenable to the idea. I gave my permission.

Providentially, Bill Van Sleet, who I had dated at the academy called, and said that he was now producing a summer stock company in Ohio and would I be interested in playing the lead in *Light Up the Sky*?

I got a copy of the play and felt the role of the wildly theatrical actress would be an interesting challenge for me, quite unlike anything I'd done before. I said, "Yes," and the rest of my whole life was changed by that decision.

For it was there I met Bill Darrid.

He was the actor who had been cast in the part of the producer.

It was an inauspicious meeting. Bill was suffering from root-canal work and seemed impossibly grumpy. He was a bit prejudiced against Hollywood actors and viewed me with suspicion as I lay on the chaise lounge, carrying on a mild flirtation with the leading man. Bill greeted me briefly and turned away.

He was a slight man of medium height with an athletic build, somewhat protuberant blue eyes, thinning light-brown hair, and a warm, snaggle-toothed grin.

I watched him as he moved through the crowd greeting members of the cast, most of whom he knew, seeing his grumpiness dissolve into affectionate banter. People seemed to be drawn to him like bees to honey, and I was curious to know the reason why.

As I got to know him, it became obvious that, unlike many actors, he was a great listener as well as witty raconteur. He listened with compassion and with the "third ear" that spots hidden nuances. He was full of a joyful curiosity about life.

As we started rehearsals, terror gripped me by the throat. I felt that I had bitten off more than I could chew and that there was no way I could get inside the psyche of this extravagant creature. The director had his hands full with a large cast and only a week's rehearsal time and so could give me no help. Bill, bless him, had an intuitive sense. He spotted the confusion under my facade of calmness and asked if I'd like to stay after rehearsal to work on areas that bothered me.

Gratefully, I jumped at his offer. He was a fine actor himself with many seasons of stock behind him. He knew how to go for the essentials quickly. He gave vivid and actable things to work on.

I remember his pointing out that I stood and moved like an athlete. Wrong for the character.

"She loves herself. She treats herself and her body like pure platinum. Fluid and loving."

I started to get it.

"Uh uh," he admonished. "Remember, the legs are platinum too."

I grinned.

"Got it."

We broke the script down into beats and intentions. It was a method of working that had not been taught at the academy, but was de rigueur at the Neighborhood Playhouse where he had studied. It was a wonderful eye opener for me. We worked hard far into the night, night after night. At any time we could cadge from regular rehearsals during the day.

It was all very professional and concentrated until one day I caught him staring down the cleavage in my oxford shirt. Casually, I did up an extra button and Bill blushed like a schoolboy caught with his hand in the cookie jar.

I found this enormously endearing in such a sophisticated man. By opening, night we had become lovers. He empathized deeply with me and my abysmal stage fright. So much so that when I had finished throwing up and sailed onto the stage, Listerined and seemingly in charge, he stumbled as he made his entrance. He had a hell of a time covering up.

The play was successful, and we both won outstanding notices in the Cleveland papers. We settled down to a blissful week of getting to know one another as our relationship moved from the professional to the personal. Chagrin Falls was an idyllic little town of leafy lanes and clapboard houses where the actors were put up. Bill and I would neck steamily on the screen porch until I figured out a way to smuggle him into my room, past the prying eyes of the landlady.

I think it was toward the end of the week that he mentioned marriage. It threw me into an instant panic. He sensed I wasn't ready for a deep commitment and backed off immediately.

I was due to go to California for wardrobe tests on a film to be shot in India in the fall, called *Monsoon*. Before I left, Bill made me promise that we would spend the next New Year's Eve together. "You will wear Arpege," he announced, "and I will bring champagne."

I agreed and flew off to the coast while he went on to another engagement at a theatre in Maine.

I moved back into our house with the boys, Doug had vacated it some time back. I shot the screen test with three other actors. Ursula Thiess, a very beautiful German model with no acting experience; George Nader, a handsome but somewhat wooden leading man; and Myron Healey, a craggy, intelligent character actor.

The screenplay was based on a play by Jean Anouilh called *Romeo and Jeanette* about two doomed lovers and a dysfunctional family. The original play was set in France. Olivier had done a version of it set in Ireland. Now the producer of the film, Forrest Judd, had decided to set it in India. This chiefly because he had been the associate producer on *The River* when Jean Renoir directed it there and he had contacts within the Indian film industry as well as some frozen funds.

The actors were to be paid one week's salary in rupees

with the rest invested in the film to be paid out of profits. My erstwhile agents nearly had a fit when I told them what the deal was, but I was determined to do it as the potentials of the script, as well as the chance to travel to India, intrigued me.

Ursula played one half of the doomed lovers. I was her sister and Myron her dissolute brother.

All through the summer Bill would call me from wherever he was working, and I grew to anticipate the sound of his deep and resonant voice. I was deeply attracted to him, so I wrote Herb that I had a serious romance going and not to expect to see me on my return to New York.

Next week a package arrived. It was a book by Stendhal, *On Love*, with an inscription on the flyleaf: "You don't seem to realize-this is only the beginning of our love affair. — Herb."

I called Barbara and Win Levine and asked them to convince Herb that there was no way we could get together, that I had found the man I wanted to be with. Eventually Barbara called me back and said that she had finally convinced him that there was no point in his waiting around for the romance to be over. I was vastly relieved.

Doug had kindly arranged for me to buy a new car at a reduced price due to a contact of his in Detroit, but the car had to be picked up there. Arrangements were made for the boys and Mrs. Doubrava to move to his house for a couple of weeks while I drove it back to New York.

Doug suggested I put the house on the market as I was now settled in the East and he had no interest in living there. It and its contents had been part of my settlement in the divorce, so I had some of the antiques shipped back. When I looked for the Van Gogh lithographs, they had disappeared, only to reappear many years later on the walls of Doug's Beverly Hills house.

Next time Bill called, I told him of my plans, and he suggested that he fly to Detroit to meet me in order to drive back together. I agreed, though with a bit of trepidation. A summer-stock romance was one thing, but this smacked of something more permanent, and I wasn't sure I was ready for it.

In my sessions with Doug's psychiatrist, he had said something interesting and pertinent. "Your sense of trust has been damaged, and you may find it difficult to form any new, meaningful relationship, which is perfectly normal. If it goes on for some time, you might consider seeking some help yourself."

When I watched Bill's plane set down at the Detroit airport, my heart beat rapidly, but all my defenses were up. He stood at the top of the stairs next to the plane and lit a cigarette. "Aha!" I said to myself. "With all the signs around saying 'No Smoking,' the man's obviously an idiot. You don't want to get involved with him."

My ragweed allergy kicked in, and I started sneezing uncontrollably.

I sneezed all the way back to New York in my handsome new convertible, using up box after box of Kleenex. I peered at Bill with swollen, red eyes while he drove, sometimes glancing anxiously at me. I was perhaps the most unromantic sight east of the Mississippi, but he hung in there with caring and humor. We reached New York the best of friends, as well as lovers.

We drove out together to meet the boys when they flew in from the coast.

Michael cast a chilly eye.

"Who's he?" he said. "And where's Herbie?"

Not an auspicious beginning

Followed by Joel's reaction a month or so later: Bill was sitting in the living room of the apartment on a Sunday morning reading the *Times*. He had moved to a hotel a few blocks south of us and was spending quite a bit of time with us. The boys were decidedly cool, and he was making no particular effort to ingratiate himself with them. He was always dead honest in relationships, never pretending emotion where there was none.

As he read he suddenly realized he smelled smoke. I was cooking in the kitchen, and he called to me, asking if I had burned anything. When I confirmed that I hadn't, he realized that smoke was curling up from under his chair.

Looking over the arm, he saw Joel's chubby legs sticking out from under the chair, and he grabbed them and pulled him out. In Joel's hand was a cigarette lighter, and he had been trying to set the chair on fire.

Bill turned him over and spanked his bottom immediately. Joel's howls had me running out of the kitchen to see the cause.

"I just paddled your son. He was trying to set the chair on fire."

"Good God. Go to your room, Joel. I'll talk to you later."

I went back to my cooking.

Later, Joel came out of his room, tears drying on his pink cheeks, one hand behind his back.

"Billy," he lisped. "Billy, I have something for you."

Bill said he looked up and his heart melted at the sight of this generous child who bore no grudges.

He leaned forward.

"Do you, Joel? Thank you. What is it?"

"This!"

And Joel punched him on the nose and ran into the kitchen.

Bill was furious, and I punished Joel. Later over drinks, however, Bill and I couldn't stop laughing over the devilish ingenuity.

"I kept wishing he was twenty-one," said Bill, "so I could sock him on the jaw."

The car provided us with a way to get out of the city on the weekends. Now we needed somewhere to go.

I started perusing the ads in the classifieds, looking for a bargain in the country, and one day I saw a possibility.

"Old saltbox, three acres and a brook. Dutchess County. $6,000."

We all piled into the car and sped up there.

The house was on farmland about fifteen miles inland from Hyde Park. It had old apple trees, a falling-down barn, horsehair plaster on the walls, wide-plank pine floors, a pump in the kitchen, and an outhouse. No indoor plumbing or heat, but there were electric lines running to it.

The boys leaped out and started damming up the stream, while Bill and I walked over the property.

"It's going to need a lot of work," he said.

"Well, we can do it bit by bit," I responded. "But it gives us an escape from the city."

And indeed it did.

For the first year, we bathed in a galvanized tub in the kitchen, sometimes with leaves floating around us, as the pump had not been used in ages. We balanced ourselves gingerly on the seat of the outhouse. The boys were convinced that their bottoms were going to be bitten by spiders nesting below, but it never happened.

The boys became friends with the farmer who lived down the road, Mr. Olah, who was forever losing track of his herd of cows and would send the boys out to find them. He carried on a hopeless war with his wife. He would throw stones at her chickens, and she would throw rocks at his cows. They never spoke. They were dirt poor and getting poorer by the minute as they killed off their sources of livelihood. But something in my boys touched this farmer's bitter old heart, and he took them to see their first pig slaughter. He also fed them their first taste of homemade wine. Both, I might add, without my knowledge.

I was given the lead in a perfectly dreadful soap opera, *Three Steps to Heaven*, and out of the proceeds managed to put in a bathroom and a fireplace, making the place habitable except in the deepest winter.

I lasted six months on *Steps* which aired live on N. B. C. This in spite of unpleasantness with the producer who was a woman that disagreed vehemently with my interpretation of the character.

"You are playing her as an intellectual with an ironic

sense of humor," she said accusingly.

"That's what I'm aiming for."

"Soap opera fans don't want to see that. They want to see brave suffering. Go see some early Joan Crawford movies, see how she stands there against the wall, rain dripping on her raincoat, head thrown back, biting her lip against the tears. That's what I want."

"How have the ratings been since I took over?"

"That has nothing to do with it!"

I think she had to keep me on as long as she did because of the ratings, but eventually I was canned, and I felt a sense of relief.

Live television was nerve wracking, but soaps with one day's rehearsal, day after day, the writing being mostly pathetic, was sheer torture.

I remember one poor soul who had what amounted to a nervous breakdown on camera during *Steps*. He was in the scene immediately prior to mine, and he had some long speeches which carried the plot line. He was to relate them to Mark Roberts, the male lead. They were seated in the mock-up of a taxi, and he got as far as "I gotta tell you..."

Then he took off his hat, scrunched it between his palms, and said, "I'm so nervous, I can't remember a thing!"

Mark attempted to calm him and clue him in, though in the script he couldn't have known any of the information.

"Was it about Vince?...Vince Capelini?"

"Vince...Vince...yes! He...I'm so nervous, I can't remember a thing!"

It went on like that for several minutes while John Marley and I watched in horrified fascination on the monitor, waiting to begin our scene.

Finally John clapped his hand over my ears.

"Don't listen! It's catching!" he commanded.

Mark sweated bullets, but managed to get through it. The other poor actor left the studio and the business that day.

I had some pretty hairy moments myself doing live TV

One I particularly remember happened on a Kraft Theatre production. At the end of the first act, somebody announced that the character playing my father's secretary was dead. My line was "Not Hazel Johnson!"

As mentioned earlier, I have a dreadful memory for names. As the red lights came on and the camera moved in for a closeup, I knew that I didn't have the faintest idea of the woman's name. The only name I could think of was Gertrude Ederle, who swam the English Channel in 1926. Go figure that.

I took a deep breath and started to ad-lib, hoping for one of the other actors to come up with the name because the first act couldn't end without it. The one actor who could legitimately have known the name let me go rambling on for close to a minute (which seemed like hours) before somebody poked him and he supplied the name.
During the act change I accosted him.

"Where the hell were you? Couldn't you see I was up?"

"No, you were making a lot of sense so I thought you'd just been given new lines."

My knees shook. I wondered what would happen if I just ran out of the studio and never stopped, running up through the Bronx and Yonkers, never to be heard of again. I wasn't sure that a word would come out of me in the second and third act, but I got through it, though blind panic was not far away.

Usually, tension would make me throw up after dress rehearsal and before performance, but I was cured of it while playing Lydia Languish in the NBC Masterpiece series of Sheridan's *The Rivals*. Mary Boland was playing Mrs. Malaprop.

After dress rehearsal, I headed to the powder room for the usual regurgitation, but discovered that the wide farthingales of my costume wouldn't permit me to get inside the booth. While trying vainly to fight my way in, I suddenly realized that my stomach had calmed down, and it was time I gave up the silly habit. It never happened again.

170 In The Wings

In the fall of '51 Bill and I kissed good-bye, and I embarked on the plane for India.

It was in the days of the old propeller planes so the journey had to be broken up by a stopover in London. The company had booked me into a rather seedy commercial hotel on the Strand called the Strand Palace. As soon as I was booked in, I spent the afternoon revisiting old haunts from my childhood. Around the Round Pond, past Peter Pan's statue, down to Kensington Garden Square (the Kengar Hotel was a mass of rubble and the results of the bombing were everywhere) and into Whiteleys, where I used to visit Father Christmas.

This time I was in search of knitting needles and yarn (well aware of the time spent waiting for a shot to be set up in a movie), and I asked a saleswoman to help me make a selection.

She called to an assistant.

"Would you please help the Yankee lady?"

I turned around, looking for an American.

"The Yankee lady needs some yarn."

With a shock, I realized they were talking about me. I glanced in a mirror, half-expecting to see myself at eight, with dark braids hanging down my back, but instead saw "The Yankee Lady," blonde sophisticated and all grown up. Coupled with the jet lag, I felt totally disoriented. I walked slowly back to the Strand, getting lost in Covent Garden along the way. By the time I reached the hotel, I had covered about eleven miles. It was five o'clock in the evening.

I had some tea and scrambled eggs, left a call for 6:00 A.M., took a sleeping pill, and hit the sack.

Through deep fogs of semi-awareness, I heard the phone ring.

"Madam," chirped the voice. "It is six o'clock."

I groaned myself into a conscious state, rolled out of bed, and started packing my few belongings. My stockings and panties were still wet from last night's laundry.

"Goddamn damp British climate," I muttered peevishly

as I stuffed them into my sponge bag.

My eyes and mouth felt like blotting paper, and there was a thudding going on in the back of my head.

"Never again," I promised myself, "will I touch a sleeping pill."

I carried my suitcase down to the lobby, and as the elevator doors opened, I viewed a hallucinatory scene from hell. Masses of people rushing back and forth, name tags pinned to their fronts, were greeting one another with boisterous slaps on the back and loud North Country accents. Lights blazed and cocktail glasses clinked as I made my way to the front desk to pay my bill.

As the desk clerk handed over my bill and I attempted to figure the pounds into dollars, a faint suspicion crossed my mind. I glanced at the clock above us.

"What time is it?"

The clerk looked at the clock, then at me, assuming that he was dealing with an idiot or a drunk.

"It is six thirty, madam."

"A.M. or P.M.?"

"Why, P.M., of course, madam."

With a groan, I grabbed my suitcase, went back to my room, and fell across the bed, not to surface for another ten hours.

Myron and I were on the same plane, and when he saw me, he burst out laughing.

"Did you see that mess of a test we made?" he asked. "Thank God we had been cast already, or no one would have hired us. I stunk up the screen pretty bad, but you…you…well, I've never seen such scenery chewing. It was hysterical."

"Really?" I said, cooly.

But when I saw the test in Bombay, I could see that he was right The flamboyant character I had just played in *Light Up the Sky* had bled over into the repressed sister in Anouilh's screenplay. The head tossing and nostril flaring were not to be believed. I cringed with embarrasment.

On the other hand, Ursula and George, who did very little but stand there looking soulful and enigmatic, came off rather well. Next lesson in film acting…when in doubt, do less. Myron was an amusing companion and an intelligent actor, so we had some fruitful discussions about the script, specifically, how we saw our characters. There were different layers of interpretation that Anouilh had written into the play, and the relationship between brother and sister was mysterious. It could be interpreted as incestuous.

When the plane stopped for refueling at Riyadh, I peered out the window at a bizarre sight. Huge bonfires were burning along the runway, and airplane mechanics, porters, and some crew were dancing wildly. They whirled among the smoke, laughing hysterically. I called Myron over.

"What's going on?"

Myron watched for a few minutes.

"Damned if I know, but it looks to me like they're all stoned."

And indeed they were.

The government had uncovered a huge cache of marijuana and had decided to get rid of it by burning it up, not reckoning on the smoke giving everyone in nearby a free high.

The area around the Taj Mahal Hotel in Bombay was awash in beggars. Skeletal mothers held up babies with running sores. Amputees lifted shaking palms. The air was heavy with the smell of rotting fruit and tropical flowers and feces. One longed for a breath of air that didn't smell of something.

The poverty was heartbreaking, but all members of the company were warned not to give even an anna to the surrounding throng as it would lead to a stampede and no one would be able to leave the hotel.

It was four years after independence, but racism was still rampant. All the faces on the veranda sipping drinks were white, all outside were black.

A night or two after I arrived, shots were fired followed by a stifled cry. A drunken Australian had fired an elephant gun in one of the corridors of the hotel, and the bullet ricocheting down the hall wounded three bearers stationed outside their master's door overnight. No arrest was made. The Aussie merely forked over some money before he left.

Sitting up during the long flight over had aggravated a sacroiliac problem. I awoke the next morning stuck like a turtle on its back. Every movement in agony. Eventually I reached a telephone and explained my predicament to the company manager, who said he'd send a masseuse and, if needed, a doctor. He would reschedule my scenes to the end of the week.

The masseuse was beautiful and exotic in her silken sari, and it was a bit of a shock to hear a clipped, British games-mistress kind of voice coming from her.

"Now then, what seems to be the matter? Can't turn over, can we? Well, we'll soon fix that!"

I recoiled in horror as she pushed her sleeves up and advanced on me, but after much pushing and pulling, she strapped me up, and I was able to maneuver.

"Got to keep those tummy muscles strong. That's what keeps the back in place. Don't go more than a day or two without sit-ups or swimming."

I've followed her regimen ever since.

The director was a blithe young man who seemed to treat the film as an excuse for an extended vacation. When I asked him about the possible incestuous relationship, he looked startled.

"Where did you find that?"

I mentioned the scene.

"I don't remember that scene."

Half-kidding, I said, "Rod, you have read the script, haven't you?"

"Actually, no," he replied. "I don't believe in over-studying, it takes the freshness away. I had my wife read it through to me on the plane coming over so I'd get the overall feeling. I like to wing it, day by day."

I had a horrible sinking feeling. I was meant to shoot for five weeks. I had the premonition that not only would it go over that time, but that the whole film would be a disaster. I was right.

To incorporate local color, scenes were arbitrarily switched around. I recall being close to tears one day. A scene that called for me to confide shameful family secrets in a small room was shot in an open market, so that it was impossible to keep one's voice lowered. I was directed to shout all the information to the world at large. My protests were in vain.

Illness was rampant in the company. The director ended up in the hospital for ten days, and Ernie Haller, the cameraman who had shot *Gone with the Wind*, took over for part of his absence, so we made some progress.

The crew and cast were part British and part American, with some Indians helping out. We shot in the Modi Studios, which were like covered airplane hangars with corrugated iron roofs and makeup quarters roofed in cow dung. Ursula and I were lying on our raincoats, trying to catch a nap on the lunch break once when cow dung came flying through the air as they repaired the cracks. We had to cover our heads and run.

The British crew were inordinately proud of their new color cameras, which were the latest thing. They would cringe when the Indians hung wreaths around them, then cracked them smartly with a coconut as a morning blessing. A collision of cultures was always in the offing.

It surprised me that four years after independence, so many of the British customs were followed. We were invited to dinner at a British club by some of the Modi family, and the latent snobbery in the conversation could have been heard in one of the Stately Homes of England. I was seated next to the Maharajah of Kaputhala. He mentioned his string of polo ponies and invited me to visit his "little kingdom," saying his mother would love me and he would send his plane to pick me up.

It so happened that Jimmy Vining, our English makeup man, had been born in the palace of Kaputhala (I would imagine his father had been with the British army). The next morning while he was making me up, I asked him if any other members of the cast had been invited to visit the "little kingdom."

Jimmy snorted with laughter.

"No, darling. You're the only one. Jid Kaputhala has been asking around about you, so I imagine it's like being invited up to see his etchings. I know he's handsome, but watch your step."

My spirit of adventure said, "Go," but caution prevailed, taking into consideration my two small chaps at home. I recalled a conversation I had had recently with a Pakistani actor.

The actor had taken me sailing out to Elefanta Island and brought along a picnic of Punjabi chicken. Along the way we had discussed acting and our lives in general. He was very knowledgeable about Stanislavski, was up on the Method, Arthur Miller, and Tennessee Williams. He seemed completely Westernized in his ideas.

When it came to discussing his personal life, however, there was a divergence. He mentioned his wives and when he saw me blink, laughed. He said that by law, he was allowed three, but who could afford more than two?

When we landed back on the quay and he helped me out of the boat, several heads turned.

"I can't stand their staring at you," he muttered. "I should like to kill them."

"But you said your second wife was German and blonde," I said. "Don't people stare at her?"

"They did. So I never let her out anymore."

I stared at this handsome, modern young man.

"Never?"

"Never. It's too upsetting for me."

This memory was reason enough to turn down Jid's

invitation. I could imagine my kids wailing at home while Mommy was in purdah, up to her eyes in a yashmak, shaking the bars and yelling to be let out.

With so much of my salary frozen in *rupees*, I went on a buying spree. I brought back some beautiful saris and scarves, as well as some primitive sculpture and Indian music which, with it's whining, repetitive melodies drove my friends crazy in the U.S.

Eventually the shoot was over, much to everyone's relief. I was thankful to be able to give up the diet of powered eggs and tea that had kept me healthy while the rest of the cast succumbed to various intestinal ailments. I ate the airline food with relish.

When the plane landed in Cairo, I spotted someone swaggering back from the first class cabin with a camel-hair coat slung over his shoulders. I slunk back in my seat, hoisting a magazine in front of my face, for I recognized a face from my past—Johnny Meyer. He was the man who had first introduced me to Errol Flynn at the Beverly Hills Hotel. It was an episode in my past that I had no wish to revisit, and I prayed he wouldn't see me. But there was no escape.

"Hey, kid!" he hailed. "Long time no see! You going to Rome?"

"Just for a day or two. Actually I'm going to Malta to see my sister and then back to New York."

"You staying at the Excelsior?"

"No, I'm not."

"Well, where are you staying?"

I hesitated.

"Come on. Where?'"

"The Hassler."

"Great. You want to meet the Pope? We'll pick you up."

My jaw dropped. The combination of Johnny Meyer and the Pope was too much to envision.

"What did you say?"

"The Pope. Glenn McCarthy and I have tickets to go see him at his summer place, and we got two more for our lawyers. But I say screw the lawyers. There's only going to be twenty people. Want to come?"

I considered for only a minute. It was irresistible.

"Well...don't you have to wear a hat and veil and gloves and everything? I don't have..."

"Don't worry about a thing, kid. We're meeting Lois Andrews in Rome and that broad has a wardrobe you wouldn't believe. She'll lend you something."

"Okay, sounds great."

"You're on. The limousine will pick you up at the Hassler, five A.M. Lois will bring a hat and gloves."

At five the four of us were seated in the car and on our way to the Castello Gandolfo. There were Lois Andrews, ex-wife of Georgie Jessel and a flamboyant character; Glenn McCarthy, a Texas millionaire, middle-aged and taciturn; and the very chatty Johnny Meyer.

I donned Lois's little black hat and veil, which, with my dark grey suit, looked appropriately somber. We wound our way up past the Swiss Guards as dawn broke behind the walls of Castell Gandolfo.

We waited for the arrival of the pontiff in a paneled room hung with exquisite tapestries. The other Americans in the group were all carrying rosaries and murmuring with downcast eyes. I hoped that our foursome wouldn't do anything disruptive.

As the Pope made his entrance, "Jesus!" Lois breathed in my ear. "Dig that cape! What an evening wrap that would make!"

"Sssssshhh!" I hissed. But she was right. It was gorgeous.

Pope Pius XII had a lean, ascetic face. He had been vilified for not taking a stand against the Fascists in the Second World War. Many felt that he could have spoken out in defense of the Jews earlier, and throught the weight of the Catholic Church saved many lives. But none of this seemed to matter to the rosary-toting tourists, they gazed at him with pure adoration.

As he passed down the line to greet us, they dropped

to their knees and kissed his ring, and he asked each one in turn where they had been born, where they live now, and how long they had been in Rome. His English was very halting, and he appeared to have a slight hearing problem.

"Oh, God," I thought, "When he gets to me...Bermuda. How am I going to explain that it's a small island in the Atlantic?"

When he arrived opposite me, I shook his hand, and when he inquired as to where I was from, I found myself blurting out

"Perth Amboy, New Jersey."

Which happens to be my mother's birthplace.

"Ah!" he said, his face lighting up. "I know Newark. Do you know Newark?"

"Yes," I said. "My dentist is in Newark."

Which happens to be true.

"Your dentist? Ah, how interesting."

And he passed on, leaving my fellow travelers staring at me in puzzlement.

"You talked to him about your *dentist*?" they said later. "What are you, nuts?"

"Now," said Johnny as we drove back to the Hassler, "Glenn wants you to do us a favor."

"Oh-oh," I thought. "Here it comes."

"You speak French, don't you?"

"Some."

In fact I had been quite fluent when I was in my teens, having spent some time in France, as well as having six years of it in school, but I hadn't used it for some time.

"Well, we got a business meeting with Count Miani. We don't speak Italian, he doesn't speak English, but he does speak French. So, we figured you could translate for us."

"'Migod, I don't know how I'd cope with all the legal terms. Why don't you get a regular interpreter?"

"We're only here today, and we've got to have somebody we can trust who won't go to the papers. I told Glenn you'd be okay. Will you do it?"

"Well, okay. I'll do the best I can."

A few hours later, the limo picked me up again, this time without Lois, and we drove up one of the seven hills of Rome to an immense estate. The floors of the villa were marble. Priceless statuary stood in the niches, and formal arrangements of flowers were everywhere. Count Miani's footsteps echoed down the hall as he approached.

He had shrewd eyes and slicked-back hair. He led us into the dining room to a delicious lunch and one of the most exhausting I have ever been through. By the end of it, having translated terms from French into English and back again, trying to get every nuance correct, I was ready to put my head down on the table and weep. But they seemed satisfied.

It was with joy that I heard an English voice approaching when we got back to the drawing room. It was an English nanny escorting the count's two small boys, who bowed formally and kissed my hand. They were all of three and five, solemn and attentive.

"Who do they play with?" I asked her.

"Unfortunately, just each other," she replied.

"But I saw some children on the driveway on the way up."

"They are the gardener's children. As children of the nobility, the boys are not allowed to associate with them and, sadly, all the other noble children have French nannies, so they speak only French. The count and countess wanted their children to be brought up speaking only English."

"But they speak Italian? To their parents?"

"A little. They don't see that much of their parents."

I watched them go over to bow and shake hands with their father and his guests and leave, as quiet and well behaved as when they entered. I thanked God for my noisy and rambunctious two.

Malta, with Fan and Jock, was a wonderful tonic. Jock was stationed with the British army there and, we went to several regimental dinners and cocktail parties. We went sailing and had a grand old time gossiping and catching up.

Ian, Fan's eldest, was off at boarding school. Tom, aged four, was around and showed himself to be a wonderfully self-sufficient child who would play for hours with a block of wood and a bit of string, making up imaginative games. Fan was pregnant again. She confided in me that she hoped it wouldn't be another boy, as she wasn't sure they could afford the expensive education that was necessary for boys.

I didn't question her, as I remembered the old English class system that made it mandatory for sons of the ruling class to go to the "Right" public schools. Higher education was not considered that necessary for females. As it turned out, the following spring, her wish was granted when Joanna was born.

Back in New York, I had no sooner hugged my boys and greeted Bill than my agent called, saying that it was the last day of auditions for a play by Herman Wouk. Otto Preminger was going to direct and would I please get my self down to the theatre posthaste to read for the role.

I tore down to the theatre and read with the stage manager for the female lead in the play called *The Koenig Masterpiece*, later changed to *Modern Primitive*.

Travel-tired and somewhat at wit's end, I had no idea how the audition had gone. I was stunned when Otto Preminger called me later that night and told me I had the part.

"Mr. Preminger," I said. "Are you sure?"

He laughed.

"Very sure, young lady. Rehearsals start next week."

It was almost too much to grasp. I had never acted on Broadway and here I was being offered a starring part in a play by a well-known author (*The Caine Mutiny* had come out a couple of years earlier) as well as an infamous director. The play was about a painter who embezzled money to finance his time to paint. He goes to Mexico with his mistress, a not-too-bright chorus girl, who in the third act turns out to have the moral strength that he lacks.

Anthony Quinn had been Preminger's first choice as the artist, but when he backed out, Otto cast Murvyn Vye in the part. He then proceeded to make his life miserable.

Murvyn was a competent actor, but had all of an actor's insecurities. Knowing that he was a second choice didn't help his confidence.

Otto picked on him unmercifully during rehearsals, which only made him falter more. It was painful for everyone concerned. I had hoped to divert it by appealing to Otto for more direction for my character, sorely needed anyway, but he brushed aside my concerns.

"Darling, you are lovely," he said in his Viennese accent. "Your instincts are all perfect. Just keep coming up with all those lovely original things."

"But Mr. Preminger, I've done the scene six or seven different ways. You've got to say what you want. We've got to set it sooner or later."

"Don't worry, darling, you'll be marvelous. Do you suppose Murvyn will ever get his lines?"

And that was all the direction I got.

Meanwhile he would scream at poor Murvyn, the veins standing out on his forehead, literally foaming at the mouth. I had never seen such terrifying rage in anyone. He had Murvyn trembling and incoherent.

Murray Hamilton and Paula Lawrence were in the cast as well, and we'd confer about the horrible scenes that Otto threw.

"Ain't nothing to be done," said Murray. "Otto's known for this. He always has to have a whipping boy, and this time it's Murvyn."

Nevertheless, it was sickening. I am sorry now that I was too chicken to challenge Otto directly over his cruelty toward a fellow human being, but I was craven and determined not to jeopardize my job.

Opening night in Hartford was a nightmare.

Murvyn had what we found out later was a complete nervous breakdown. The form it took was eerie. When he got to a line that he had had trouble with in rehearsal, he would turn to the audience and gag. When some cues were given, he would just stare back stonily at his fellow actor and sometimes reply, sometimes not.

After the second act, Paula grabbed me backstage.

"Thank God you carry the third act," she said. "He has practically nothing to say, so we'll get through it somehow."

I just shook my head wildly.

"Your first Broadway show, isn't it?"

I nodded. I couldn't seem to talk.

"Well, kid, I promise you that in all your professional life, you'll never have a worse experience."

And she was right. I never have.

The play was a strangely constructed one. The first two acts were light, romantic, and comedic. Suddenly in the third act, it turned into a morality play. The character I played discovers the embezzlement, delivers her ethical judgment, and leaves the artist. Murvyn's character answered in monosyllables while I went on and on.

At one point, when I am pointing out the ethical questions involved, his line was a terse "Maybe."

When he didn't say it, but stared at me blankly, I took a deep breath and went up the stairs delivering my final speech. It ended with something like, "And this is it. It's final. Good bye."

Suddenly Murvyn's eyes lit up.

"Maybe," he said.

With my hand on the doorknob, I froze. Could not leave on that final word. What to do?

Taking one step down the stairs, I revamped the final speech, then, keeping a close eye on my co-star, worked my way back to the door, making sure I could make it out by my final line.

At the party, or should I say "wake," after opening night, Murvyn was completely out of it. He kept telling me of visions that he had had where the Virgin Mary had told him that we belonged together. Frantically, I signalled Bill to stay by my side. Then Otto approached me, asking if I would appeal to Doug to come in and replace Murvyn.

"He would do it if you asked him. I'm sure he would."

I flatly refused.

Doug had recently been hospitalized for pneumonia. And the idea of appealing to him on a sentimental basis to rescue a play in trouble that had been turned down by Tony Quinn was the ultimate in lunacy.

With that, Otto and Herman Wouk left, and we played out the rest of the week praying that Murvyn would make it through. He did, bless him, and was ultimately carted away to spend the next four months in a sanitarium.

After closing late that Saturday night, Murray, Paula, Bill and I took the milk train back to New York, fortifying ourselves with brandy all the way. As I remember, it took about five hours. It was as dawn broke that we staggered our way back to our respective homes. For the next month ,the posters mocked us outside the Playhouse Theatre.

Written by Herman Wouk. Produced and directed by Otto Preminger. Starring Murvyn Vye and Diana Douglas…Big deal!

Through the next year, Bill and I pursued our various television commitments. While we delighted in each other's company, we studiously avoided any deep commitment to each other. Both basically loners, renouncing any neediness, we were nevertheless mutually drawn together.

His needle-sharp intelligence, compassion, and humor made him the ideal companion. In all the years we spent together, I was never bored.

In the summer, the boys went out to California to spend the holidays with Doug. Bill went back to Chagrin Falls to be in the U.S. premiere of a new Emlyn Williams play, and I went to Lakes Region Playhouse in New Hampshire to do two plays; *The Little Foxes* with Ruth Chatterton, and *The Happy Time* with a then-unknown Cliff Robertson. Michael

Howard was directing both of them and was of great help to me when Miss Chatterton challenged my being cast in the part of her daughter.

Though I looked young for my twenty-eight years, she had envisioned a child in the part, so my problem was to bring as much youth as possible to the part without being "Shirley Temple" cute. Michael helped me work out an adolescent gangliness that served the play well without being cliché. He was a fine director and is now heading up the Michael Howard Studio in New York, the best of the acting coaching schools.

That fall, Joel began at Allen Stevenson, enrolling in the kindergarten class. I went to Bermuda for a couple of weeks to act in two series that were being shot there. The company had taken over an airplane hangar on Darrell's Island left over from the old Pan Am clipper days and had transformed it into a sound stage. There was mismanagement galore. No one had counted on the tidal difference or the constantly changing light in Bermuda. Every sequence ran overtime and overbudget. The company went broke before completing the thirteen shows that were needed in each series.

While there, an unexpected thing happened. I had noticed that the set designer, an intense, handsome young man standing behind the camera, watched all my scenes intently. We were thrown together a couple of times coming over to the island on the ferry and were seated next to each other at a dinner party. Suddenly there was an overwhelming attraction, a "coup de foudre" as the French say. As we worked and moved around the island, we were intensely aware of where the other was.

He was married, and his wife was expecting a baby. I had no intention of getting involved with him, but the strictures placed on our relationship and the impossibility of any physical culmination only seemed to fan the emotional flames higher. It was like a delayed adolescent crush with all its palpitations and pain.

It shook both of us deeply, and we knew it had to end

The Wedding with Kirk, New Orleans, 1943.

With Kirk in Beverly Hills, 1946.

My parents, Thomas and Ruth Dill, 1902.

With my brother, Sir Bayard Dill, and Kirk at the Royal Bermuda Yacht Club, 1948.

The Dill family. Top row, L to R: Margaret Dill, Peggy Dill Truscott, David Dill, Daphne Dill Stobo, Laurence Dill. Bottom Row: Bayard Dill, Ruth Dill (mother), Diana holding John Truscott, Tommy Dill, Bill, and Clare Dill.

Kirk and Michael at Burt Lancaster's place in Malibu, 1947.

With Kirk, Michael, and Joel, Laurel Canyon, 1947.

With Anne Seymore and Lloyd Bridges in *A Whistle at Eaton Falls*, Portsmouth, New Hampshire, 1950.

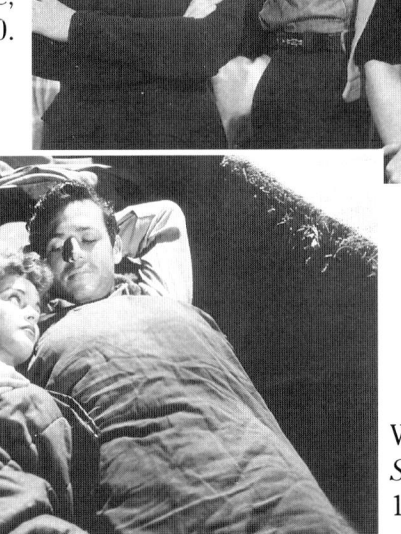

With Rex Reason in *Storm Over Tibet*, 1951.

With Michael and Joel in New York, 1952.

Kirk greeting Michael and Joel on arrival in Paris, 1954.

With Kirk, meeting me at the Orly Airport in Paris, 1954.

With Barney Kates and Bill in *Light Up the Sky,* Woodstock, New York, 1954.

With Kirk and Michael Winkleman in *The Indian Fighter*, 1955.

Michael in High School.

With Bill Darrid at our wedding in Westport, Connecticut, 1956

Sailing on Martha's Vineyard, 1958.

Michael and Joel in Westport, 1960.

With Barry Nelson in *Cactus Flower*, Royale Theater, New York City, 1966.

Bill Darrid in Yugoslavia, 1969.

With Bill in Westport, Connecticut, 1970.

With the cast of the TV series *The Cowboys* with Moses Gunn, A. Martinez, Jim Davis, Bob Carradine, and Clint Howard, 1974.

With my grandson, Cameron, Coldwater Park, Los Angeles, 1979.

Michael and Joel working on *Jewel of the Nile* in Morrocco, 1985.

With David Birney as Hamlet, me as Gertrude, in *Hamlet*, Slovang, California, 1985.

With Barney Kates in *Painting Churches*, Santa Maria, 1985.

With John Houseman in the TV series *The Paper Chase*, 1986.

With Michael Gross in *Hedda Gabler*, Doolittle Theater, Los Angeles, 1986.

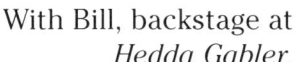

With Bill, backstage at *Hedda Gabler*.

With Bill in Los Angeles, 1989.

Above: With Roy Dotrice in *The Best of Friends*, Westside Theater, New York, 1993. Right: New York Times ad for *The Best of Friends*.

At a ceremony for Michael Douglas's prints in front of Grauman's Chinese Theater, Los Angeles, 1998. (L to R: Joel Douglas, Peter Douglas, Jack Nicholson, me, Kirk, Karl Malden, Michael, Rob Reiner, and Eric Douglas.)

With Cameron, Sherman Oaks, California, 1982.

With Howard Keel and crew members of *My Fair Lady*, St. Louis, 1996.

With Patrick and Francesca Dill, Joel Douglas, Cameron Douglas, and Michael, Sherman Oaks, California—Christmas, 1997.

With Michael, Los Angeles, 1994.

before something irrevocable happened. I flew back to New York as soon as my scenes were finished, and a day or so later, a letter arrived from him "eating his heart out" to quote. There was also a beautiful little watercolor of storm clouds over Bermuda that he had painted for me.

I was determined to say nothing about the episode to Bill, but I had not counted on his extraordinarily sensitive antennae where emotions were concerned.

Driving up to Hyde Park, I responded absent-mindedly to a remark of his when he looked at me sharply.

"What's going on?"

"What?"

"What went on in Bermuda?"

"Nothing, really."

"Oh, yes. It was something, really. Your mind has been somewhere else ever since you got back."

"Well, there was this guy I was attracted to, but nothing happened and it's over. So that's that."

"Strikes me that it was a damn sight more than a passing attraction."

He pulled into a gas station and turned the car around.

"What are you doing?"

"Going back to town. I'm not hanging around while your mind is on someone else."

"Don't be ridiculous."

"I'm not. I love you, but I'm too old to play games. I think we should stop seeing one another."

My jaw dropped.

"But...but..."

"That's it."

I started to seethe.

"Don't tell me that you haven't been attracted to anyone else in the year or two we've been together."

"As a matter of fact, I haven't. But even if I had, I wouldn't go mooning about like..."

"I'm *not* mooning about!"

"I don't want to discuss it. Let's stop seeing each other,

and if you decide that it's me you're interested in, maybe we'll get back together. Maybe not."

"Great."

The rest of the ride went in silence. I got out of the car with my chin held high.

"I'll leave the keys with the doorman!" he shouted after me.

I didn't deign to turn around.

It lasted about three weeks.

During that time, I was asked to a reunion party for those of us who had been in the ill-fated Bermuda series. My set-designer friend was there with his wife, who fixed me with a steady stare while Dick spent an inordinate amount of time filling and refilling his pipe. I left after a short time, thankful that it was not as painful as I had anticipated and knowing that I could put an end to that chapter.

I was still angry at Bill, but I missed him more and more. I rode with the children in the park, took them ice-skating at Wollman's, and went to the movies with friends, but there was still a large, aching void in my life.

I half-expected him to call, but when he didn't, I realized the first move would have to be mine if I wanted the relationship to go on. I knew that I did want it, quite desperately and, somewhat to my discomfort, that I needed him.

Finally, one rainy night, I could stand it no longer. I put on my raincoat and trudged down to the theatre where he was appearing in *Reclining Figure* and leaned against the brick wall next to the stage door, waiting for him.

Soon Martin Gabel, an acquaintance who had one of the leads in the show, came by.

"What are you doing here standing in the rain? You look like Michele Morgan in *Quai des Brumes*."

"I'm waiting for Bill."

"Well, for God's sake, come on in and wait for him in my dressing room. I'll give you some hot tea."

And so it was that I was mournfully sipping tea in

Marty's dressing room when Bill came up the stairs and did a double take at the sight of me.

"Thanks, Marty," then, "Do you want to wait in my dressing room?"

I nodded, blinking back tears, and he put his arm around me and led me upstairs. I think it was the first time in my life that neediness had overcome my pride. Bill never gloated or rubbed it in. He was gentle, warm, and loving and, I think, knew how much it cost me. Dick was never mentioned, but because of him we moved to another plateau of commitment though marriage was still not mentioned.

The next summer we were asked to do *Light Up the Sky* again. This time at the Woodstock Playhouse. Michael Howard was going to direct. It sounded like a breeze, we'd done it before and were both somewhat smug, having received superb notices. So poor Michael (who had also just stopped smoking that week) had two maddeningly superior actors to deal with questioning every change in "our" play. At one point, he stomped out of the rehearsal hall and went home. It's a wonder that our friendship survived that summer, but it did and has thrived over the years.

It served me right that I got one of my few bad reviews for that performance.

"Miss Douglas," it said, "seemed a trifle giddish in the role."

"What do they mean 'giddish'?" I demanded angrily.

"Misprint, darling," said Michael. "Should have been 'yiddish.'"

While there my agent called and said that I had been offered a small part and understudying Margaret Sullavan in a new play, *Sabrina Fair*. He suggested I take it, even though it was a comedown from being starred myself as it had the makings of a hit and a long run. The Playwrights company was producing it, with Joseph Cotten in the other starring part and Hank Potter directing. I liked the idea of having a play lined up for the fall, so I agreed.

That fall, my son Michael showed his first predilection for acting. I spotted him limping down the hall one day, a bandanna stuck in his pocket. He was concentrated and frowning, then thought a bit and limped back.

"What's up, darling?"

He gave me an embarrassed smile.

"Nothing really, Mom. I was just trying to figure…"

"What?"

"How it felt to be that old man who lives downstairs."

Oh, boy, I thought, he's got the bug. The curiosity to want to know how it feels to be in someone else's skin is the hallmark of the actor, and perhaps of the writer.

Rehearsals for *Sabrina* were fascinating. Margaret Sullavan was word perfect at the first rehearsal and gave a complete performance. Flashing her charming smile, she was totally captivating. Joseph Cotten, on the other hand, seemed barely familiar with the script and mumbled his way through the first reading, looking worried.

The rest of the cast were in various stages of preparation, but were all fine actors and gave intelligent readings. They were Cathleen Nesbit as the mother, John Cromwell as the father, and Scott McKay as the younger brother. Lorraine Grover and I played a pair of debutantes who danced on in the arms of our dates (mine was Gordon Mills) and had a few lines of dialogue.

Before dress rehearsal in New Haven, John Cromwell came up to me and said, "You are making the classic mistake of playing a small part like a small part. You are capable of much better work than that."

A few months earlier, he had directed me in a starring part on television in which I played an alcoholic. He had been wonderful, and I had total faith in him as a director.

"Okay, John. I can't think of a damn thing to do with this part. I'll welcome any suggestions."

"Something that's individual. Perhaps she's a bad dancer. Perhaps she's had a little too much to drink."

"Okay!"

I reeled on merrily in the next run-through, tossing quips and peals of laughter, only to be silenced by Hank Potter thundering from the back of the theatre.

"Diana! What in hell do you think you're doing?"

I stopped, blinking out onto the darkness.

"You don't like it?"

"Like it? You're ruining Miss Sullavan's crucial scene. All the audience attention is meant to be on her while she's sitting quietly. Everyone's going to be watching your crazy fandango, so just say your lines and get off. And don't do it again."

"Thanks a lot," I muttered to John as I passed him in the wings. "Maybe next time you can get me fired."

"Well, he's wrong," he replied, "but you don't have to tell him that."

While in New Haven, Miss Sullavan was not feeling well a lot of the time and although she never missed a performance, felt she was not up to rehearsing the new changes as they were put in, so I got to do the new blocking and changes with Joseph Cotten. He eased his way gently into the character until it fitted him like an old glove and was a delight to work with.

Once he said to Hank, "I'm enjoying doing this, but it's probably a waste of time. I'll just end up in Joe's corner."

"What's 'Joe's corner'?"

"Down right, with my back to the audience, while Mag does her thing center stage."

"That won't happen," assured Hank.

"Wanna bet?"

And he was right. As soon as she returned, she quickly assessed the situation and restaged it to her advantage. Joe gave me a wink and a tired smile. Hank said not a word.

Later he said to Joe, "We have to be patient with her. She's having troubles…down there."

"Down there?" said Joe incredulously. "You mean she's got one?"

The play opened to strong notices and seemed assured of a long run. As I didn't have much to do, I felt I could take on the daytime run of a soap opera, particularly as we needed a bathroom in the Hyde Park cottage. That's when I did the aforementioned *Three Steps to Heaven*. However, the double duty did take its toll, and I sometimes fell asleep in the theatre dressing room with my head on the makeup table.

I had hoped to have a crack at playing the part when Miss Sullavan went on her week's vacation at Christmas. Joe said he'd be comfortable doing it with me, but the powers that be decided that she, not he, was the starring draw, so they closed the show for Christmas week, and I decided to turn in my notice after the first of the year.

It was sometime during the winter that I ran into Brother Rat again, a sad, sad moment. I was at El Morocco with some friends when he approached the table drunk, bloated, and looking far older than his forty-odd years.

"Pickle, darling," he said, weaving and trying to focus. "What good times…what very, very good times. Remember how you used to sing this?"

And he went into a rendition of a calypso number I had taught him called "Mango Walk." People turned and stared. Those at my table looked uncomfortable. I had a hard time blinking back tears.

Finally I hushed him with, "That was great, Brother Rat. You remembered every word."

"Good times," he repeated, as someone led him back to his table. "Good, good times."

We left shortly after that, and I never saw him again.

Later I went to the Bahamas to play Sabrina. Conrad Bain, who was exactly my age, played my father and was brilliant. Even then he was a fine, fine character actor. On opening night, I had two surprises.

A well-dressed matron in a sable stole came back to the dressing room and threw her arms around me I hadn't a clue as to who she was.

"Darling, it's Squidge!"

"It's what?" I said blankly.

"Squidge, darling. Upper Chine. Don't tell me you've forgotten!"

Slowly it came back to me. When I was a lowly junior, she had been an unapproachable senior named Patience. Only her very close friends were allowed to call her Squidge. Now she glittered with diamonds, sported fashionably streaked hair and a suntan and chirped away in her upper-class British accent as though we had been the best of buddies. I made vague noises about our getting together while I was in Nassau, but privately decided against it.

Next, Lawrence Langner and Armina Marshall of the Theatre Guild showed up, congratulating me and saying how they wished I could have done it on Broadway. I thanked them, but discounted it as mere politeness until several years later when their interest really paid off for me.

Bill and I also worked in winter stock at the Palm Beach Playhouse, though in different plays.

I was cast in a play with Steve Cochran that was meant to be in its pre-Broadway tryout. Bill was in a musical by Lerner and Loewe, an early one called *The Day before Spring*. He protested in vain that he could not carry a tune, but was told that he could talk his way through a patter song, "Where's My Wife?"' Cloris Leachman, who had a lovely soprano voice, played his wife, and all the rest of the cast were accomplished singers, so rehearsals were sheer hell for him, made worse by a martinet of an orchestra leader.

On opening night, he was a bundle of nerves, unusual for him. He made the mistake of looking directly into the follow spot and blinding himself. He then leaped off the stage as planned, but right into the lap of a Palm Beach dowager. With that, all the lyrics of his lengthy song went clear out of his head, and he raced up and down the aisles spouting total gibberish, but with such confidence and verve that the elderly audience were checking their hearing aids and the rest were trying to translate.

I watched, incredulous. Full of conflicting emotions: terror for what he was going through, my usual response to disaster of nervous hilarity, and sheer admiration for the professionalism he was displaying.

We sat on the beach together the next morning going over the whole night, while I cued him once again through the miserable song. A fellow actor arrived with a special-delivery letter. It was from Doug, who had been in France the better part of a year and was missing the children. He suggested that I fly over with them for their spring vacation. "No point in wasting a first-class ticket to Paris on Mrs. Doubrava."

I read it out loud to Bill. He didn't comment.

"Well, I'd have to think about it," I mused. "Of course I'd insist on separate accommodations. What do you think?"

"It's up to you."

"Well, would you mind?"

"It's all really none of my business. You'll have to do what you think is right."

I had already had word that the pre-Broadway tryout I was in was not going to make it to Broadway. Paris in the spring sounded like a pleasant adventure, so I wired Doug that we would be over the following month.

I had not counted on catching one more childhood disease from my offspring.

On account of my siblings being older, I had missed all the childhood diseases save whooping cough. After the age of twenty-five, I contracted measles, German measles, mumps, and finally chickenpox, the latter shortly before I was due to shepherd the boys over to Paris.

Doug had kindly purchased first-class tickets with sleeping berths for us for the flight over, but the boys were much too excited to bed down. As soon as I turned in, they were sprung, headed for the bar in the belly of the plane where a group of raucous traveling salesmen made them welcome.

I had just dropped off to sleep when a loud burst of male laughter, followed by Joel's piping treble had me sitting bolt upright and rushing to check on their berth, which of course was empty. I went down to the bar and seized both kids by their shoulders. I marched them upstairs to the disappointed catcalls of their drunken buddies.

We arrived at Orly to be met by Doug with a handsome young woman in tow who he introduced as his assistant, Anne Buydens. She was reserved and watchful, and I assumed that there was something more than a professional relationship going on. We drove to Doug's house, rented in Auteuil, and there it was explained to me that the separate quarters were not going to be forthcoming. The boys would be in the bedroom next to his and that I would be upstairs, four flights, in a maid's room.

If I had felt better, I would have registered some strong objections, but all I wanted to do was lie down as the chickenpox had entered my lungs. I was coughing and miserable so I turned the boys over to Doug and Anne and crawled into bed.

After a couple of days, the cough was worse and I was running a fever. Anne sent for a doctor, who administered some antibiotics, but who also wanted to slap a mustard plaster on my chest. I fought him off, as the scabs were still healing all over me and I could imagine nothing worse than mustard on my raw flesh.

When I was on my feet again, Doug and I entered into the most antagonistic and controversial phase that we have ever had. I felt angry and trapped. I felt I had been duped, and was receiving no letters from Bill, who was obviously not happy that I was there. Doug, on the other hand, felt I was not giving enough credence to the "success" that he had become, and many bitter words were exchanged, which we may have regretted later.

Anne tried to be a peacemaker, and I sensed that she was a fair and decent woman caught in a very difficult situation. We had lunch together, and I was able to reassure her that there was no possible way that I could reconcile with Doug and that the field was open as far as I was concerned.

She told me that he was about to announce his engagement to Pier Angeli, a young actress barely out of her teens and that she, Anne, knew it could never work out. He needed someone who could take charge and manage his life, which was growing ever more complicated.

I smiled at her.

"You could."

"Yes, I could," she admitted.

I sensed that she loved him. I only hoped that she had an idea of what that entailed.

Doug says he remembers Michael putting his and my hands together one day in the bois and saying, "Now we are a family again." That I do not remember, but I recall the boys playing in the bois with some French kids, realizing cowboys and Indians was a universal game as they shouted, "Boom! Boom! Tu es mort!"

The three weeks in Paris seemed endless. The strained relations between Doug and me combined with the fear that my insensitivity might have wrecked my life with Bill. Fortunately, upon my return, he greeted me with warmth and affection, never an "I told you so." The man was incapable of any pettiness. Since he has been gone, I've been deeply aware of the precious gifts he gave me.

One was to restore my sense of trust in men. It took a long time because I was understandably skittish, but he would not settle for a superficial relationship. He demanded the very best that I had to offer and returned the same, and more...total devotion and a strongly upheld moral code.

The second gift was restoring my sense of self as a desirable woman. After we were married, he told me that he was deeply in love from the time that we met, but he was never sure that it would work out. I thank God for his patience and his deep understanding.

It was sometimes stretched to the breaking point.

Some months later, while we were having drinks at my apartment, I got a phone call from Doug.

"Are you sitting down?" he asked. "If not, you'd better."

"Okay," I said. "Shoot!"

"I'm in Las Vegas. I just got married."

"Oh? To whom?"

"Anne Buydens."

I gasped. "You did? Oh, my God, that's marvelous! Congratulations, you clever chap! That's great news!"

"Well…" he sounded a little taken aback. "I'm glad you're pleased. I wasn't sure how you'd take it."

"I couldn't be more pleased. Give her my love."

"I'll do that." I walked back into the living room.

"Darling," I said to Bill, "such good news. Doug has gotten married to…to…to…"

And I burst into floods of tears.

Bill stared at me with shocked eyes, and I couldn't understand my reaction myself. Later we talked it over, and I tried to make sense of it. I realized that what I was mourning was the death of a young marriage.

Logically, Doug and I could never live together. The heart creates reasons that can torpedo logic.

Later, thoroughly composed, I told the boys. Michael reacted with equanimity—remembering Anne as a very nice lady—but Joel looked at me his eyes filling with tears.

"He won't want us anymore."

"Of course he will," I reassured him. "You'll always be his children, and he'll always love you."

"Even if he has more kids?"

"Even then. No one's going to take your place."

Joel nestled deeper into my lap, tears drying on his cheeks, but he still looked doubtful.

Michael gazed out the window in seeming indifference. I wondered what went on in his deep and stoic soul. He had a core of sensitivity that he guarded jealously. Being another who valued privacy, I could empathize without intruding, but I sometimes wished that we could reach out more to one another.

Bill and the boys were growing closer. On our trips up to the Hyde Park cottage on the weekends, he would involve them in the various tasks to be done. Michael, being older and more responsible, formed an especially close bond with him and rejoiced in the male companionship.

It wasn't until Joel had pneumonia that I saw the depth of Bill's feelings for him. A simple cold suddenly turned deadly, and Joel's temperature shot up to 104. Calling Bill's friend, Dr. Frank McCormick, we bundled him into the car and raced over to Lenox Hospital, where Frank could get him admitted immediately.

Waiting outside the room while he was being prepped, we gripped each other's hands tightly, while I fought to keep back the tears. At last we were summoned inside to see the tiny figure inside the oxygen tent. Joel turned his head toward us.

"Water," he croaked.

Bill reached for the water carafe by the bed.

"It's okay, Billy," Joel rasped, barely intelligible. "I'm a big boy. I can get it myself."

Bill raced out of the room and later, I found him in the hall, weeping.

"He's just so goddamn brave. So goddamn brave!"

We seemed to be coming together more as a family, and I began to think of marriage, but now Bill was not ready to commit. I think it was partly the practicalities that had him uneasy. His earnings as an actor were sufficient to keep him in a decent style of bachelorhood and he had plans to become a Broadway producer, having optioned Budd Shulberg's novel *The Disenchanted*, but that was in the future and there was no way we could maintain my current lifestyle without the $1,000 a month I received as alimony.

However, Arnold Krakower, my lawyer in the divorce, had added an interesting item. It had seemed impossible at the time of the divorce, but had suddenly started paying off in the last two years. I would be entitled to 10 percent of anything that Doug made over $100,000. That is until my remarriage, when it would stop. Doug's salary as an actor had shot up, so I was enjoying the benefits and socking it away in a savings account.

I figured that it, along with the proceeds of the sale of the Hyde Park cottage, would be enough for a substantial down payment on a house in the suburbs within commuting distance from New York. The public schools in Princeton, Westchester county, and Connecticut were good, and even with the vagaries of our profession, I reckoned we could make it with our combined earning power. We had been together four years, drifting together and apart, but always coming back to a relationship that was sustaining and nourishing for both of us, filled with love and respect.

I knew that with the uncertainties of the acting profession, I would be giving up financial security, and I did some deep thinking about that. I also knew that this was the man I wanted to spend my life with, that I loved him deeply, and that he was an outstanding role model for my children.

I was not a woman who needed luxuries to be happy, and I was willing to work hard. When I presented all my arguments to Bill and he still was not ready to commit, it seemed some drastic change was needed in my life. It was impossible for me to drift along in our old pattern indefinitely.

A former agent of mine, Pat Harris, had recently relocated in California as a casting agent. She would call me every now and again to chat. It was apparent that most of the television companies were moving out to the coast and she felt that I would work a lot more if I were there. I wasn't ready to uproot, but I kept it in the back of my mind.

Then came a surprise call from Doug. He was about to start production on the first film of his newly formed company. It was to be called *The Indian Fighter*, and Anne, who was helping cast it, had suggested that I might be right for a role in it. It was that of a pioneer widow with a small child who was husband hunting. She had set her cap for Doug, the Indian fighter. He, however, was smitten with an Indian maiden played by Elsa Martinelli.

Doug said that the director, Andre de Toth, felt that I might be too refined looking and could I send out some stills that emphasized a plain and rugged look. I had some shots made in daylight, with no makeup, hair pulled back severely. Evidently they passed muster, for the next thing I knew I was summoned to the coast for wardrobe fittings.

Chapter 11

CALIFORNIA ONCE MORE

It was the start of summer vacation, so the boys flew out with me. Anne was expecting her first child and said that the boys could stay with her while we were shooting on location in Oregon. They seemed quite comfortable with the idea. Bill was about to start rehearsal for a role in *Inherit the Wind* starring Paul Muni on Broadway, so our professional and personal lives seemed to have come to a fork in the road.

We bade each other good-bye, both of us wondering whether it was the beginning of the end of our relationship and neither of us commenting on it.

Working on *Indian Fighter* was not the happiest experience in the world. Doug was nervous about this, his first production under the "Bryna" banner (the company was named for his mother). He dealt with it by being quite officious in every department, giving other actors line readings, and changing camera shots set up by de Toth and the cameraman. Generally throwing his weight around.

Walter Matthau and some of the other actors came to me and asked if I couldn't persuade him to desist, but I told them that I was a hired hand just like the rest of them. Any suggestion I made would probably have the opposite effect. I had already had my run-in when Doug tried to give me specific line readings. I told him that we'd both come out sounding like him and suggested that he leave the direction to Andre. It did not go down well. Aside from our scenes together, we had very little to do with one another socially.

When I wasn't working I would still drive out to the location fort, ride the available horses, and watch the stunt men work. They were extraordinary, daring but precise, and I never ceased to marvel at them. I earned their respect when I managed to drive a six-horse team at breakneck speed through the gates of the fort and pull them up on the camera marks. They had stationed one of their crew under the seat of the wagon in case the team stampeded, but it wasn't necessary, and they gave me a round of applause.

Aside from that, I wasn't too thrilled with my work. I couldn't seem to get a handle on the lady, and Andre had his hands full with Elsa. She was beautiful, but inexperienced. I went back to the old precept "when in doubt—do less" with the result that I found the final product on the screen was bland and less than interesting.

Michael and Joel came up in the final weeks of shooting. Doug wanted them in the picture, so he told Andre to give them some lines; "The Indians are coming!" and place them on the lookout tower of the fort. The boys were thrilled. Unfortunately, their thespian powers had yet to be developed, and the scene was cut out.

As the picture ended, I was offered a play in La Jolla. It was another "pre-Broadway tryout" called *Native Uprising* to be directed by Norman Lloyd. He was an actor-director for whom I had great respect. Marjorie Lord and Howard Duff were also to be in the cast, so it sounded like an interesting project even if it never made it to Broadway.

Doug and Anne wanted to have the kids for the summer and the boys were again amenable, so I headed down to La Jolla in happy anticipation. A lot of rewriting was done on the script, both during rehearsals and after we opened, but the playwright was never to get all the problems solved. However, it was good to be working on stage again, and there was a sense of generous community effort on everyone's part that made it an exciting exploration.

Toward the end of the run, Doug called and asked if I would consider moving to California and putting the boys in school in there for a year. Now that he had a more stable homelife, he wanted to see more of them, rather than just on holidays. It seemed a reasonable request. I thought the change might be good for all of us. It would give Bill and me chance to test the strength of our relationship and see if we could stand living apart from one another.

On my return to L.A., I signed a nine-month lease on a small house in Westwood, arranged for an English couple that I knew to rent the New York apartment, and investigated the local schools. In a sad but honest conversation with Bill, we gave each other permission to date others and to try and make a new life for ourselves independently.

The day after the boys started school, Michael at Emerson Junior High and Joel at Bellagio Elementary, I came back to the house with a sense of foreboding. Looking at the calendar, I saw the many months before I would see Bill again and felt that I had made a dreadful mistake. Already I missed him terribly.

And indeed much seemed to turn sour in the months ahead.

Joel was found to be dyslexic, a condition that no one knew much about at that time. At Dalton, where he had spent the first and second grades, his clowning around had been labeled hyperactivity, and his memory was so retentive that he could reel off pages of a book out loud to fool us that he was actually reading. When confronted by new material at Bellagio and panicked by his lack of comprehension, he would run home as soon as the teacher's back was turned.

I would bring him back and have long conferences with the teachers. I took him to a child psychiatrist, but nothing seemed to help. He was a deeply confused, unhappy little boy. The one thing he seemed to enjoy was the Cub Scouts.

Michael, on the other hand, was thrown in with a bunch of kids far older and more sophisticated than he. Allen Stevenson was so superior academically to the California public schools that he was placed, at the age of not quite eleven, with peers who were in their early teens, sporting black leather jackets. They wore Elvis pompadours, duck's ass hairdos, and motorcycle boots, cleaning their nails with lethal looking knives and sassing their parents.

Wanting to be one of the gang, Michael tried to outdo them in machismo. He went from being a polite, tractable kid to developing into a hood, rebelling against everything, challenging me at every turn.

On top of this, Doug's rapidly changing plans made a quietly structured routine difficult to maintain. He would call up at the last minute, wanting to take the boys to Palm Springs or Catalina without regard for plans they might have made. We had one humdinger of a row when he wanted to disrupt a Cub Scout outing that Joel had been looking forward to. I refused, precipitating a lot of abuse.

In November of that year, Anne gave birth to Peter taking some of the frantic attention off my two. Doug used to say that he couldn't live with them and couldn't live without them. He would spoil or punish them arbitrarily, which had them confused and insecure.

As Christmas approached, I knew that some change would have to be made in Michael's schooling before things got totally out of hand. I tried to find a private school that was more structured and academically challenging. None would take him halfway through the year except a military academy called Black Fox. It was not the ideal choice, but it was the better of two evils, as I felt that Michael was headed for serious trouble if there were no intervention.

I worked on and off in several television shows and dated on and off with some pleasant fellows. Most of my energies were taken up with my children and their problems. I was coming to a realization of the vastness of the mistake I had made in disrupting all our lives.

I watched the building of the freeway system from the window of my bedroom and saw the 405 sneaking on over the Sepulveda Pass while I checked the pages on the calendar, quietly yearning for Bill. Our infrequent phone conversations were friendly, but stilted. There seemed no way out of the impasse.

Then, with the the new year, he called. He hated life without me. It was bleak and drab and profoundly miserable. He had come to the decision that we should be married, if I still wanted to.

"Yes!" I shouted. "Yes, yes, my darling!"

We started to make our plans.

He would fly out when *Inherit* went on hiatus and announce our engagement. Then he would start looking for houses within commuting distance of New York, sending me snaps of the possibilities.

Overnight my spirits changed. There was a future. There was hope. Together I felt we could lick any problems that came up. I knew that we could provide a more stable atmosphere for the boys, and they seemed to sense a change in the air and were more cooperative.

I had ruled out any pets, save hamsters, as we were in rented quarters, but when a cleaning woman introduced a sad, dirty, stray pup to the household, the kids pleaded with me to keep him. So Penrod joined our lives. He was intelligent and adaptable and brought us all a lot of joy for the next thirteen years.

Bill flew out as planned, and we had a big party to announce the engagement. He had brought me a ring that his father had designed for his mother in 1912, a pearl surrounded by diamonds. The day that he gave it to me I happened to be engrossed in the *New York Times* Sunday crossword puzzle. I heard him murmur something that I didn't catch.

"Hmmm?."

He cleared his throat.

"I was asking if you would do me the honor of being my wife."

With the formality of the phrasing I assumed he was joking.

"Not if you were the last man on earth," I replied.

There was a silence, and I looked up to see his stricken

expression.

"Oh, my God, darling, I'm sorry. Yes, of course, I'll marry you. Yes! Yes! Please ask me again!" The boys were happy to see him and reacted positively to the marriage. They joined in the plans for the future.

We narrowed down the house hunting to Princeton and Westport, principally because of their excellent school systems. I wanted a safe, semirural community where the boys could ride their bikes to visit friends and pursue their own interests. Princeton was high on my list because of the academic community and its proximity to New Brunswick, where my sister Ruth lived. Bill favored Westport, where he had summered as a child, but we were both open to change.

Bill's plans for the *Disenchanted* were moving along. Budd Shulberg had agreed to work with Harvey Breit on adapting it to the stage, and after *Inherit the Wind* closed, Bill was looking forward to spending all his energies in production. He confided that acting was becoming boring to him. With his brilliance and far-ranging curiosity, I could see how that might be.

After he went back East, the Polaroid photos arrived in droves. Quaint houses, ugly houses, farmhouses, Victorian houses, all with Bill's notations and preferences on the back. Luckily before a decision had to be made, I was cast in a TV film called *The West Point Story* which was going to be shot at the academy on the Hudson. We planned a whirlwind tour of prospects on my weekend off.

We saw one charming, perpendicular house that fronted on a river. Bill was an avid fisherman and lusted after it, but the fact of a steep ladder between the kitchen and dining room as well as minuscule closets ruled it out. There was one last house Bill had saved for me He felt it was somewhat depressing, but had the right amount of rooms and was within our price range.

It was a simple farmhouse, built in the middle of the nineteenth century, white clapboard with a red barn, only half a mile from the Post Road and shops. It was also within a good school district in Westport.

The interior looked depressing. Everything was painted a uniformly ugly shade of grey and lit by forty-watt bulbs, but it had two acres in back, fronted by a nursery and dominated by a couple of enormous weeping willows. We decided that was it and put in an offer before I rejoined the cast at West Point.

The whole cast was housed on the premises of West Point and were given various "dos" and "don'ts" to be observed while there. One of them was "No visitors overnight in the room." Well, I was damned if I was going to be parted from my newly affianced, so we doubled up happily in the spartan single bed, rejoicing in being together again.

Come the dawn, we found ourselves in the middle of a French farce. The production manager, a fierce Teutonic type who never bent the rules, suspected that I was harboring someone in my room. He banged on the door at six in the morning, saying that there had been some change in my wardrobe and demanding to be let in.

Bill bounded into the closet, and I threw his shoes and underwear in after him, opened the door, yawning elaborately while the gentleman pushed his way into the room, his blue eyes darting suspiciously.

I spotted Bill's pipe on the desk and sat on it, swinging my legs casually while Erich stood, holding up the dress he said I was to wear.

"Shall I put it in the closet?"

"No!...No, that's all right. I'll do it later."

"Nein. It should be done now. You don't want wrinkle."

"Oh...okay. Give it to me."

I sidled over to the closet, praying that Bill was well back in the shadows, opened the door a few inches, and slid the dress in.

I leaned back against the closet door and smiled, fingering Bill's pipe in my pocket, as Erich stared at me coldly, seeming to debate as to whether he should demand I open the closet door. I talked fast.

"How kind of you, carrying my clothes all the way up here. That really was the wardrobe department's job, wasn't it? You are really on top of everything, aren't you?"

He narrowed his eyes to let me know he wasn't fooled, opened and shut his mouth a few times, then turned suddenly and left. I let Bill out of the closet, and we fell into each other's arms. Tears streamed down our cheeks as we howling with laughter.

I flew back to L.A. and began making arrangements for our move back to the East Coast. There were some uncomfortable scenes with Doug, who liked to remain in control. However, when he saw that there was no turning back as far as I was concerned, he conceded. I think he was secretly relieved that from now on he would just have the boys on vacations.

My happiness was infectious, the kids picked up on it, and the last months in California were the best. We went riding with Lloyd Bridges and his kids and deep-sea fishing off Santa Monica Bay. Then we took a trip down to Rosarita Beach in Mexico with Mary James, an old friend, and visited the newly opened Disneyland.

Shortly before we left, Penrod had disappeared, causing us all a great deal of worry.

He was an unusually amiable dog with one unfortunate characteristic, which the boys and their friends found highly amusing. He was continually tumescent, and, while not given to making advances or mounting one's leg, he would sit a straddle with a large pink, glowing erection that riveted the attention of our guests.

On our way to Mexico, we stopped in San Diego to have tea with a cousin of Mary's, and an exceedingly proper naval officer stationed there. As Mary poured, she remarked, "Diana, I've been meaning to ask you. Did Penrod ever show up?"

"He did, thank God. Just before we left."

"In his usual condition?"

"Oh, sure. I heard scratching, opened the front door, and there he was with his usual erection." The cousin visibly paled.

"Good Lord, ladies, who may I ask, is Penrod?" Due to our hilarity, it was some minutes before we could impart the information that he was a dog.

I arranged for Penrod to be driven back across country in my car, and the boys and I flew back to New York. We bunked in over the weekend at Bill's vacated apartment on Fifty-fifth Street.

He had flown to London to try to get Tyrone Power to commit to the starring role of Manley Halliday in *The Disenchanted* and while there, got to meet my sister, Fan, for the first time. There was instant liking on both sides.

There was a lot to do, but everything seemed easy due to the rosy future. Closing the apartment on Eighty-fifth Street and putting the furniture in storage out in New Brunswick, and arranging for the sale of the Hyde Park cottage while we stayed there for the summer months. (I was so anxious to unload it that I gave the buyers an interest-free mortgage, for which I took an unholy ribbing from Bill and all my family!) However, as it was sold for exactly twice as much as I had paid for it we didn't do too badly.

We could take possession of our new home in Westport the day before school opened. I had the boys registered, Michael in junior high and Joel in elementary. We spent the first night sleeping on mattresses on the floor and ate breakfast in a local diner, as the utilities had yet to be hooked up, then I took the boys on their first day in school.

We planned the wedding for December for various reasons, some monetary. Waiting until then would assure that I would receive the 10 percent of Doug's '56 salary, which would be a large help. Now that there would be no more alimony, the $540 that I received in child support each month didn't stretch very far, particularly now as the kids were growing up. The December date held a tax advantage for Doug as well. To get the mortgage on the house, I had to apply alone, showing my income from the alimony as well as from my earnings as an actress, giving no hint that it might change.

Bill came up on weekends during the fall, sleeping in what we called the "monastery room," which became his office after we wed. Upstairs there were three modest-sized bedrooms with two baths, one bedroom so tiny it could barely accommodate bunk beds. That was assigned to Joel. Michael was in the slightly larger room next to mine.

Another reason for the December date was that it would allow us a honeymoon in England. Bill had arranged a meeting with Tyrone Power to finalize the contract for *The Disenchanted*, and Doug and Anne would have the boys for the Christmas vacation.

The boys seemed to settle in well in Westport. They made friends readily. Mike's was Jerry Crosby, a shy, sweet boy who lived within walking distance. Joel rediscovered a friendship with Nicky Prince, who he had known in second grade at Dalton. Joel was still having problems with his studies, and Bill and I would try to coach him through his homework. It was a frustrating experience for all of us as we hadn't the faintest idea of how to deal with dyslexia and couldn't understand why Joel didn't "get it." We could have spared the boy a lot of agony and loss of self-esteem if it had been correctly diagnosed and the proper professional help available.

As it was, the problems deepened and eventually led to psychiatric treatment. The problems were furthered by his trips to California and back. He was a warm-hearted, sensitive child who hated partings. When he left me for California, or left Doug to return to Connecticut, it was a wrenching, painful experience. Michael seemed to weather it well and was protective of his younger brother. We hoped in time that Joel would get over his separation anxiety, however, once established, it is almost impossible to dislodge. A flight attendant once became concerned over Joel and his wracking sobs, only to be advised by Michael.

"Don't worry. He always stops crying over Kansas."

A few weeks after we moved in, the boys came running in, gasping excitedly.

"Come and see! We've built an enormous tree house way, way up!"

They led me out and across our property line into the woods of our neighbors.

"Oh, Lord!" I said. "This is the Liebling's land. You must take it down immediately, being very careful not to mark up the tree. And then you must go and apologize to Mr. and Mrs. Liebling."

A note here: Mrs. Liebling was better known as Audrey Wood, a top literary agent. She and her husband, Bill Liebling, had had a theatrical agency together for many years. While studying at the academy, I'd had reason to go there and recalled her being a most formidable lady, stern and hatted behind her desk. I still regarded her with some awe and was nervous about starting our neighborly relationship on the wrong foot.

Pouting, my boys disappeared. But the smart little devils went first to the Lieblings' house, no doubt turning on their considerable charm. The upshot was, not only were they invited to share blueberry pancakes with the Lieblings, but Bill Liebling made out a deed, inscribed and signed, which he baked in the oven to give it an authentic aged look. It deeded the tree to "Michael and Joel Douglas and their heirs in perpetuity." The boys returned, proudly waving their permission and resumed the business of completing the tree house.

Wedding preparations continued. We had chosen a white, steepled Congregational church and went to meet the minister, Gibson Daniels, for his permission to marry us. Bill was Jewish and had been brought up mostly in the Unitarian church, and I in the Church of England, similar to Episcopal.

Reverend Daniels was not too happy about the fact that I was an actress and divorced, but I convinced him that I was not into "serial Hollywood marriages." He turned his attention to Bill, who, with his usual forthrightness, said that he didn't believe in God, and I thought to myself, "Well, there goes the whole ball game." But Reverend Daniels was intrigued, and they had a long and interesting discussion about the merits of faith. I think Dr. Daniels sensed the depths of Bill's moral fiber and honesty and respected him for it.

Our wedding day was cold and rainy. Friends and relatives drove for some distances to attend the reception after the ceremony. We figured around eighty in all, but had turkey, ham and champagne ordered to be served in our still bare house.

John Blum, Bill's brother, was best man and my sister Ruth matron of honor. Bill's father, Morton Blum, drove over from South Norwalk with his stepmother, Edith. Johnson relatives turned up from New Jersey in force. With our actor friends from New York, we did number just a little more than eighty.

We arranged for the boys to sit with Dr. McCormick and his wife during the service, with instructions to keep a weather eye on Joel, who wasn't sure he liked the impending change in his life. When the time came in the service for the minister to ask if there are any objections to the marriage, they could be ready to clap a hand over his mouth.

As it was, both boys were caught up in the excitement of the event and threw rice, laughing hysterically. Later, during the reception, Joel was found sobbing on his bunk bed. I comforted him as best I could and brought him down to my niece, Diana, who was to drive them both to New York to meet Doug and Anne. It was a time fraught with high emotions for all concerned, but it was toughest on the children.

We were to spend our wedding night at the Silvermine Tavern and leave the next day for London. However, as we were getting in the car, wedding guests waving merrily, John bolted out of the front door, flagging us down.

"Urgent phone call from London!" he yelled. "A Mr.

Power says he must talk with you!"

Bill sighed, and we returned to the house.

I watched him while I made small talk with the guests. His knuckles holding the receiver were white.

"But, Ty, I don't understand…"

"No, Ty, the production cannot be postponed…"

"Yes. Well, I'm sorry too. Good luck with the film."

He hung up and turned to me with a rueful smile.

"Not good. I'll tell you in the car."

We left John and Pam, his wife, in charge of the sixty guests remaining and drove the few miles to Silvermine.

"I'm afraid London is out, my darling. Ty said that his agents had pulled a fast one, as they really didn't want him to do a play. But that if I waited four months he would get rid of this commitment. What if after four months, something else comes up? I can't take that chance." As a business trip would be paying for part of our honeymoon, we could no longer afford it.

We sat in our room at the Silvermine Tavern, sipping champagne and wondering what to do. The idea of going through lengthy explanations to friends and relatives when we showed up back at the house was anathema. Suddenly I had an idea.

"How would you feel about Bermuda?"

"Bermuda? Fine, I guess. Why?"

"I told you, my brothers have a cottage colony called 'Ariel Sands' on the South Shore which opened a couple of years ago. It's the off-season now, and we probably could get a good rate. That is, if you can stand being on an island where I'm related to just about everybody." I called Bayard, and he arranged for a cottage at Ariel immediately, saying that would be the family's wedding present to us at no charge.

Not an easy way for Bill to meet the extended family as a whole, but with his innate dignity and their sensitivity, it was managed well.

My mother, who had adored Doug, liked and respected

Bill. "He seems a good, steady sort of chap," she said, to my amusement. She didn't know the half of it. Bill believed in risk taking, in exploring all the possibilities in one's cultural and artistic life, in stretching one's talent to the utmost and never settling for the mundane. He was generous to a fault, with his time and with worldly goods. I knew we would never be wealthy, but I knew that we would have a hell of a good and exciting life.

Our first night in Bermuda, the whole family gathered in the bar at Ariel. Having many drinks, as was their wont, they sang Irish ballads and English music-hall songs, the proverbial "sing-songs" that I remembered from my childhood. Bill was game and went along with the jollity, though he was tone deaf and couldn't join in. Later he would flee when he sensed a sing-song was coming up, but now he just looked bemused.

After they went home, we sat out on our balcony at "Wild Waves," the cottage furthest from the clubhouse, which had been reserved for us to gaze at the moonlit water. The same thought seized both of us—why not go for a swim?

Of course, it was December, not the best of swimming weather. Of course, we had not brought bathing suits, given the season, but in our slightly inebriated state, a dip in the pool seemed the perfect way to start our honeymoon.

The grounds were deserted, we being the only guests in the hotel, so we made our way down to the large saltwater pool at the ocean's edge. I was in my wedding-night dress and negligee, and Bill was in his undershorts.

Once there I threw off my clothes and dove into the chilly water, Bill following immediately after. We raced to the end and back, hauling ourselves out quite blue with cold and with Bill fetchingly draped with bits of seaweed.

As we ran back to the cottage, teeth chattering, Bill volunteered to get us some brandy from the bar while I ran in to get warm. I was drying myself off in the room and wrapping up in a warm towel when I heard a yell coming from the direction of the clubhouse. I'd started to throw on some clothes when Bill appeared, quite helpless with laughter.

He'd found the clubhouse door locked and was circling the building looking for an open window when he ran into the night watchman coming in the opposite direction. Glistening from seawater in the moonlight and draped with seaweed, he looked like an apparition of a drowned sailor, and the night watchman had dropped his flashlight and screamed bloody murder.

Christmas passed pleasantly and uneventfully, with Bill joining my brothers at their usual target practice off the back of Newbold Place, though Bill did mutter quietly to me that he would prefer to declare open season on Cousin Mabel, an ancient gorgon of a relative who glowered from a corner during the festivities.

One thing that had me watchful was the unthinking anti-Semitism that pervaded most of the families in Bermuda. But I guess the word had gone out and all were careful about comment. That is, until our last day.

We were waiting with my mother for the taxi to take us to the airport, my brothers were there and also Lloyd Meyer, a family friend who was in the process of writing a biography about my father. He was not one of my favorite people, both a snob and a toady, leeching onto the family.

He asked where in Connecticut we had bought a house. Informed it was Westport, he said,

"Oh, you really should have bought in Wilson Point. It's a very distinguished area. Restricted, you know."

My brothers shot alarmed glances at Bill, who smiled and asked, "Restricted? Really? Now who would they be restricting?"

Meyer paled, realizing he'd stepped in it.

"Oh...," he said, waving his hands helplessly. "Oh...houses...the kind of houses one can build. That must be it."

Bill continued smiling.

"Are you sure?"

Now the man, red, eyes darting from side to side, turned to my brothers who were carefully looking the other way. He got to his feet.

"I...uh...think I left something on the stove..."

Just then the taxi arrived and we made our farewells.

In the cab, Bill kissed me.

"Well, they tried awfully hard and they almost made it," he said. "I really do like your family and they must be puzzled that you insist on marrying one Jew after another. But I'm glad you did."

"Me too."

Chapter 12
WESTPORT

Looking back on the Westport years, one is tempted to see it all in a misty glow of uninterrupted happiness, but of course this was not so.

There were problems to deal with. Problems of adjustment for the children and for us as a newly married couple. Our sex life suffered a bit with the close quarters, children's nightmares, and calls for "Just one drink of water more, Mommy." Tutors were hired for Joel, but he was still having a bad time with schoolwork.

We were taken up with a fashionable and flirtatious group that had given Westport a certain notoriety. I had to fend off some unwanted attentions as the males jostled for position, circling the newest female in the pack..

Bill was working with Budd Shulberg and Harvey Breit on drafts of *The Disenchanted*, and I was commuting into the city a few times a week, doing some TV and a few commercials. Michael joined the Downshifters Club, a bunch of car aficionados and the local Little League, where he instantly became a star player. Then Joel joined Little League as well, and the results were disastrous. His form of dyslexia also affected his coordination, so catching and throwing were difficult for him to master. My heart broke for him. He sat so patiently in the dugout, hoping to be called in, waiting in vain.

Penrod slept with Joel and followed him behind his bike everywhere he went. Both boys took great comfort from the animal.

We entertained a lot, drank a bit too much, had a weekly poker game with the McCormicks. The kids joined in and were counseled to "breast your cards and sit up straight if you want to play with the grownups." We bought an outboard power skiff called "The Lark," in which we'd go tooling around the sound, out to Cockenoe Island and back. We picnicked and beached ourselves on sand bars with regularity. Bit by bit, we settled into a family life.

Bill was consistent and firm with the boys, but had a sense of fun, and they responded well. Michael says he remembers that I eased up a lot after we were married and was no longer as rigid with the rules as I had been as a single parent. He also remembers how well Bill listened to him when he was responding to some query about school. He told me that it was the first time that an adult male had listened seriously to him. He was so shaken by it that he ran upstairs weeping.

As Michael entered puberty, we had a few nose-to-nose confrontations. He resented taking orders from a mere woman, and I figured that part of the problem was his burgeoning sexuality. I felt it was time for Bill to have a "Birds and Bees" talk with him to answer some of his questions. At first Bill objected.

"I'm not his father."

"Look, his father is 3,000 miles away. Anyway, I'm not sure he would give the best advice on the subject. The way Michael resents me right now, I couldn't get to first base."

"Well, okay, but first you'd better fix me a strong Scotch." That done, he called for Michael to come downstairs to his small office. Instant alarm from Michael.

"What did I do? What did I do?"

Bill waved me away and ushered Mike in, closing the door. I returned to the living room and sat by the fire trying to concentrate on my needlepoint. All was quiet till I heard a sudden burst of raucous male laughter and slapping of thighs. Not quite what I'd had in mind for sexual education, I decided. Obviously they were having a whale of a time, but I hoped some pertinent information was being dealt.

After about an hour, they emerged, arms around each

other's shoulders, both looking vastly relieved.

"That wasn't so bad," Bill confided to me later. "He had some misinformation that I was able to clear up, then we told each other some dirty jokes. He's going to be just fine."

A year or two later, it was time for Joel to have the talk.

Confidently, Bill led him into the office and sat him down. To Bill's chagrin, he couldn't seem to make any headway. Joel kept fidgeting and glancing away.

Finally, Bill said "Are you finding this embarassing? Is that what it is?"

"No," said Joel. "It's just that I'm missing *Gunsmoke!*"
Bill shooed him back to the television set. Any information on the subject must have been imparted by Michael.

The next winter, when Bill was in Florida with Harvey and Budd Schulberg, the boys came back from skiing with Doug in Lake Placid and persuaded me to have a go on the local slopes. I was instantly enchanted, called Bill, and told him that I had discovered a sport that he would go bonkers over.

Initially suspicious, he soon became an addict, and we would go with the boys and sometimes with the Prince family up to Mohawk Mountain. Joel did not fare well on the slopes. He was a strong skier, but was inclined to be reckless and ski out of control. One winter he broke his left leg. The following winter, his right. It didn't stop him from tackling the sport after that.

Bill now had a producing office in New York and a secretary, Shirley, who never tired of telling me how much she was in love with my husband. I found her tiresome. Strangely enough, given my background with Doug, I never entertained any suspicions about Bill or their relationship. One time, when Bill missed the last train and announced ingenuously that he stayed over in Shirley's apartment, I did hit the roof. He was honestly surprised at my reaction, but promised not to do it again.

"Better to sleep in Grand Central," he muttered. "Boy, oh boy!"

I would go into the city on jobs and appointments, but mostly I played the part of the fifties, suburban wife; meeting the train in the station wagon, attending P.T.A. meetings and Little League games, and being happier than I had ever been in my life.

Bill was a joyous soul, and he spread joy around him, which is one reason he attracted so many friends. His humor and wit continued to delight me. I counted myself one lucky woman. Surprises and treats that I arranged for him were always given great appreciation and some astonishment, as he wasn't used to such treatment. A female friend said that I was going to spoil him.

"I hope so," I said, "considering the way he spoils me."

It sounds icky, but for us, it worked.

I think one reason he reveled in the affection he got from me was that he had been emotionally deprived as a child. His father had consistently rejected him, favoring his brilliant older brother and his twin sister. No matter what he did, he could never please his progenitor. Shortly before our marriage, I was witness to a horrific fight between father and son because Bill had chosen to legalize his professional name of Darrid. It was obvious that there were deep, unspoken angers that had festered for years.

He had adopted the name Darrid at the age of sixteen when he had his first summer-stock job as an actor. His natal name was Blum, and one of the other actors said that Billy Blum sounded like a borscht-circuit comic so he looked for one more suitable to the classic actor he hoped to become. On his library card, someone had printed his middle name, David, as Darrid, so he immediately rechristened himself.

Though his anger was never directed toward me, it was always there like a time bomb waiting to explode. It made for a complex man, one who did not suffer fools gladly. He used words with deadly accuracy. This, coupled with his compassionate nature, warmth, and charm made for an interesting kaleisdoscopic character.

One adjustment was made early in the marriage. Bill was not a talker in the morning, whereas both the boys and I woke up shinyeyed and jabbering. I solved this by serving the boys breakfast downstairs before they went off to school, then bringing a tray up to the bedroom, with breakfast and the paper. I tried to keep my mouth shut until he had shaved and showered, but sometimes the editorials became too much for me.

The day that China invaded Tibet started me spluttering. I ranted on while Bill shaved, I shouted through the noise of the shower, and continued my nonstop tirade in the car all the way to the station.

"You see. This could be Armageddon!"

Bill sighed.

"Yes, well, Ah'm a gettin' out!"

The production of *The Disenchanted* was underway. Bill had taken on a partner, Eleanor Saidenberg, who brought in some of the financing and signed Jason Robards, Jr., for the part of Manley Halliday and Diane Cilento for Jere. The script was in good shape, if overly long, but Bill felt that a lot of that could be taken care of out of town. In the summer of '58, life was sunny indeed. The boys went out to California, and Bill and I went to Martha's Vineyard for a vacation before rehearsals started in the fall.

We took sailing lessons in Edgartown, and the instructor remarked that I must have raced boats before as I instinctively picked up every breath of wind. As far as I remembered, I never had. It must have been something passed down by seafaring ancestors.

We walked back up the streets to the hotel tanned, happy, and salty to be greeted by the news that Diana Cilento would not be in the play. She had contracted tuberculosis. Rehearsals were due to start in two weeks.

We tore back to Westport, and frantic calls were made. From the beginning, Bill had not wanted me to read for the part. He was looking for an intrinsic quality in the actress who played Jere, an underlying hysteria and neurosis that he felt I did not have. I could not deny the truth of that and decided not to push it, though privately I felt that I could play the hell out of it.

Bill enlisted the help of our next-door neighbors, the Lieblings, in his search for the right actress. Bill Liebling came up with the right suggestion, a young English actress he had just seen playing Shakespeare on Broadway, Rosemary Harris. Rehearsals started on time directed by Dan Petrie. The play ran overly long, and Bill had a hard time convincing Budd to make the necessary cuts.

"If O'Neill can run five hours, Shulberg can too," Budd was said to have announced.

I visited New Haven while the show was being tried out, fascinated to see it all come together. The costumes and the sets were outstanding. I had to confess that Rosemary had exactly the right quality of barely suppressed hysteria that Bill felt was essential for the part, and as for Jason, one could not take one's eyes off him. He always carried with him that element of danger that is one of the requisites for a star. George Grizzard had had an innocent and touching quality so right for the young man. The cast as a whole was excellent.

There was a bit of a run-in with the musicians' union when the armistice scene was staged, as they insisted that a harmonica could not be played on stage without two or three musicians standing by, sitting downstairs in the green room. As I remember, they were forced to settle for one when Bill said that he would have the soldiers whistle on stage rather than bust the budget.

By the time I visited in Boston, Dan had been replaced by David Pressman. I don't think I ever found out the reason why as Bill was closeted with Budd and Harvey at every available minute going over rewrites. I barely saw him.

Opening night in New York was like the culmination of a dream, one that Bill had been pursuing for the past five years and one that held the key to our future in the business. Excitement was high, and when the notices were read, they were excellent, so we settled down to anticipate a long, healthy run.

It was not to be. A newspaper strike caused it to close prematurely after a few months, and we were back to facing financial insecurity.

However, it wasn't long before Bill came upon another script he loved, and even though *The Disenchanted* had not completely paid off its investors, he had no trouble raising backing for *The Andersonville Trial*, a fascinating courtroom drama based on history and written by Saul Levitt.

Chapter 13
BROADWAY

*I*t was at one of Alex Cohen's parties that my chance meeting with the Langners paid off. They had remembered my performance in Nassau in *Sabrina Fair* some six years previously and told me that they were co-producing a play, *The Highest Tree*, with Dore Schary that he had written. They had read several actresses for the lead, but had yet to find the right one. They suggested I come in and read for Schary, who was also directing the piece. Needless to say, I was on the train the next morning.

Dore Schary was a dear, warm man who made me comfortable right away. I was able to do my best without my nerves going awry. When the reading was over, he came on stage, held both my hands, and kissed me on the cheek.

"Thank you," he said. "I've found my Mary. Rehearsals start in two weeks."

I couldn't believe my luck. Dore Schary had been almost a mythical figure in Hollywood. He was deeply respected for his liberal politics and the moral fiber to back them up, particularly during the time the House Un-American Activities Committeewas riding roughshod over civil rights. He was a talented filmmaker, had been the head of M.G.M. and had written a hit play, *Sunrise at Campobello*. It had played on Broadway a year or two earlier. The next few weeks were happily frantic with costume fittings, photographs, and interviews. At the same time Bill plunged into rehearsals for *The Andersonville Trial*.

When the cast assembled for our first read through, I thought I recognized one of the young members of the cast who had a walk-on part, but I couldn't place him, so I forgot about it. Kenneth McKenna was a fine actor who had been a matinee idol back in the 1930s and subsequently an executive at M.G.M. He played an atomic scientist who finds that he is dying of leukemia. I was playing the part of his mistress and to my delight, Dore decided to star me as well. A few days into rehearsal, the young man I had noticed before came up to me and said, "You don't remember me, do you?"

"Well," I hedged, "I know we've met, but I can't remember where."

"No," he said, "we've never actually met, but I used to live across the way from you in Westwood. I used to watch you and your boys go in and out, but I never had the guts to speak to you. So I spent a lot of time washing my car out in front and hoping you'd say hello. My name is Robert Redford."

He was good in the part, though he didn't have much to do, and Dore predicted a stellar future for him, however he was a far cry from the devastatingly handsome man that he was to grow into.

He and his young wife had a terrible tragedy shortly after we opened. They lost their firstborn to sudden infant death syndrome. One's heart bled for him as he moved through his days like a sleepwalker, so young and so very sad.

Bill and I were having lunch at the Madison Hotel one day, shortly before *The Highest Tree* was due to open out of town, when a fortune-teller approached our table.

"Go ahead," said Bill. "Can't be anything but good times ahead. Let's hear it."

The fortune-teller studied my palm.

"I see you surrounded by famous people, but you will never be famous yourself."

Bill and I exchanged a surreptitious grin for hadn't it just been announced that I was about to star on Broadway?

"You have two children," she went on, "one of them will not be well. It will cause you much pain."

"Okay, that's enough. Thank you very much," said Bill,

dismissing her. He squeezed my hand.

"You know they're all phonies," he said.

"Yeah? Well how come you tell everyone about the fortune-teller you went to when you were sixteen who predicted that you would be an actor, but leave the profession for another. That you wouldn't get married until you were in your thirties and that you'd marry a divorced woman with two children? She sure hit it on the nose."

As it turned out, this particular fortune-teller also predicted correctly.

Although I have made my life in the entertainment business, mainly theatre, fame has eluded me. Granted, I never sought it avidly and treated it as a tool to play interesting parts, but I have certainly been surrounded by the famous. The latest being my son, Michael, who has achieved superstardom.

What has made for the better life? I wonder. Stardom and celebrity or the quieter joys of the journeyman actor? To some it would seem obvious. Stardom is what it is all about. But having observed it from the wings, I am not sure.

There is a terrible hunger in people's eyes when they look at a star, as if they want to devour him. He ceases to be observed as a human being and has become instead an icon.

People behave differently around a celebrity. Sometimes they appear to have taken leave of their senses and babble on in the strangest fashion. Of course, there is the coterie that surrounds a star, protecting him from many mundane chores that anchor the rest of us to reality. They tell him only what he wants to hear, like a modern day "Roi du Soleil."

It is no wonder that so many succumb to drugs and drink. What is amazing is the ones who don't. Who, through striving, manage to lead normal and productive lives.

Of course, I would be a liar if I didn't admit to the joy I get out of performing on stage. The give-and-take with the audience and, yes, the applause at the end when you know you've done a good job. But it is a far cry from the invasiveness of celebrity.

I am proud of Michael, fine actor that he is, for his levelheadedness and for his commitment to making a difference in the world in which he lives. His work with the UN, antiproliferation, and gun control, as well as his loyalty and love of family and friends. There are few who have coped with celebrity as well as he.

Joel has had other problems to deal with. Fending off opportunists who hope to get to his father and brother through him. Keeping his self-esteem when odious comparisons are made. Through it all, I think he is the one who has benefited most from Bill's influence, he truly "listens with the third ear" and has deep compassion for the walking wounded.

When he was in the College of the Seven Seas, sailing around the world, one of the faculty told him that a student was up in the crow's nest threatening suicide. They were at a loss as to how to get him down. Joel climbed up and, after an hour or so, persuaded the troubled boy to come down.

His quiet kindnesses have not met with enough acknowledgment.

Back to 1959. Rehearsals were a joy under Dore's direction, and the cast truly had a familial feeling. The day came when we headed out of town. Our first stop was Boston.

"Treat yourself like a star, for heaven's sake. Stay at the Ritz," said Bill and I took him up on it, though he couldn't join me. He was deep in rehearsals for *The Andersonville Trial*. We were due to open at the Colonial Theatre.

My first inkling of trouble came one day when Dore was walking with me across the Commons after I'd had a fitting. Dore was not only the playwright, but the director and co-producer of the piece. As the Langners had not come to Boston with us, he had no one to discuss his rewrites with. He was visibly uneasy and kept talking about the first act, which I was not in.

"I think I'm going to have Ken do such and such, huh?"

he said, looking to me as if for approval. My heart sank.

"Oh, God," I thought, "he's meant to be the daddy. He's meant to have all the answers. All is not well!"

Indeed, all was not well. Though the writing and acting got respectful notices, the critics were noticeably cool, compounded by the fact that *The Sound of Music* had just opened to ecstatic reviews around the corner.

Rewriting went on all during the Boston and into the Philadelphia run. Ken was getting visibly exhausted, and the whole company was on edge, though Dore did his best to keep our spirits up. Ruth and Mother came to see it on a matinee, and Mother was quite disturbed by the reality of my performance. In a scene with Bill Prince who was playing the doctor, I was informed that my lover was dying. Each time it hit me in the gut; sometimes I wept, sometimes I didn't, but the emotion was full always. On that particular matinee, I happened to weep, and my poor mother was still shattered when she came backstage.

"Darling, do you have to put yourself through that every night? I simply can't bear it!"

Being in a play that is having problems out of town is something like being a patient who has been told he may have a terminal disease. Denial plays a very large part, anger is there too. Determination to beat the odds, a false cheeriness, any hope you can hold on to.

Bill called, saying that Joel was having a really rough time with his homework and that he was going to hire a special tutor for him if that was okay with me.

"Fine," I said, guilt washing over me. The kid needed me ,and I wasn't there. Was the satisfaction of working really worth it?

Opening in New York, the notices were, for the most part, respectful but poor. While acknowledging Dore's high-mindedness, they found the play talky and undramatic. The most painful and incisive critique came from Kenneth Tynan in *The New Yorker*, who wrote "With his feet on the soap box, his head in the clouds and his talent firmly in escrow, Dore Schary has committed *The Highest Tree*."

We closed two weeks later.

The fortune-teller's next prediction, sadly, also came true.

When the children arrived back from their holiday visit with Doug, I noticed that Joel was staggering a little, as though his balance was off. We put it down to a plugged ear, made worse by the flight, but the next morning he could not make it down the stairs and had to navigate on his bottom. Now seriously alarmed, we called Dr. Frank McCormick who suggested we take him to Lenox Hill Hospital for a complete evaluation. That began four of the worst months I have ever experienced. What they must have been for Joel, I can only imagine. He became unable to walk.

As soon as he was hospitalized, he withdrew more and more. His voice shrank from a croak to a whisper and finally he stopped communicating altogether. Meanwhile, test after test was being run on him. Medically they could find nothing wrong, so we assumed it must be a psychiatric problem. However, the psychiatrists insisted that the cause was medical, and so it went round and round.

Bill and I moved into New York to be closer to the hospital. (Michael had started boarding school at Eaglebrook by this time.)

After a few months with no improvement, it was decided that he would do better if forced to interact with other children, rather than being in a private room. So plans were made to move him to a children's ward in Presbyterian Hospital.

All the way up in the ambulance, he stared at me with fury in his eyes, and when I delivered him into his bed in the ward, he turned his face to the wall. Any attempt to make him stand or take a step resulted in total collapse. I went home and wept bitterly on Bill's shoulder, wondering if we'd done the right thing.

The new team of doctors and psychiatrists started in on Joel, and after the first week, it looked as though he might be making some progress. He had begun communicating with the little girl in the next bed, which was a hopeful sign. First, the nurses told me, they waved to each other when they thought they were not being observed. Then they seemed to be working out a sign language known only to them. Suddenly the girl's condition worsened, she was moved to intensive care, and in a matter of twenty-four hours, she died. He turned his face to the wall again, silent in his grief.

Weeks stretched into months as we tried to reach him, but the doctors were as baffled as ever.

One night I rolled over and said to Bill, "One thing hasn't been tried. Hypnotism. I know the psychiatrists are loath to use it, but won't his muscles start to atrophy?"

"Let's bring it up and see what they say."

The next morning, I met one of the doctors in the hall before I went into the ward and asked if hypnotism had ever been considered. His jaw dropped.

"How did you know?" he said.

"Know what?"

"We had the whole team going over Joel's case last night. And we decided as a last resort to use hypnotism. But when you see Joel, be sure you don't let him know what we are planning."

"Of course not."

But something in my attitude must have changed and something in the attitude of the attending nurses must have changed too because late that night I got a call.

"We have just run the flag up over Presbyterian Hospital. Joel has taken his first steps. He's bouncing off the walls like a drunken sailor, but he's moving, and I think the sooner you can get him out of here and home, the better."

"I'll be down first thing in the morning…and…and…thank you."

We bundled him into the station wagon and headed up the Merritt Parkway homeward. It was spring, and the fruit blossoms and dogwoods lined the roads, and I could see color returning to Joel's cheeks, interest returning to his eyes and then he spoke.

"How's Penrod? Did he miss me?"

And I knew we were going to be all right. The next day, Jerry Crosby came down to visit Joel and stopped me in the hall on his way out.

"Mrs. Darrid, there's something I'd like to do with Joel. I think it would be good for him."

"What's that, Jerry?"

"I'd like to take him on a long bike ride. Maybe even overnight. Sort of an adventure."

"But, Jerry...my God, he's just out of the hospital. His balance is still very shaky. I don't think..."

"We won't go until he's ready. I'll come every day after school and work with him riding around the driveway."

"Well, okay. I'll check with his doctor. But I guess you can do that." True to his word, Jerry was there every day, holding onto the back of the bicycle seat. He encouraged Joel as he wobbled his way over the tarmac. Finally, the day came.

"I think he's ready. I think he can do it."

I was conscious of Joel watching my face closely as I tried to keep calm.

"If Joel feels okay about it, then it's fine with me too."

I sent up a few prayers as they mapped out their route to the falls, almost seventy miles away. I knew that Jerry was an extremely conscientious boy and would call immediately if there was a problem.

They made it up and partway back. When I picked them up with their bikes, there was no mistaking the triumphant glow on Joel's face. I marveled at the miracle that one kid can perform on the other, the leap of faith that adults are often too chicken to make.

Meanwhile, Bill was out of town with *The Andersonville Trial*, and I went back to my suburban wifely chores of PTA meetings and Cub Scouts. Joel was continuing to have trouble with his homework because of what proved to be his dyslexia, and I often found my patience running thin as I tried to cope. This was the first year that Michael was away at boarding school, and I think that affected us all. We all missed him, but Joel had lost his staunchest ally and was totally disconsolate.

We had decided on boarding school for Michael after his second year in junior high in Westport. The reason for it was that he was being subjected, according to the guidance counselor, to a lot of aggressive female attention. She told us that the girls in the class were continually passing him notes, vying for his attention, etc. She said he was like catnip to the girls, and she thought he would do better in an all-male atmosphere for the time being.

At first I was incredulous. My skinny little fourteen-year-old a Lothario? Then I began listening to his end of phone conversations that went on every evening and realized he was sounding like a blase and bored Don Juan.

"Yes," he was saying, " I thought about taking you to the movies, but I changed my mind...No, no particular reason. That's just the way it is."

After he hung up I said, "Mike, that wasn't very kind. What's come over you?"

"Mom, you just don't know. You just don't know how it is."

After another consultation with the guidance counselor, we asked Michael how he would feel about an all-boys' boarding school, and he seemed amenable to the idea. We started making the rounds of the various New England prep schools.

We all liked Deerfield, but Michael's grades weren't high enough for acceptance. The headmaster suggested he go to Eaglebrook, a pre-prep school located up the hill from Deerfield and then transfer after a year. Michael liked Eaglebrook so much, he stayed there three years before going to Choate and later sent his son Cameron there.

The Andersonville Trial opened to spectacular notices. George Scott was magnificent as was Herbert Berghof, and

Jose Ferrer's direction had never been better.

Bill described a scene to me that had taken place while they were in Philadelphia.

They had all come to the conclusion that the show would play better in two acts rather than three. This would normally call for an extensive rewrite, and they had only three weeks to go before opening. Jose called him into his suite at the hotel and proceeded to tear pages out of the script, positioning them around the floor. He then shuffled scenes around until they could fit nicely into two acts, like a jigsaw puzzle. It probably would only have worked in a courtroom drama, which this was. Bill was in awe at his ingenuity and had the new running order posted on the callboard so the actors could refer to their new entrances. It all came off without a hitch.

Bill had been warned about George's drinking problems, but for the first few months, all was well and he continued to give a riveting performance. Then, one night came a call from Irving Cooper, the company manager.

"I've put Bobby Burns [the understudy] on. About a half-hour ago, I get a phone call, some guy asking if George Scott isn't meant to be in the show."

"Sure he is," I told him. "He's backstage right now."

"Oh no he isn't. He's sitting here at the Theatre Bar with shots of brandy lined up in front of him, and he's downing them as fast as he can."

"Well," Irving went on, "I trotted down to the Theatre Bar as fast as I could, and George spotted me through the window. When I got to the door, he looked up with murder in his eyes and said, 'Irving, you're a very nice man. But you take one step through that door and I'll throw you through the plate-glass window.'"

"And," added Irving, "he meant it."

Now, Irving stood about five foot two and perhaps weighed 110, soaking wet. George was an ex-Marine and approximately twice his weight. Built like a bull. Irving did the smart thing and retreated.

"Oh boy," I said when Bill relayed the news to me. "You sure can pick 'em."

Bill had had difficulties with Jason's drinking during the run of *The Disenchanted.*

It was a strange thing. The three most talented young actors on Broadway at that time were Jason, George, and Christopher Plummer. They were all brilliant, and they were all drunks, though later in their lives they solved their problems. Now Bill had to deal with George and hope that he could keep his alcoholism under control as his was the performance the public was flocking to see.

He had a quiet talk with him in his dressing room, reminding him that he could be brought up on charges to Equity, that the fate of thirty other actors in the cast lay in his hands, and that he, Bill, was not going to make a report to Equity over this one slip-up. If it happened again, the boom would be lowered.

There were no more alcoholic episodes, but a few months later, after the actors' strike had affected all the productions in town, an agreement was reached between the producers and actors that each cast would vote on a temporary reduction of pay until some restitution could be made to the investors. The whole cast of *Andersonville* agreed with the exception of George, who used it as an excuse to break his contract. So much for gratitude.

The understudy was put on, but the show closed within weeks.

The start of the sixties brought a reversal of fortune for us. Bill's next show *A Cook for Mr.General*, got generally poor notices in spite of good audience reaction,and closed in a matter of days. Steve Gethers, the writer of *Cook* loved to tell a bittersweet story of the closing night. He and Bill were getting quietly drunk together in a neighborhood bar, and Steve was overcome by the beauty of their friendship

"Do you know how many people end up not speaking after a production?" he enquired solemnly. "Even when it's successful, they can tear one another to bits. I just think it's

234 In The Wings

wonderful that after all we've been through, and the play flopped, we've ended up such good friends."

Bill fixed him with a cool gaze.

"I'd rather have had a hit."

On my agent's advice, I had turned down the second lead in a play with Margaret Sullavan. He felt I should hold out for starring roles. Nothing else was offered till the summer when I went to Stratford, Connecticut to play Hermione in *The Winter's Tale*. Incidentally, the play with Miss Sullavan was her last. She died during the tryout period in New Haven, amid rumors of a suicide.

I thoroughly enjoyed the summer at Stratford. Douglas Watson was a fine Leontes, and Mariette Hartley a lovely and touching Perdita. Will Geer played the old shepherd and Fred Gwynne, Autolycus. But the pay was certainly not up to Broadway standards, and things were getting financially tight at home. Our savings were dwindling at an alarming rate; no more alimony, of course, and the boys' expenses were increasing as they got older.

Bill called his fellow producers asking for a job, any job, in the theatre. Unfortunately the only reaction he got was one of acute embarrassment. I think it made them uneasy to realize that a producer who had had such a "success d'estime" with two plays on Broadway could be reduced to asking for a job to pay the mortgage. Later that year, 1961, Otto Preminger called and asked if I would "standby" for Virginia Gilmore and Georgann Johnson in *Critic's Choice*. I was back to understudy status again.

It was amusing, however, to be covering two such different characters. One week, they both came down with the flu. I alternated from night to night, depending on which one had the highest temperature, slapping on a red wig for Virginia's character, blonde for Georgann's. Henry Fonda was playing the male lead. He looked quite befuddled at times.

It wasn't the most satisfying job in the world, but it got us through the winter. Bill, meanwhile, had always wanted to write. He had written some good poetry as an adolescent, so he started work on a script for a television drama called *Go Slowly to the Sea*, set in Scotland in the last century. It was a lovely, haunting story. When it was finished, he let Audrey Wood read it. Although she wasn't sure where she could place it immediately, she was impressed enough with his talent to want to represent him.

As the summer approached, we had used up all our savings and were in debt. Something drastic had to be done. The boys would spend the summer with Doug and Anne, so they were well taken care of, but we were at a loss as to how to generate some income. Then I got a call from my brother, Laurence. He said that the time had come for him to find himself a wife, and that he was going to England to find one.

His house in Bermuda would be empty for the summer if we would care to use it while he was on his quest. Would we! It was the answer to a prayer. We rented the Westport house out for the summer, which took care of all our debts, and embarked for Bermuda.

Bill continued his writing while on the island. Soon we were joined by John Newland, who wanted to collaborate on a script with him. It was an unbelievably hot summer. The two of them would pace the length of the living room, pouring sweat, and exchanging or negating story-line ideas.

Members of the family would come over for barbecues, all highly amused at Laurence's venture. They speculated how he would go about finding his mate. An ad in *the London Times*? Hooking a shapely ankle with a brolly handle in Hyde Park? The possibilities were endless and hilarious. But, bless him, he knew what he was about and met and married Mary Kerr. She was an attractive woman in her thirties, with a penchant for music similar to his. Later they adopted a little girl, Susan, who was to become the light of their lives.

During the summer, Mother told me that she had advanced Fan some money so that she could buy a trailer to travel around Europe on their holidays. She asked if we needed any assistance.

"Better now than after I'm gone," she said.

I checked with Bill, and we both felt it would be an immense relief not to have to worry about making the mortgage payments each month, given the insecurity of our profession. She advanced us enough, against my eventual inheritance, to own the Westport house free and clear.

When we returned in the fall, Audrey approached Bill with a proposition. She had not been able to sell his script, but had a job in mind for him that he might find interesting. Universal Pictures, the parent company of M.C.A. was the agency Audrey was with. They had to divest themselves of the ties to the agency, and were setting up a New York office to look for material for the studio. With Bill's background, both as a writer himself, as well as a producer concerned with redrafts, she felt that he would be an ideal choice to join their fledgling story department. After an interview with Lew Wasserman, head of Universal, the job was his.

Our lives now did a complete turn around. Bill began commuting regularly to New York. He would catch the 8:05 at the Westport station, returning around six thirty. I met him in the station wagon like all the other suburban wives. For the first time, we had a stable income. We almost didn't know how to react to it all.

Typical of his generous heart, Bill was given a Christmas bonus and immediately spent it on a new suit for me at De Pinnas. I sashayed around town feeling frightfully chic. He had to cover all the new plays in town, we had a glut of theatre going. This delighted me because I could never get enough of theatre; good, bad, or indifferent. There were dinners out at fine restaurants, and a newfound sense of freedom. Both boys were now in boarding school. Joel was at the Forman School in Litchfield, Connecticut, and Michael was at Choate.

I felt the need to expand in my work. I knew that I was a better-than-competent actress, but I also knew that I had fallen into the habit of using things that were effective and easy for me. I was neither digging deep nor growing in my talent. I remembered what Bill had said about Sandy Meisner when he had studied under him at the Neighborhood Playhouse. That he was difficult, but inspiring. I read he'd started a class only for professionals in a studio down on Twenty-third Street, so I went down and signed up.

It was a far cry from when I had joined the American Academy. Now I knew how much I didn't know, and I was nervous as hell. Glancing around at the other actors, Jon Voight and Dina Merrill among them, I realized we all were. We waited for the word from the unprepossessing, bespectacled man who sat hunched over his desk, his eyes like lasers cutting through any false vanity we might possess.

He allowed me to prepare and perform two different scenes, both of which were greeted enthusiastically by my peers, but said nothing until I had completed the second scene. Then he sat back in his chair.

"My, you do direct yourself well, don't you?"

"Huh?"

"So well that it's hard to let your talent come through. You see, you professionals who have been acting for quite a few years remind me of a safecracker who had developed calluses on his fingertips. He could no longer feel the sensitive movements within the locks. My job is to sandpaper down those calluses. Get it?"

"Um. I guess."

"You will. You will, but it's not going to be easy. No more scenes for you. Nothing now but improvisation, so you won't be able to plan anything. We will try to get back to the pure instinct."

He was right that it was not easy. Sometimes, choreographed by Sandy, my fellow actors were brutal and jeering in their attacks. I felt naked and vulnerable and often very, very angry. Poor Bill had to put up with my rantings when I got home.

"Who needs this shit? How do I know I'll be able to act at all again? I'm losing all my confidence. Why do I have to go back there?"

Bill sipped his martini. "You don't."

"Oh."

And, of course, I went back. After about six months, Sandy allowed me to do another scene, but demanding total honesty, total openess. I felt like a snail without its shell, but when it was over, he gave an approving nod.

"I think I can safely guarantee that you will never indicate again. Unless, of course, you have to, but then you will know that you are doing it and will indicate well. Now do you get it?"

I did. I found his principles enormously insightful and helpful, but he was not for everybody. Some in the class were too fragile emotionally for his cutting wit; he could be ruthless.

"I am not your psychiatrist," he would say. "Tell your insecurities to him, they don't interest me. If this class is too rough for you, you are free to leave." And we did indeed lose a few. Some left weeping, and for a moment, I hated him.

At home, there were still the children's problems to deal with. A child psychiatrist, Dr. Herbert Saks, had diagnosed Joel's problems as being based in dyslexia, exascerbated by other symptoms, separation anxiety being one of them. He had begun treating him in Westport three times a week. The following fall, he felt that he had progressed enough to try a boarding school which was when we chose Forman. It was run by Dr. Forman, who seemed kindly and was a devout Christian Scientist. As Joel had started going to Christian Science Sunday school on his own, it had seemed an appropriate choice.

Joel did not have an easy time at Forman. It turned out that Dr. Forman, the school principal, did not believe in any kind of psychological therapy and refused to let Joel come to Westport for treatment. I voiced my concerns to Dr. Saks. The dear man would drive up to Litchfield each week and drive Joel around in his car while they had their sessions. He got Joel through the year, but it was evident that he needed a smaller and more specialized school. We started researching, eventually coming up with a small school in New Hampshire that had special training in dyslexics called Pembroke Place.

After inspecting the school, we decided to drive back via Vermont and stop at Stratton Mountain for some skiing. We had both boys with us, and all agreed that rural Vermont was one of the loveliest places around. This led to another change in our lives.

By the end of Bill's second year with Universal, we had paid off our debts, built up a tidy savings account, and even bought a new car. It was a Volkswagen bug to replace the aging station wagon now that the boys' bikes didn't have to be schlepped around.

"Wouldn't it be wonderful," we dreamed "to own some land up here. Perhaps one day to put up a log cabin." The boys agreed enthusiastically, so a week later we drove up again and started looking.

We met a realtor named Fred Malone, who was to prove a good friend. He showed us some lovely land on a ridge between Londonderry and Weston. It was about eighty acres, mostly pine woods, with some overgrown apple orchards. There were two views: Magic Mountain on the left, Stratton Mountain straight ahead. It could be ours for ten thousand dollars. That, we didn't have, but we could manage five, so we schemed to offer Bill's brother a half interest. We figured forty acres apiece would be ample for both of us.

We turned up at the Blums full of enthusiasm, but it turned out that they weren't interested. Somewhat dejected, we limped back to Westport. But the dream wouldn't die. When we rode the train into Manhattan, we talked about it, cogitated over dinner, and bored our friends silly with descriptions of the beauty of the land. We generally showed all the symtoms of having fallen hopelessly in love.

Finally, Bill said, "Fuck it. I've got a steady, grown-up job for the first time in my life, and it doesn't look like I'm going to get fired. Let's take another mortgage out on the house and buy the land ourselves." So we did.

Now, we went up almost every other weekend to walk the property and gloat. One day Fred Malone joined us.

"So when are you going to put up a house?" He queried.

We hadn't even considered that. We'd thought maybe we would put a tent up in the summertime, but the dream of a real honest-to-goodness house was way in the future.

"Tell you what, go see this friend of mine in the bank over by Manchester. He will figure out a way so that you can get started on construction right away. Bill, you go talk fishing with him. Guarantee you'll get a loan."

We looked at him as though he were mad, but Bill decided to check it out anyway. I waited in the car while Bill went into the bank. A half hour-later, he came out shaking his head in bewilderment.

"It's true. The guy figured what the cost of the land with the house on it would be and said that one third of that would be the amount of our loan. That exactly covers the cost of building. Fred was right."

Fred took us to see a model chalet he had built for Commander Whitehead of Schweppes fame. It was slightly larger than we would need, but both of us liked the simplicity of design, the use of wood throughout, and the large glass doors leading out to the balconies. Fred said he could modify it to suit our taste and pocketbook.

We could hardly wait to tell the boys. They were as thrilled as we were. There were bunk beds planned for downstairs in case of an overflow of guests. A powder room. A large living-dining room and an open kitchen. Upstairs was a guest room, a full bath, and our bedroom whose balcony looked straight across to Stratton Mountain.

That summer the boys joined their father in Israel, where he was making a movie, *Cast a Giant Shadow*. They both had jobs on the production so Michael had saved quite a bit of money. He immediately purchased some land a bit north of us, and has it to this day. He seems to have inherited the real-estate gene.

During this time I plied my trade, going out to California to do a *Ben Casey*, a popular TV show starring Vince Edwards. In Florida I did a guest stint on a TV series with Walter Matthau. Walter was wooing Carol Saroyan, and their courtship was a stormy one. He had been trying to persuade her to join him in Florida, which she was loath to do. One morning, as we prepared to start shooting, he had a grin as wide as a Cheshire cat.

"Okay, it's all set. She will be down tomorrow. You know how I did it?"

I shook my head.

"I told her you and I were having an affair. That got her attention!"

Annoyed as I was, I couldn't help being amused at his glee. Carol was noticeably chilly to me upon her arrival, in spite of Walter's admitting his falsehood. The chief thing I remember about that stint was playing Liar's Poker on the boat, while we waited for setups. Walter taught it to us and was invariably the big winner.

I worked on *The Defenders* and various television shows in New York while Bill commuted daily to his office at Universal. One evening, he brought back the first sixty pages of the galleys of a new novel that he was convinced would make a fantastic movie. He let me read them that night, sitting up in our fourposter bed. As I read the last chilling page and dropped it to the floor, I could barely breathe.

"A horse's head in the bed…Jesus!"

It was, of course, *The Godfather*. Bill flew out to the coast the next day to try and convince the powers that be to move quickly on optioning it. But the machinery of bureaucracy moved ponderously, and no one could seem to sense the urgency, to Bill's frustration. Paramount moved in on it, and the rest is history. I think that was the beginning of Bill's disenchantment with his job.

With Michael's graduation from Choate, college options had to be addressed. John Blum said that he could probably get into Yale, but would find it hard going with his C average. Other Ivy League colleges were discussed, but Michael's ultimate decision was for the University of California at Santa Barbara. He had had enough of "preppyness," and opted for a different life style, which he embraced with a vengeance.

I joined the cast of *Cactus Flower* in New York, playing a small part, and understudying my old fellow classmate at the American Academy, Betty Bacall. I stayed with it six months. That, added to Bill's earnings, made it possible to furnish the Vermont house, as well as toy with the idea of a different future. Bill was now head of the story department at Universal, but was increasingly frustrated by the lack of cooperation from the West Coast.

He knew that he wanted to write. For a time, we planned to move to a Greek Island. With that in mind I bought a book, *How To Teach Yourself Modern Greek in Twenty Lessons*. I would study it backstage during the run of *Cactus Flower*. When I reached lesson number seventeen, the fascist colonels moved into Athens and took over the government.

"Well, we are not going there," said Bill.

"But I've almost finished the book!" I wailed.

"Well, why don't you try Italian."

I almost hit him.

Chapter 14
THE SIXTIES

The sixties. They began with that glorious inaugural address, "Ask not what your country can do for you." Our handsome young president standing bareheaded in the snow, his wife beside him, both of them from our generation. Robert Frost on the podium with them signified a renewed interest in the arts.

It's hard to remember now what hope we had for the country on that day. We knew of old Joe Kennedy's machinations behind the scenes, but Jack Kennedy seemed cut from a different cloth. The sleaze seemed to have been taken out of politics. The Peace Corps made our hearts leap; the future seemed to hold boundless possibilities.

Through the Cuban crisis and the backing down of Khrushchev, the magic seemed to hold. We followed the informal press conferences and the weekends in Hyannis with fascination. Then that terrible day in November. Walking along Twenty-third Street on my way to Sandy's class, I was aware that the streets seemed unusually empty and quiet. A knot of people were huddled in front of a television store, silent. When I got to the building, there were students sitting on the steps outside, openly weeping.

"He's been shot. He's dead."

Somehow, I didn't even have to ask who it was. We met in the classroom, and all decided to go home immediately. Even Sandy looked lost and bewildered.

Two days later when Jack Ruby shot Oswald, it confirmed that the days of mayhem were here. And so it went. The children torched to death in a Southern church. The Martin Luther King and Bobby Kennedy slayings. The brutality of the 1968 Chicago convention. We all lost our innocence and a lot of hope during that decade, while the Beatles sang "Lucy in the Sky with Diamonds."

"That means LSD" my kids confided to me.

And, yes, it was the advent of drugs, as everyone seemed to know except me.

Michael's letters from college spoke of joining friends trampling grapes in the local vineyards, surfing, dating, a little about schoolwork. Mostly blithe and happy missives that gave no inkling that he was into the drug scene like so many young folk in the sixties. I found that out much later. When he mentioned that he was going to move in with a girl, but that they were both going to date other people, I was a bit concerned. I thought maybe he had not considered her reputation seriously enough, that she might be considered "easy" because they were living together. But his generation were coming up with a whole new set of rules. Some gains, frankness and lack of hypocrisy, as well as, I felt, some definite minuses. They missed out on that wonderful anticipation as friendship turns to lust, and sometimes love.

Toward the end of the spring term, a letter was sent to Doug and me, suggesting that Michael take a year or so off from college. His grades were pretty abysmal, and he seemed directionless. At that point, it was suggested that a university education would be wasted on him. We were both shocked.

"Does this mean that he is out?"

"Not necessarily. We feel that he is immature in his attitude and does not really know why he is in college. Perhaps a year of work will help it become clear to him."

So Mikey came back to Westport and went to work as a grease monkey at the local Mobil station. He was conscientious and worked hard at the job. He became Mobil's "Man of the Month." I am pretty sure he was not doing drugs at that time, though with my lack of sophistication in those matters, it's possible.

Later that winter, Doug was making a movie in Norway, *The Heroes of Telemark*, and he asked Mike to come over to work on it in the wardrobe department. On his return, Michael was sporting a magnificent sheepskin coat as he came through customs. With his long hair and huge coat, he must have looked like the quintessential drug smuggler, for they took his coat apart and subjected him to an intimate body search. He was still shaky from the experience when he visited me down in Atlanta where I was playing in *Gigi* and *Once More with Feeling*.

At the end of the school year, he reapplied for admission to U.C.S.B., changing his major from English to drama, finally admitting to himself where his real love lay. He did well from then on. I think he even made the dean's list.

I was in California doing a *Ben Casey* when Michael called and said that he was going to be in a play by Michel de Gilderode called *Escurial*, and would I come up to Santa Barbara to see it? Would I!

He met me on his motorbike and ran me over to his dorm so I could freshen up, then pointed out the direction of the theatre. I took my time strolling over, trying not to feel queasy about my neophyte trying out his wings for the first time (or rather, the first time I had seen him play).

As I sat in the darkened theatre, I offered up a little prayer that he prove talented.

The curtain rose on dim and ancient battlements, with an elderly man in royal robes emerging from the darkness. He quietly assessed where he was, and when he spoke, it was with tired authority. There was no doubt that this was the old king. I first surmised that this must be the drama professor and was glad that Mike was working with such a pro, when, suddenly, a turn of the head in the beam of light and I realized it was Michael!

I fought back tears as I watched my son, proud as a mama, but deeply admiring as a fellow professional. Backstage, he came up with the usual actor's line.

"I think I was better last night."

I cuffed him gently.

"Don't give me that old actor shit, 'Shoulda caught me in Philadelphia.' You were wonderful. Some cats got it, and some cats ain't. You've got it. In spades."

I held him tight, trying not to cry.

Later, at his dorm, Doug called. He had seen the performance a week earlier.

"So, what did you think?'

"I'm stunned. God, what a Henry V he will make!"

"And Hamlet? What about Hamlet?"

The two of us were babbling like idiots, laughing and kvelling with joy.

When I got home, I told Bill what an extraordinary talent I had witnessed in Michael. On the strength of that, he recommended Mike to George White to apprentice at the Eugene O Neill Foundation Theatre the following summer.

Unfortunately, Michael was miscast in his first play. That, coupled with a bad attack of nerves, made his debut less than interesting. He was uptight and stiff. When it was over, Bill looked at me with compassion.

"I know you love him dearly, darling, and want desperately for him to do well. But you have to face it, sweetie, the kid is not an actor."

Needless to say, he has endured a lot of kidding about his remarks as Michael's career took off into the stratosphere.

During this time the Vietnam War was escalating. From a minor engagement, it was reaching into all the families in the country, disproportionately so to the poor and less educated as college deferments bought some time from the draft, and compliant doctors attested to injuries that would preclude the sons of wealth from carrying a gun.

Early in the war, I was torn in my sympathies. On one hand was the injustice of the system, on the other was my upbringing, which had stressed duty to one's country as a major virtue.

As it inched closer to home, along with the real possibility that my sons might die in an Asian jungle, I became as nonobjective as a female panther when her young are threatened.

Plus, the more I read about the war, as we became more involved, the more the sheer stupidity of the morass became evident. I joined the marchers and protesters outside the library in downtown Westport. We were subjected to some abuse, but it being a civilized community, there was no violence.

Earlier, I had marched in front of the White House with other women, protesting the testing of nuclear weapons and the fallout of the deadly strontium 90 on future generations. At the time, the Women's Strike for Peace was viewed by many as a soft-headed leftist movement. Thirty-five years later, it turns out that our fears were justified. Cancers and genetic faults keep showing up near the test sites.

I have continued being an activist in liberal causes throughout my life, supporting Amnesty International, Handgun Control and Human Rights Watch, among others. We do what we can, though often it seems fruitless.

Doug was instrumental in arranging medical deferments through a Beverly Hills doctor who found an old football injury in Michael's spine and later, a psychiatrist to attest to Joel's emotional problems.

Michael has told me recently that he still feels guilty that he didn't go to jail, as his friend John Arvenides did to protest the war. There was never any question of his going to Canada or Scandinavia as did so many of his generation.

It was a time when many of us questioned our old values, and many of us behaved in a hypocritical fashion. None came out with clean hands. It was devastating for the country, most of all for the soldiers fighting in Vietnam, disproportionately drawn from the minorities, many of whom were treated with scorn upon their return. The war continued to escalate through the early sixties under President Johnson, though Barry Goldwater offered no viable option in the fall of '64.

In November of '64, my brother Bayard asked if I would like to sail with him to Bermuda, as part of the crew. He'd had a racing sloop built in Germany for the Newport-Bermuda Race in which he participated every other year. However, it had not been completed in time for the race. It was delivered to Luders Boatyard in Stamford, Connecticut, in the fall. Not the ideal time to brave the Gulf Stream and the North Atlantic, but he wanted to get the boat down to Bermuda so he could break her in at leisure.

I had never done any ocean sailing, and the whole idea sounded like high adventure to me, so I signed on eagerly. Bayard's sons, Nicky and David, were also part of the crew. Nicky as navigator, two Scotsmen from Luders, and two other men—one an experienced sailor and the other not. I was the only female, in charge of the galley.

We started out at sunset from Luders, Michael and Bill waving good-bye from the dock, and headed north up Long Island Sound. At around midnight, the running lights went off, and we found that the refrigerator was not working as well. So we reversed course and headed back to shore, the waves soaking us all to the skin.

At around two in the morning, I crawled in beside Bill, who swore that he had never felt anyone as cold, even in Alaska.

A day or so later, we started out again, with everything ostensibly in working order. Indeed, we made it past Montauk and were two days out in the Atlantic when disaster struck.

Again, all the electricity went kaput, including the Conistan direction finder based in Newfoundland used to keep us apprised of our course. On top of which, we ran into bad weather with waves cresting at forty feet. It was impossible for Nicky to get a sighting since there was no horizon visible.

Before we were out of the sound, Bayard had issued all of us seasick pills, which were very effective. The only one who refused to take them was the inexperienced sailor, who claimed that he "never got sea-sick." I thought we were going to lose him before the end of the voyage, he became so dehydrated, couldn't even keep a sip of ginger ale down.

My bunk was directly below the hatchway, and for the first few nights, I relished the songs that the Scotsmen sang while on watch. They were wonderful wild ballads, with the monotonous wail of bagpipes in the chords. By the end of the voyage, I was ready to put a rope around their necks to shut them up.

A lot of the food had to be jettisoned for lack of refrigeration. Thank God we had a supply of canned goods that would last for a few days as well as a battery-operated radio, that one hoped would pick up a signal from Bermuda. As it turned out, we missed the island entirely, heading straight for Portugal on our sixth day at sea, when we heard a crackle from the radio. Eagerly we crowded around it to hear a faint Bermudian voice.

"The *Duchess of Devonshire*, Sir Bayard Dill's yacht, is still missing, and there is no trace of her. However, Lady Dill assures us that there is no cause for worry, her husband said they might be late."

We all turned and stared at Bayard.

"A little late? It's meant to take three days!"

Bayard was his usual, unruffled self.

"How much food have we left?"

"Enough for a day or so."

"Well then, why don't you go below and cook us all a good meal. We seem to have missed the island, so we're going to put up the spinnaker, reverse course, and go like hell. With any luck, we should see St. David's lighthouse at around three tomorrow morning."

We stared at him blankly, wanting to believe, wanting desperately to believe.

I went below, opened cans of Chinese food, and dumped then in a large skillet while Nicky sat across from the stove, working on his charts. As we came about, the boat heeled over quite suddenly. The stove top swung on its hinges to accommodate it, and I did the unforgivable. Without thinking, I grabbed for the top of the stove, a no-no every galley cook knows.

The entire mess of chow mein crashed to the deck, splattering Nicky and me.

We looked at each other in horror. Then Nicky put his finger to his lips.

"Ssshh. Don't say a word. Just scoop it up, heat it, and serve it. What they don't know won't hurt ' em." As that was the last of our food, there was nothing else to do. I only hoped that Bayard's prediction was correct.

At three the next morning, even those who were not on watch were awake. I lay in my bunk, figuring how many bottles of soft drinks we still had available. Then we heard the call.

"There she is! There's St. David's!"

I turned over and faced David, in the next bunk.

"When three of them spot it, then I'll believe it," I said.

With that, David scrambled up the ladder and joined his voice to the others.

"It's true! It's true! Come see!"

And there it was, a tiny revolving light, our link with home, our saviour.

Actually Bayard was our saviour. I marveled at his skill getting us through the reefs as we approached the island. One dim flashlight was still functioning, and David sat up on the bow directing our path through the jagged rocks. Finally we were safely in the North Passage and making our way up the North Shore, past the Dill houses.

"Do you know Morse code?" Bayard asked me.

"I think I remember some from my Girl Guide days."

"There may be someone watching for us to come in. Get the flashlight and flash 'Duchess of Devonshire heading for the Yacht Club.'"

"Okay."

I did as bidden and watched carefully for an answering

flash. For a moment, I thought I saw one high up on the hill, but when I looked again, it was gone. We limped into Hamilton Harbor just before dawn to hear a hail from the Yacht Club steps.

"Ahoy, Duchess of Devonshire!"

Laurie Truscott, married to my niece, Peggy, had been sitting out on his balcony, high on the hill when he caught our signal. He had raced inside for a flashlight, started to signal back, but thought better of it and tore up to the Yacht Club. He had been waiting anxiously, wondering if he'd hallucinated the whole thing.

Clare had called Bill asking if he wanted a seat reserved on the coast guard plane that was to begin searching for us that morning. So the first thing I did upon reaching Newbold Place was to call him and let him know that we were safe. I caught him just as he was walking out the door. Next, I had the longest, most luxurious hot bath that I can recall. After tea and toast prepared by Mother's companion, Dorothy Fetigan, I fell into bed for eighteen hours flat out.

There was a special bond formed among those who had been through the voyage. We had all behaved well, rationing ourselves as to liquid intake without comparing notes, saving our strength when not on watch, and keeping our fears to ourselves. We did not talk much, but generally tried to maintain a cheerful face toward one another.

A strange phenomenon happened the last day or two on board. I suddenly developed a strong sexual attraction for one of the Scotsmen from Luders boatyard. It sprang out of nowhere and disappeared as fast as it had come once we hit land. No one was aware of it except me. Having heard the stories of coupling in the Underground during the blitz, I surmised that danger and the imminency of death arouses a strong need to procreate.

When I got home, my agent told me that I had an audition for a musical. It was *Henry, Sweet Henry*, based on the movie *The World of Henry Orient*, so I rushed down to my singing coach, and quickly prepared a song "On the S.S.

Bernard Cohen" from the musical *On a Clear Day*.

I was a little nervous for the first go-around, but they seemed to like it, and I was called back for a second audition. That was more fun, and by the third, I was having such a ball they could barely get me offstage...so I got the part. I was the mother of one of the schoolgirls who followed Henry Orient around. Henry was played by Don Ameche. Rehearsals were to begin in a month.

I had been plagued for a time with a copious menstrual flow, perhaps aggravated by the birth control pills I had been taking. It suddenly became worse, and I consulted a gynecologist in New Haven, who recommended immediate surgery. She had located an ovarian cyst as well as fibroid tumors and suspected that the cyst might be malignant.

In vain I protested that I had just too many things to do, kids coming home from school and college, the musical for which to prepare for, but she was firm.

"I'm booking a room for you at Yale-New Haven tomorrow. If I call you tomorrow morning and say you are to get in there, I want you in there by noon. Surgery will be scheduled for early afternoon."

I sat at my desk, trying to compose a letter to the boys, in case I didn't make it through surgery. I couldn't think of anything to say except that I loved them and I hoped they would always be good to one another and to Bill.

They told me later that I went into postoperative shock and that my blood pressure dropped dangerously low, which might have been the reason for the vivid dreams I had under anesthetic. I was surrounded by a white light, and friends and relatives both past and present came trooping down to embrace me, each wearing a mask that looked like somebody else. There was much laughter as each took off their mask and became who they were, and I woke up feeling warm and comforted.

Bill was there holding my hand.

"It was benign, darling. See?"

He held up a note left by the surgeon on my pillow.

"In case I'm not here when you wake up. There was no malignancy. You have had a total hysterectomy. Also your appendix has been removed."

"Wow, they really cleaned me out." Bill kissed me on the forehead, tears gleaming in his eyes.

"You know I didn't want kids, anyway. I just thank God that you're all right."

I made a fairly fast recovery, though I was stunned when I tried to do my usual sit-ups to find myself stuck on my back, like a turtle. The abdominal muscles had been cut through in the operation. I probably pushed myself a bit faster than normal, as I was conscious of the imminent rehearsal date, but I felt fine.

On the first day of rehearsal, I went charging into New York, full of high hopes and anticipation. Waiting at the corner of Fifty-seventh Street, my knees suddenly turned to water, and I sat down on the curb involuntarily. A knot of passers-by stopped and offered help. After sitting there for a few minutes while my head cleared, I accepted a hand up and stumbled into a taxi. I was okay all through rehearsal, but I realized I would have to learn to pace myself.

I found certain changes had been made in the script since the audition. Originally my part was in four scenes and had three songs. Now they had cut my part, and also that of Carol Bruce, who played the other mother, to two scenes and two songs. I was not particularly happy about it, but I could see the logic behind the decision.

When I got home, a quiet bombshell awaited me. I had known for some time that Bill was becoming increasingly frustrated with his job at Universal, but they were happy with his work and kept promoting him. He was now a vice president and in a few months would have stock options and all sorts of perks. But something had happened that day which triggered an immediate decision, so he quit.

Lew Wasserman, the head of the company, tried to dissuade him and asked him to take a leave of absence while he reconsidered, but Bill was adamant.

A few months before this, Bill had told me that Doug made him a job offer that he was considering. This had triggered one of the few serious disagreements we'd had. Knowing Doug's penchant for control, I begged Bill to turn it down.

He took my pleas as a signal that I thought he couldn't stand up to my ex-husband.

"If I can tell Lew Wasserman to go jump in the lake, I sure as hell can do the same with Doug."

"Then please do. I know you are well qualified for the job, but so are many others. Why do you think he picked you?"

He scratched his head, but set his jaw in a manner I knew well.

We didn't speak for three days. At the end of the time ,he came to me.

"I've never known you to be so adamant and to feel so strongly about something. I still feel that I could work with him with no problems, but obviously you don't. I'll go along with your wishes. Back to the grind at M.C.A. Universal."

I felt lousy putting him in that position and interfering in his line of work, but I felt strongly that we should keep Doug at arm's length, and eventually Bill agreed with me. However his time at Universal grew more and more rankling. I could see that he was becoming unhappy there and felt his time was being wasted.

He knew if he didn't make the break and start writing now, the time would never be right, and he would be stuck in the business world forever. We would be returning to the insecurities of the artistic world financially, but we had some savings, two houses, and no debts. Both of us believed in exploring all possibilities in life and expanding our talents wherever possible.

Family and friends were pretty aghast at what they felt to be an irresponsible move, but both boys were in college by now. We had no one to answer to but ourselves, and the look of relief and anticipation on Bill's face made it all worthwhile.

I told him about the cuts and changes in rehearsal.

"If there are any more, why don't you quit too?"

"Whaaat?"

"Quit."

Such an idea had never occured to me.

"Think about it," he said. "We can rent this house and move to Vermont. Living there is cheap, and it'll give us a breather."

I continued on with rehearsals and traveled to Detroit for the out-of-town opening.

There is nothing quite so thrilling as being in a musical and hearing the overture play. No matter how down you may be feeling in the dressing room, the first chords send a surge of adrenaline through you, and you're pawing the ground like an old fire-horse heading for the blaze, so eager to get on that stage.

However, due to the many changes made during the tryout, another scene and song were cut, so I took a deep breath and turned in my notice. Probably not a good professional move. George Roy Hill, the director, never hired me again.

Now the die was cast.

As we drove up north, both of us were somewhat silent. We found later, the same thought was occurring to both of us. In our eleven years of marriage, we had never been totally alone with one another for a long period of time, with no outside distractions or friends. We hoped we both liked each other enough to stand the strain of being snowed in together, dealing with unfamiliar rural chores together, and not running out of things to talk about.

Bill set up his typewriter facing away from the window, as the view over the valley toward Stratton was too distracting. At the local post office I ran into Millie Humphries, an old actress who lived about three miles down our road. (She had toured with Walter Hampden as Roxanne to his Cyrano.) She was thrilled that theatre folk were moving in and ran down to the farm that bordered our acreage to spread the good news to 'Hezzie,' the ninety-year-old farmer.

"Aye-a," he said, in typical, dry Vermont fashion, "It's going to be a long winter."

We vowed then that we would not seek help if we got into trouble, like other city folk, and all in all, coped pretty well. The nearest farm was more than two miles away, we were on a dirt country road so quiet often we were snowed in for days before the plows got to us. We had snowshoes and cross-country skis, as well as downhill, so we could get some exercise, but we had to keep a backlog of canned goods for emergencies.

I kept my downhill skis in the car at all times, for when I would make the run over to the laundromat or market in Manchester, I would pass the slopes at Bromley. If the lift lines were short, as was usually the case during the week, I would take a few runs down the mountain. My skills as a skier were rapidly improving. The exhilaration when one is skiing well is almost indescribable. Like dancing down the mountain to a Viennese waltz.

One day I had an experience that Bill used later when he was writing his novel, *Solomon Moon*. I was walking alone down the dirt lane skirting the woods near our house when I heard a strange, howling noise. It sounded more human than animal, and I debated as to whether to respond, thinking that someone might be lost or hurt in the woods. I was about to call out when I heard it again, this time directly above me. Looking up I saw a figure that looked almost Biblical, a tall man with flowing grey locks and beard, dressed in tattered green work clothes. Arms outstretched, he was howling at the sky.

He was standing on top of a rocky hill that poked out of the woods on my right, and as I watched, the keening started again, sorrowful but terrifying. When I backed away, a dislodged rock attracted his attention and he looked directly at me. For a moment, I froze. I don't think that ever in my life have I sprinted so fast. I covered the half-mile home in a few minutes, hurling myself through the door and bolting it.

I related the incident to Bill who was bemused as he had always thought of me as a fairly fearless person, but talking to our neighbors, the Humphries, they told him of a mountain man that lived in a cave in the hills who had chased their daughter a few years back.

"He hasn't been seen for a year or more, so we thought maybe he was dead," they said.

That was the birth of Riodan Flynn in *Solomon Moon*, Bill's second novel.

The Vermont house was a sanctuary for the whole family. When the boys came on the weekends, we played endless games of Scrabble and Monopoly while listening to the Beatles or Tom Lehr's brilliant satirical records, "The Vatican Rag" and "Whatever Became of Hubert?," a plaint for the vice president so hogtied by LBJ.

Once we were all snowed in for three days. I called the boys' schools to let them know there was no chance of their getting back in time, and when I surveyed the living room, it looked like the Sleeping Beauty's palace. Everyone was snoozing where they sat, board games forgotten, while the snow softly fell outside. I realized how much we all need for time to be suspended in order to fall in with the rhythms of nature.

But after a time, I felt the need to be in the fray again. I had tried to occupy my time with studying a book on archeology and cooking casseroles for the local church suppers. But as winter wore on, Bill said he detected a manic energy that made him uneasy, while I carved chess pieces at the dining room table.

When my agent called early in the year to see if I could replace an actress in Edward Albee's *Everything in the Garden* on Broadway, everything in me screamed "Yes!" However, I told him that I would call him back with my decision.

Bill was wonderful.

"Go!" he said. "Get an apartment in New York, and I'll come down and visit on weekends."

He was a wonderfully self-sufficient man, and, having been a bachelor until the age of thirty three, was efficient at housekeeping as well as being a gourmet cook. I had no doubts that he could survive on his own. He could have made me feel guilty for running out on him, and this he refused to do. I think one of the reasons that our marriage was so successful was the freedom we gave one another to pursue our artistic dreams wherever they made lead either one of us. Picking our projects solely because they interested us probably would have been impossible had we been locked into stardom. Fame tends to keep one on a prescribed path.

The cast of *Everything* included some old friends: Jim Karen, who had been at the Neighborhood Playhouse with Bill; Augusta Dabney, who I'd met on several auditions in the past; and Beatrice Straight. I only needed a couple of rehearsals to fit in and found a rather ratty apartment near the theatre in the same building as my friend Carole Shelley. True to his word, Bill came down almost every weekend, and the unfamiliar surroundings lent a pleasantly illicit glow to our meetings.

That summer and the following, I worked at the O'Neill Foundation in Waterford, Connecticut, which proved to be one of the most stimulating and rewarding experiences of my professional life. It was called The Playwrights' Conference, and a host of talented young playwrights were there to have their plays read and partially staged. There in '67 were John Guare, Lanford Wilson, and Israel Horowitz, among others.

It was a truly cooperative experience. If the playwright was having difficulty with a scene, we would be asked to improvise. This sometimes proved helpful, the give-and-take was exciting and fruitful.

At the end of that time, Bill had a writing assignment

from Sam Northcross, his former boss at Universal. Sam had been shot down over Yugoslavia during WWll and had been rescued by the partisans. He had told his story to an executive at NBC who felt there was a television movie to be made out of it. So Sam, a longtime fan of Bill's writing, felt that he was the one to do it.

"How would you feel about spending three weeks in Yugoslavia?" Bill asked me.

"I'm packing!"

We flew into Belgrade and passed quickly through customs. We didn't realize until we were outside the airport that we had not cleared immigration. When we went back to get our passports stamped, the officials were effusive in their apologies and thanks. The Iron Curtain seemed to have several chinks missing. Of course Tito's form of communism differed from that of the USSR, and the people to whom we talked to felt it was closer to the Chinese brand. Instead, the Yugoslav version had a pleasant insouciance and casualness about it.

Our interpreter and guide was an intriguing woman named Eva, supplied by the Yugoslav film board. She spoke seven languages fluently and understood Bill's need to contact partisan veterans. She introduced us to the other members of our party: an Austrian director NBC was considering hiring for the film and his girlfriend, a photographer for *Life* magazine. We had dinner together the first night at the Writers Club. Even though glasses were raised and toasts made to the project, I sensed a certain tension and hostility between Bill and the director, a "take-charge" sort of fellow who was determined that the script would go his way.

Bill was pleasant, but firm.

"Why don't you wait until it's written? Who knows what we are going to find on our way?"

Andre, the director, shot him a glance of pure hatred, and I foresaw a rocky few weeks ahead.

The next day, we flew in a tiny plane to Dubrovnik, perhaps the most beautiful city in the world, and swam in the emerald waters of the Adriatic. Women in native costume and an old man sitting on a wooden-saddled donkey passed us along the walled city. The streets were of highly polished marble, and from the battlements hung balconies alive with geraniums. We had a few days to ourselves before our tour into the interior to interview the partisans, and we walked the battlements, attended a concert and enjoyed just being tourists.

Eva had arranged for two cars with drivers to be available. Given the hostility between Bill and Andre, it seemed like a reasonably good idea. We drove down the coast, heading south to the Bay of Kotor. It was a dramatic inlet with mountains rising six thousand feet above the water. Here, Illyria's last queen, Teuta, drowned herself rather than be taken prisoner by the Romans in the third century.

History leaps out at you everywhere you turn. This is partly because Yugoslavia has been overrun with so many different cultures. Austrian watchtowers vie with Turkish minarets, and the Venetian influence is felt throughout in architecture. Napoleon's armies occupied Kotor in 1807.

We drove inland to the old capital of Montenegro, Cetinje, then on to Titograd, where we met two partisan generals. One, a woman who told us harrowing stories of their long fight against the German troops. As Eva translated, Bill wrote rapidly in his notebook while Andre stared out the window, drumming his fingers and sighing with impatience.

Somehow we made it through the three weeks without fisticuffs between Bill and Andre, though it came close to it at times. I wondered how they would cope once production started. It didn't bode well.

After driving back up the coast, we visited the lovely old town of Mostar with its Eleventh Century bridge. (Now, alas, destroyed in the recent hostilities) and Sudjeska, which was the scene of a dreadful massacre of the partisan wounded by the Germans. It was after this massacre that Tito gave the order that no wounded were ever to be left behind even while surrounded by Red Cross flags, as the Germans could not be trusted to abide by the Geneva agreements.

Our driver, Mustafa, picked some wildflowers and gave them to me.

"Keep them always," he said, "they are nourished by the blood of heroes."

I pressed them in a book and took them home, then made them into an arrangement that I hung on the wall in a Victorian frame above my dressing table.

On our way back, we stopped in Rome, Florence, and Venice, spending our last days in Europe at the Cipriani Hotel and using up our last monies. But what memories we came back with! My favorite recollection is that of opening the heavy window shutters at dawn to see a lonely gondolier silhouetted against the rosy mist of sunrise, poling his way across the water.

Sadly, Sam's project was dropped by the network before Bill had completed his script. We were told that a change in the higher-ups of development at the network was responsible for its cancellation.

It was disappointing, but it had enabled us to have a wonderful adventure. Upon our return, a surprise awaited us. Joel had been circumnavigating the globe gaining his college education with College of the Seven Seas together with students from many different universities. While on board, he had met a young woman from the University of Montana at Missoula and had fallen in love. Her name was Susan Jorgensen, and her parents lived in Montana. He had arranged to transfer to Montana U. for his junior year and informed both his parents of the fact.

It probably could have been dealt with in a more tactful fashion, particularly in mind of Doug's penchant for control, but I felt Joel was making a decision as an adult. I saw no reason why we should not respect it.

All seemed well the first semester. Given his dyslexia, he was keeping up his grades pretty well, had an after hours job with a veterinarian and was happy in his relationship with Susie. Then he announced they wanted to get engaged, and all hell broke loose.

Doug called me to read a letter he had written to the Jorgensen parents, which said that he and I were in agreement that an engagement was out of the question, and he expected them to comply. I was appalled by the arrogance of the tone, but mostly that he had assumed that I would agree with him without consulting me and told him so in no uncertain terms.

There was a dead silence at the other end of the line when I finished my tirade.

Then, "Fine! I had thought we could cooperate, but obviously that is impossible. You don't have to worry about me misquoting you again. I doubt that we will ever speak again."

"Fine by me!" I retorted and slammed down the phone. And, indeed, we had no further communication for the next several years. I had been afraid that if we took too adamant a stand against the romance, we could panic them into a Romeo-Juliet elopement. As it was, they only waited until they had reached twenty-one and went ahead with a winter wedding in Great Falls.

Bill and I flew out for it and met Susie and the Jorgensens for the first time. They were plain, unsophisticated folk with a house full of religious icons. Susie seemed a pleasant and practical girl whose eyes followed Joel with a worshipful gaze, while he blossomed under her attention.

Michael was slated to be his best man, but a last-minute call informed us that Michael was bedded with pneumonia and the doctor had forbidden him to fly. Bill was hustled into the breach, outfitted with a rented dinner jacket several sizes too big, the sleeves held up with elastic and his desert boots peering out from under the oversized pants.

I was the sole person sitting on the groom's side of the church, while the bride's side was filled to capacity, and had started to feel a little maudlin for poor Joel. But then I caught sight of my meticulous husband, the delight of tailors in London and New York, looking like a baggy-pants comic, and I fell in love with him all over again.

The young couple left for Banff for their honeymoon, and Bill and I flew back home. A little apprehensive, but praying for their happiness.

Toward the end of the sixties, I played a small part in a film called *Loving*, starring George Segal and Eva Marie Saint, directed by Irv Kirchner. It was a crucial scene—part written, part improvised—of a woman in the throes of divorce trying to sell her house. I had felt the scene went well, but was quite unprepared for the attention it got in the reviews. Rex Reed saying that I was "a brilliant actress," etc., and a rave from Charles Champlin in the *L.A. Times* which caught the attention of a Hollywood agent.

Wally Hiller saw the movie and asked whether I would be willing to sign with him for representation on the West Coast. I thought we should meet, so I flew out to California, liked him on the spot, and signed with the office.

It has now been twenty-eight years that I've been with the office, a tenure lasting longer than many marriages, in spite of being told repeatedly that one should change agent. Wally died early in 1998, but I like and respect Dick Bauman and Clare Miller, who now head the agency. Truly decent people in a sometimes indecent business. I'm not working much these days, but as long as they keep on asking me to sign every few years, I guess I'll go on doing it.

Chapter 15
THE SEVENTIES

No sooner than I had signed with Wally then Michael Thomas, my New York agent, called saying that I was up for a part in a soap opera called *Love Is a Many Splendored Thing*. When I went in to read for it, I discovered the part was that of a Polish grandmother in her early sixties, playing opposite Judson Laire, who was well into his eighties.

I read well, but doubted I would get the part, as it seemed too much of a stretch. I was only in my mid-forties, but to my surprise they called up the next day and offered it to me. I donned a grey wig and dresses several sizes too large. I did what I could about a Polish accent, and we were off to the races.

Ann Marcus, the head writer, came to New York a few weeks later and as we rode up in the elevator together, gave me an appraising look.

"You are not at all what I had in mind," she announced. "You are far too uptown for the part. But now your character is established, I guess we will have to tailor the writing to you. First, get rid of those dreadful clothes and that lousy accent."

In spite of that unprepossessing beginning, Ann and I have been friends for several years, and she is now a neighbor here in Sherman Oaks, a tennis and golf partner, and continues to be a fine writer.

A few months after I started the soap, I got a call from Wally. Blake Edwards was in the process of shooting a movie called *Wild Rovers* near the Mexican border, and they had run into a problem. The actress Kim Stanley was having emotional problems, whether fueled by alcohol or not was a moot point, but she was unable to work, and they needed a replacement in a hurry.

"It would only be a few days," he said. "But it is a good showy part and could do you a lot of good. Check your soap schedule, and see if you could fit it in."

By contract, we were not meant to take any other employment. But looking at the following week's schedule, I realized that it would be possible for me to fly out on the Tuesday. I would not be working again till the following Monday, and filming would be completed by Saturday, so I took the chance and flew on out.

Upon arrival, I was hurried to my room and told to stay there while my costumes were being fitted. Blake Edwards arrived and asked if I would mind having dinner served in my room, too, as they did not want me to run into Kim Stanley, still in the hotel. I began to feel like the company fink, but complied.

The next day, a limo whisked me out to the set where I met the other actors. Karl Malden, an old friend, was playing my husband. William Holden and Tom Skerritt were also in the cast, and everyone made me feel welcome and comfortable. We shot for the next four days, finishing up at sunset on Saturday with much congratulations all around. There had been a few electrical problems that seemed minor, so with a clear conscience I flew back East on Sunday. Tired, but pleased that I had pulled it off.

As of Monday, I was in every day of the soap for the next two weeks. When Wally called and said that retakes were needed because the electrical problems had caused scenes that did not match, I damn near fainted.

"They didn't realize it until they saw the dailies," he said. "Can't you get some time off?"

I went to the producer of *Splendored Thing*, confessed what I had done, and threw myself on his mercy. He was kind, but adament. There was no possible way they could write me out. I called Wally, and once more the part was recast. I believe Leora Dana ended up playing it.

I settled into a comfortable routine doing *Splendored Thing*, though my hours were a bit wacky. Rehearsal started at 7:00 A.M. at CBS on Fifty-seventh Street. That meant rising at 4:30 so that I could be on the road no later than 5:30. However, this worked well for Bill, as he discovered that he got a lot of writing done in the early hours before the phone started to ring.

The cast, for the most part got on well. Andrea Marcovicci played my daughter and Vincent Bagetta, my son. Judson Laire was my ancient suitor who came with a ready-made family, daughters Leslie Charleson, Donna Mills, and son-in-law Edward Power. There was one member of the cast, Susie, who was heavily into drugs. It was always a bit nerve-racking playing with her when she was spaced out. She tended to come off calm and beautiful while the rest of us were nervous wrecks trying to anticipate her flights of fancy with the dialogue. Judson also had some difficulty with lines, certainly allowable at his age, but I would watch him carefully, and when I saw a certain blank look come into those beautiful blue eyes, was alerted. One had to be careful helping him out, as he was a proud man who didn't want to admit to his failing memory.

We had two regular directors, but the one I remember most is Peter Levin, who made us all dig deep in our character work and not settle for any cliches. For the first time, I really enjoyed working in a soap, and I stayed with it for three years until it went off the air.

During this time, Michael was working on *The Streets of San Francisco* with our old friend, Karl Malden. It was a very lucky break for him as Karl was a professional totally devoid of jealousy, and acted as a fatherly mentor to Mike. He would counsel him to run up the hills in San Francisco while reciting poetry to give his lungs the necessary workout to do the long Shakespeare soliloquies that he foresaw in Michael's future.

To date, his career hasn't taken that turn, but we live in

hopes.

He was living with a charming and funny girl, Brenda Vacarro, a highly talented actress. He brought her back to visit us in Westport when his show went on hiatus. They were together almost five years, and today she and her charming French husband Guy, are frequent guests at my house here in Sherman Oaks.

We had some disturbing news. Joel's marriage was in trouble. Susan had fallen in love with someone else, and Joel had left college just before graduating to move down to L.A. In our phone conversations, he seemed unhappy and lost, unsure as to what he wanted to do with his life, but decided to stay on the Coast and pick up some work in film. Which he did, working on *Posse* with his father, among other films.

Love Is a Many Splendored Thing went off the air shortly after my fiftieth birthday, and I felt at loose ends without a regular job. I wandered about the house, trying not to distract Bill in his writing. He had started research on the life of Hart Crane, which he was to turn into a lovely and touching screenplay.

Then Wally called me and suggested I come out to L.A. for the summer to see what work they could dig up for me. Bill was willing, so we rented the house out to Arthur Kopit, the dramatist, and his wife and flew to California, taking an apartment in Westwood. We ran into many friends from the East Coast who had also made the exodus, so we figured it was probably not a dumb move.

Shortly after arriving I got a role co-starring with Arthur Hill in his series, *Owen Marshall*, and after that a good part in James Stewart's series, *Hawkins*. A strange thing happened while working on it. Stewart played a lawyer who was cross-examining me on the stand. During the examination, I was to break down in tears. I had noticed that he was very quiet and subdued while we were preparing for the scene, but certainly hadn't anticipated what eventually came about. As I started to weep, he started to weep. The director called a halt, and Jim blew his nose, apologized and suggested we start again. Again he wept, and after trying three or four more times, he said he had to go home, promising we would try again on Monday.

Later, I found out that a dear friend of his, John Ford, had died that day. He was quietly distraught. He was a sweet and sensitive gentleman. Monday, we got through it just fine.

Next I had a part in *Kung Fu* that I really loved. A slightly crazed missionary lady, preaching and singing "Amazing Grace"at the drop of a hat. Wally wasn't sure that I should take it, as it was such a far-out character part, but it turned out to be a good choice. It led directly to my being chosen to star in *The Cowboys*, a new series being developed at Warner Brothers due to start shooting early in the year.

Meanwhile, Bill had gone back to Westport to see to the changeover in tenants. While there, he started to have chest pains, and our friend Barney Kates called me to say he had just taken him to Norwalk Hospital. I flew back immediately, but by the time I got there, he had been released. They had done an angiogram on him and could find nothing wrong. It was put down to a possible hiatal hernia, and he flew back with me to California.

Once there, I went to work on *The Cowboys* with Moses Gunn and Jim Davis, the only two other adults, and seven boys. We worked mostly on location at a ranch built for us out of Thousand Oaks. We started shooting in January of '74. As I remember, it was cold as hell and rained incessantly so we spent a lot of the time up to our knees in mud, but the kids were great, and I loved working with them and the horses. Moses and Jim were fine actors, and we all became great buddies.

We shot thirteen sequences and got generally good notices, but when option time came, the network failed to take us up. Alas.

At home we caught up on our social life and renewed aquaintances with old friends, who became very fond of

Bill, the Seltzers and Lillian and Stan Margolies. In fact Walter Seltzer optioned the screenplay dealing with the last few months of Hart Crane's life and tried to get it produced, but the time was not right for it given Hart's homosexuality and the temper of the times. The script, however, did get Bill several more assignments.

Michael, meanwhile, had taken over the rights of *One Flew over the Cuckoo's Nest* from Doug and was trying to get a director as well as a star for it. He got and lost several directors and stars before he was able to sign both Milos Forman and Jack Nicholson and get the project underway.

He and Brenda were living in a house on Benedict Canyon, and it was here that Bill and I had our first brush with drugs, excluding alcohol, of course. A joint was being handed around when we got there, and several people seemed quite stoned, some seemed to be having a whale of a time, giggling like mad. When it was passed to me, I looked at Bill with raised eyebrows, and he shrugged, and I took a fast hit. I wasn't mad about the taste and felt no effect whatsoever so when the joint came around again I declined.

Bill, however, took several hits and when the time came to drive home, realized he was affected and asked Brenda for some black coffee.

"Honey, that works with booze, but not pot. You going to be all right, baby?"

Bill drew himself up.

"Of course. I'm perfectly fine."

I eyed him as we got in the car.

"Sure you're okay?"

"Positive."

We made our way slowly down the driveway.

"Funny," said Bill, "I didn't think Benedict Canyon was this long."

"God! Move over. I'm driving."

Bill complied, amidst fits of giggles as we drove back to Westwood. That night we made love, and in the morning, he was still ecstatic.

"My God that was glorious. It seemed to go on for ever and ever!"

But that was the last time we tried it. Pot, that is! With alcohol we knew where we stood. Besides, it was illegal.

Michael was still working on *The Streets of San Francisco* with Karl Malden at this time, and the casting man, John Conwell, called me in one day to say there was a part he felt I was right for. It was a guest star in the series, but he thought it would be fun not to let Michael know I was going to be on.

I flew up to San Francisco, checking into a hotel, and showing up early for makeup. When Michael walked onto the set, his jaw dropped.

"Mom! Whatever are you doing here?"

"Guesting, silly. Pity we don't have any scenes together."

He watched my scenes from behind the camera like a mother hen, and one time called on the makeup department to pluck a hair he had spotted picking up the light.

Michael had gotten *One Flew over the Cuckoo's Nest* into production, and they were shooting in an actual insane asylum in Salem, Oregon. Joel was working on the production, Milos Forman was directing, and Louise Fletcher was playing the part I would have given my eyeteeth to play, that of the evil Nurse Ratchet. I went to visit them during the shooting and watched Jack Nicholson's work with fascination. An old pal from the O'Neill Theatre, Danny de Vito was also in the cast. Milos was shooting with three cameras at once so that he could pick up the reactions of all the inmates at the same time.

Speaking of inmates, the actual patients in the hospital were in a different part of the building, but when I made a wrong turn, I ran into some young girls whose hands were restrained by leather handcuffs attached to a waist belt. They were making their way downstairs. I said "Hi!" but they only glared at me and pushed on past. It shook me up and depressed me for days.

When I returned to Westport, Bill and I discussed the

possibility of finding a permanent place in L.A., perhaps a house with a guesthouse. Renting out the main house could help cover the mortgage payments, and we could reserve the guesthouse for us, as a pied-à-terre whenever we were out there.

At the beginning of the summer in 1975, Joel came back to Westport for a visit. He was divorced and had started dating a tall, red-haired woman called Judy Corso. It didn't seem to be particularly serious. He said he planned to join us in California in a couple of weeks, so Bill and I packed up the car and prepared to embark on our first cross-country trip by car. Bill had contracted with a travel magazine to keep a diary of the journey, and we took our time, exploring the byways as well as the highways. I remember being deeply moved by a marker denoting the start of the Oregon Trail, the land stretching away endlessly, thinking of the loneliness and the courage of those early pioneers.

At Cheyenne we headed north, a bit out of our way, but we wanted to see Jackson Hole, Wyoming, and experience river rafting on the Snake River. That was an experience never to be forgotten, exhilarating and terrifying in equal amounts. We bounced down the rapids as in a mad roller-coaster ride, hanging on to the "chicken strings" on the gunwhales of the raft. I had been warned to take off my sunglasses, for they would be lost when a wave hit, so I tucked them in my bra, zipped up my windbreaker, and tied the lifevest tightly over all. Well, when the first wave hit, my glasses shot out of my pants leg. This gave me some respect for the force of the water!

Arriving in California, we checked into an apartment complex near Warner Brothers in Burbank. We kept expecting Joel to turn up, but there was no word from him, nor did we know how to contact him, as he had moved out of our Westport house as soon as it had been rented. Finally, we got a phone call. He and Judy Corso were going to be married. Could we come back to Westport for the wedding?

I'll admit, this time I had serious misgivings. In my few

meetings with Judy, she had struck me as a determined and highly manipulative woman. She was older than Joel with a son about to enter his teens. It was hard to make a case long distance, but I pleaded with him to give it some time before they took the plunge. Later I found out that they had already married secretly, but still wanted a formal wedding. He was twenty-eight years old, old enough, one hoped, to know what he was getting into.

We flew back for the wedding, and members of my family came up from Bermuda for the event, though Doug and Michael couldn't make it. We all hoped for the best. The reception was held at the Silvermine Tavern, where Bill and I had spent our wedding night nineteen years earlier. I prayed that Joel's marriage would turn out as happy.

Back in California, Bill had started work on a novel *The Blooding*, the story of a rabies scare set during WWII. Walter Seltzer was interested in his doing a screenplay based on a novel called *Wolf Mountain*; I was gainfully employed guesting on different television shows. It looked as though the move to California had been a wise one professionally for both of us.

One Sunday, we were driving over to the Seltzers for a brunch when we realized we were a half-hour early, so we decided to drive around the neighborhood. Going up a little canyon street, we saw a woman putting out an "Open House" sign in front of a quaint little cottage.

We looked at each other.

"Let's give it a go."

We were the first ones to arrive, and the real estate woman had time to show us around. It was eerie, but I swear the house spoke to us. There was the Picasso print of Don Quixote and Sancho Panza on the stairs, identical to the one we had in Vermont. A swimming pool with a waterfall out back, and three tiny bedrooms, one with the exact dimensions of Bill's office back in Westport. And, as we came down the stars to leave, who should I see but Vincent Bagetta, who had played my son in *Love Is a Many*

Splendored Thing.

I flew down the stairs and threw my arms around him.

"Vinny! Darling, what are you doing here?"

"I live right around the corner. What are you doing here?"

"Just looking at this house."

"Buy it! Immediately!"

"Ahem!"

I turned.

"Oh, I'm sorry, darling. This is Vince Bagetta, who was in the soap with me. Vince, I'd like you to meet my husband."

"Great to meet you. Can you come over to my place for a drink?"

"Well we're due at some friends in a few minutes."

"Call them from my house. This is important."

We looked at each other.

We complied. Vinny was brimming over with excitement.

"I walk by that house almost every day, and I've always wanted to see the inside of it. It's one of those houses that was built in the 1940s with good hardwood floors and lots of little extra charming things that the newer houses don't have. This is a great neighborhood, so if you are thinking of buying, I suggest you move fast. It's not going to last long on the market."

We thanked him somewhat warily and departed for the Seltzers. All through brunch we kept looking at one another.

"Lets go back!"

When we returned, it was a madhouse. There must have been close to a hundred people rummaging through the house. I had a proprietary feeling and watched them all anxiously. We approached the real estate woman to find out what the immediate steps were to begin a sale. A few thousand down to show good faith, a list of our assets to show that we could pass escrow, and had the ability to get a mortgage. Bill and I hurriedly glanced at our checkbooks to see if we could cover the down payment. We could, just.

After plonking it down, we went back to the apartment, and Bill worked out a very comprehensive sheet of our assets, which looked impressive, though we were land-poor.

Besides the Westport and Vermont houses, we had acquired a cottage in Bermuda, and I had a third interest in Pembroke Hall, which had been left to Ruth, Fan, and me. As for cash in the bank, there was very little, but based on my earnings in television over the past two years, we saw reason for nothing but optimism in our future in California.

In October of 1975 the house was ours! We packed our suitcases, picked up our dwarf lemon tree from the balcony, and hied ourselves over to Sherman Oaks. We bought a bed and a chest of drawers for the "master bedroom" downstairs, some cheap wicker furniture for the living room, which we figured we could gradually replace with more permanent pieces, and settled ourselves in. From the beginning, the place felt like home, and we reveled in it.

In a few months, our euphoria was brought up short. Suddenly I was not getting any TV work. Wally was at a loss to explain why this should be so, other than I had run through my time of being a new face in town.

"But, Wally, we just bought a house on the strength of my working out here."

"Darling," he said gently, "I didn't tell you to buy a house, did I?"

Of course he was right, but it didn't help the fact that we had no income except the rent from the Westport house. Bill and I had a long serious talk.

"Something has got to go. We haven't had much luck in renting out Vermont. I guess it makes sense to unload it."

"But, darling, it's your favorite place in the world!"

"I know, but we've got to start acting like grown-ups, hard as it is. It's more likely we will work here, than sitting on a mountaintop in Vermont. We will go back together to say good-bye to it and then put it on the market."

Easier said than done. The first morning in Vermont, we sat on the back balcony sipping coffee and looking across the blazing autumn colors to Stratton Mountain. A little white-tailed deer came across the glade, looked up at us totally unafraid, and I burst into tears.

"Let's wait and see what happens. Something's bound to turn up. It always has."

But nothing did, so a few months later, Bill went back alone to negotiate the sale. A Swiss couple bought it; it reminded them of their homeland, they said. When I drove by the place in 1993, I was happy to see that the same people owned it. They must have loved it as much as we.

Early 1977 brought a lot of changes. Michael and Brenda had broken up the year before, and he had been dating various girls, most of whom he brought over to the house. I didn't sense any serious intentions from him about any of them, but in January, he went to Washington with Jack Nicholson and Warren Beatty to attend Jimmy Carter's inaugural. There, at an evening gathering, the three of them spotted a beautiful young woman named Diandra Luker. Michael moved quickly to cut out the competition and somehow persuaded her to fly back with him to California. He called me from the airport.

"Mom, I'm back from Washington. We just landed. There's somebody I'd like you to meet. Can I bring her over right away for lunch?"

When I hung up, I turned to Bill.

"This is it. I've never heard him like this. This is the one he is going to marry." Six weeks later, they were wed.

It was a lovely ceremony, taking place in Doug and Anne's back garden with a woman judge officiating and a quotation from a Shakespeare sonnet, "Let me not to the marriage of true minds," recited. Diandra was a tremulous, but beautiful bride, and Michael's joy in her was palpable.

Diandra did not have an easy time fitting into the life style of the movie colony. European bred, she found the lack of privacy and the arrogance of the paparazzi difficult to take. A point of view with which I sympathized.

"They don't even ask before they take your picture!" she complained in puzzlement to me.

I think Michael tried to understand her point of view, but having been brought up in "the business," he was pretty well inured to such considerations. They moved into a house he had bought on Tower Road that had a magnificent view not far from our place, so we found ourselves meeting for dinner fairly often.

At the end of 1977, Steve and Judy Gethers gave us a surprise going-away party before we left for Spain. Bill was at work on a new novel, *Solomon Moon*, and he needed to visit Spain to do research on the Inquisition, which played a part in the book. It was a humdinger of a party, with Michael and Diandra and about twenty of our friends. Everyone brought small gifts that had to do with Spain from castanets to a bullfighter's hat. We toasted and drank until the wee hours of the morning.

We landed in Madrid and were booked into the Ritz. We had been given strict instructions to not let it be known that we had any connection with show business as the Ritz had excluded anyone from the profession since Ava Gardner had, on a drunken evening, peed in the ornamental fountain in the lobby. Our room was elegant and we minded our manners. I guess I passed muster, though I saw some disdainful looks at my sneakers as we made our way down the circular staircase to the lobby. I was damned if I was going to tackle the cobbled streets of Madrid in high heels.

We did all the touristy things. Dined at Hemingway's favorite restaurant and the Jockey Club, visited the Prado with its magnificent Velazquez and Caravaggios, as well as the heartbreaking Goya war drawings. Everywhere we saw graffiti saying "Fuck Franco," and one night we joined in what we thought was a student celebration with bonfires in a square. We were holding hands in a circle, singing, and dancing, only to find out the next morning that it was considered a riot and the police had arrived wielding batons shortly after we left.

God protects fools and innocents abroad.

After visiting Toledo, we flew down to Seville, where Bill was to do his main research, staying in a small hotel on the edge of the barrio within sound of the chimes from the Giralda. We covered most of the city on foot, then, rented a car to drive to Cordoba. At Cordoba, a professor skilled in the Jewish history of the town was to meet us and show us pertinent locations. He turned out to be a lively, enthusiastic old fellow with definite ideas about what we should see. The first thing on his list was the immense mosque, with a Catholic cathedral built inside it.

It was indeed impressive, made more so by his observations. He pointed out that in the Gothic structures of Christianity, the light came from above, leading the eye to look upwards to the Deity. Whereas in the mosques, the windows were at eye level, signifying man's equality with God. He fairly danced with excitement as he imparted all the information, quite ignoring the faithful praying in the little side chapels, and when he found a Star of David on one of the pillars, he got quite carried away.

"Look, you, Jew!" he shouted at Bill "Look! Here's your Jewish star in a Moslem temple, right next door to a Catholic cathedral! How's that for ecumenical?" A few heads were raised, but nobody shushed, him and we followed him meekly out the door, grinning quietly.

At Granada, we were booked into a marvelous grand hotel that had seen better days. I think it was called the Alhambra. Carpets were threadbare, but the views magnificent, looking across the town to the mountains where the last Moor made his retreat. After dinner, Bill fell into conversation with the headwaiter, who said he wished to give us a special treat as we seemed interested in the history of the hotel. He took us in the elevator down to the bowels of the hotel, which hung on the side of a mountain, and showed us a tiny jewel of a theatre where Sarah Bernhardt had performed. Then he asked us to close our eyes while he led us into another room.

We obeyed, then heard the click of a Bic lighter.

"You may open them, now."

We gasped.

A vast, mirrored dining hall reflected a table that could seat a hundred, each place setting glittering with vermeil and crystal. In the mirrors, the table and the little flame seemed to go on and on. The effect was magical.

He flicked off the flame and led us out.

"The state dining room. It is always kept ready for the heads of state. Most people don't know it's there."

We thanked him, and I reflected once more on how Bill's friendliness had enriched my life. People opened themselves to him, and I was the beneficiary.

Back home again. *The Blooding* had received excellent notices and was selling fairly well. Bill was hard at work on *Solomon Moon* when Diandra called one morning and asked if she and Michael might come over for dinner.

I said, "Of course."

She arrived ahead of Michael and said she had some news for him, but wanted us there when she broke it. I had an idea what it was, but let her take her own time. During dinner she suddenly handed him a magazine.

"What's this?" said Mike. And then as he looked at it, "It's a baby magazine. What are...Oh my God. Is this what I think it is?"

Diandra nodded her eyes filling with tears.

"Are you happy?"

"Happy? Oh, God, oh God...I'm ecstatic!"

He was crying, too, and Bill and I were pretty choked up as well.

Diandra had a fairly trouble free pregnancy until delivery. Then, they found that the baby was in a breech position. A placenta-previa condition existed, so she had to have a caesarian. I tore down to the hospital as soon as I heard the news and raced up to the maternity floor.

On the way to her room, I passed a covey of newborns

being wheeled down the corridor. One glance and I knew which one was Cameron, he was the image of Michael as a baby. Diandra was weak, but happy and oh, so proud.

I adored being a grandmother. I had forgotten how delicious the talc smell of infants can be, the tiny mewing noises they make, the sudden focusing of the eyes and the flash of recognition.

Sometimes they left Cameron sleeping in his basket with us when they went to a concert, and it was easy to get attached to the little guy. He was so responsive and happy. Later in the early spring, I visited Joel and Judy in the lovely old colonial house they had bought in Darien, Connecticut, but was acutely uncomfortable. There was tension in the air, though they both tried to put a good face on things. I felt sure the marriage was headed for trouble, and it turned out later that I was right. Sometimes family life resembles a seesaw ride, with happiness and unhappiness going back and forth at random.

Back in California, an interesting theatre experience was offered me. A group known for innovative work, the Los Angeles Actors Theatre, headed by Ralph Waite and Bill Bushnell, were planning a production of Harold Pinter's *Old Times* and asked Rita Gam and me to come in to read for the two female parts.

We read, then Bill Bushnell, who was directing, asked us to switch parts. We did and then he asked us to switch back. He sat there scratching his head.

"It's interesting, you both bring such different values to each part. I'm damned if I know who to cast as what. How would you feel about both of you learning both parts and alternating every few performances?"

Rita and I looked at each other and shrugged.

"Okay by me. How about you?"

"Sure. Fine. Let's give it a go."

I think we both found it very stimulating. Our interpretations were entirely different. Aside from similar blocking we made no attempt to copy one another. The only person who had rather a rough time of it was James Booth, who played the man caught between the two women. He seemed a trifle schizoid by the end of the run, trying to figure out who was what, when.

The play got very good notices, and I got a Dramalogue award. Shortly after the play closed, I had to have a small skin cancer removed from my cheek, and the surgeon suggested I have a chemical peel so that the color would remain even. As I looked into it, it seemed to make sense to have a face-lift while I was at it, being in a profession that valued looks and youth to an inordinate degree. I was fifty-seven and in robust health, but I was beginning to get the grim look of Great-aunt Julia.

In the dining room at Newbold Place, her portrait glared down at us while we dined. I used to ask Mother what she was so angry about.

"She was really very pleasant," said Mother. "It's just the unfortunate configuration of her mouth and jaw."

Unfortunate, indeed, and I seemed to have inherited it, getting grimmer by the minute.

"Go ahead, if you feel you must." Said Bill. " I think you look great."

God bless love's myopia.

The makeup artists on *Knot's Landing*, the first show that I worked on after the operation, remarked that I seemed to have a very bad sunburn, and no matter how much makeup they piled on, the redness came beaming through, but, aside from that, the lift was very successful.

I worked with my old friend, Ann Marcus, on a series that she wrote with her husband Ellis called *The Life and Times of Eddie Roberts* or *L.A.T.E.R.* that was a great deal of fun, but unfortunately didn't last. However, I was kept busy doing a lot of episodic TV as well as a well-meant but agonizing production of *The Trojan Women* on stage.

The director double-cast all the characters with deaf actors and hearing actors. That had been done before with the Theatre of the Deaf, but the deaf actors would sign onstage, while the speaking ones would narrate from the sidelines. It meant that the focus would be where it should be, on the signing actors.

In this production, however, both the speaking and the signing actors were on stage simultaneously, trying to keep pace with each other and creating one hell of a traffic jam with all the characters competing for space.

I was the speaking Hecuba, and fine actress Julianna Fjeld was the signing one. I think the experience was equally excruciating for both of us, for when one had an emotional moment going, one had to be conscious of not pulling ahead or falling behind the other. It was like a ghastly three-legged race, and I felt we stumbled through the performances. However many people who saw the production were intrigued by it. As for me, I was grateful that it was only a limited run.

Michael and Diandra bought a lovely, old house in Montecito, a suburb of Santa Barbara, and began spending more and more time up there. I think Diandra was more comfortable away from the Hollywood scene, and it was certainly an ideal place to bring up young Cameron. Diandra had gone to boarding school in Montecito at just about the time Michael was going to U.C.S.B., so they had ties which went way back.

Shortly after they bought the house and were planning renovations, Michael had a bad skiing accident, severing all the nerves in his knee, and stayed in a cast from hip to ankle for many months. With his high energy level, he couldn't bear to be confined and wanted to oversee every inch of landscaping and architecture, so he was a familiar sight to the workmen, wheeling around at top speed on his crutches, his cast held out in front of him.

When the time came for the cast to be removed, the doctors were astonished at how little the muscles had atrophied and were of the opinion that all his activity and the strength it took to hold up the cast made his recovery time much shorter.

Joel, meanwhile, had broken up with Judy and was moving to California. He seemed more relieved than unhappy and was anxious to get more work in his profession. He had co-produced a small budget film in Alabama called *King Cobra*, which I was in, along with Fritz Weaver and my old friend, Norman Lloyd.

While standing by the camera observing a shot of the snake, Joel had to jump back suddenly as the cobra struck at the lens. He fell over backwards, hitting some equipment and injuring his back. So shortly after his arrival in California he had to be hospitalized and ended up having a spine-fusion operation.

He had a long recuperation period, but found a ground-floor apartment in Beverly Hills and settled once more into the life of a bachelor.

After so many trips back to Westport to repair damage done by renters, Bill and I faced the fact that our lives were centered pretty much in California. When we were in Connecticut the winter before, the car we were driving got stuck in the snow, and when we made it back to California and found ourselves playing tennis on New Year's Day, we decided that L.A. life wasn't too bad after all. So we made the decision to sell the Westport house.

This was a poignant moment for me, redolent as the place was of memories of the boys growing up, of Bill's and my wedding, of all the laughter and parties, of our departed friends, Dr. Frank McCormick and his wife Judy, and of our dear next-door neighbor, Audrey Wood. Bill Liebling had died a few years previously.

Audrey professed herself appalled that we had sold to a playwright.

"She will be nagging me to represent her!" she exclaimed.

Which reminds me of a story Audrey told us after Bill Liebling had died. He always carried a pocket watch with an alarm, which he would set to go off when he wanted to leave a party. Many was the time, sometimes when Audrey was in the midst of telling a joke, that the alarm would ring and Bill would stand up.

"Time to go, Audrey!" he would announce, and Audrey, with a regretful smile, would rise and leave with him.

After he died, she was almost paralyzed with grief. She didn't come up to Westport, but stayed in their apartment at the Royalton with the curtains drawn, not venturing out. This went on for the better part of a month, and she had forgotten that she had put Bill's watch on the mantel till suddenly the alarm went off. It hadn't been wound since he died, and the only reason she could think of for the phenomenon was that Bill was sending a message from beyond.

"Time to go, Audrey."

And time for her to get on with her life, which she did.

Alas, a year or so after we sold the house, Audrey was felled by a stroke and never regained consciousness. She lingered on for four years, a great tragedy. She had stipulated in her will that she wanted to set up a trust for young playwrights, and she had also stipulated that she did not want any heroic measures to save her life. They took her off the lung machine, but under New York law, they could not take her off intravenous feeding as that would constitute starving her to death. So all the money that she had hoped would be left to fledgling playwrights was eaten up in medical expenses.

We arranged for our antique furniture to be packed up and sent out to California and walked on Compo Beach for our final farewell to Westport, which had served us and our family so well. The air was crisp and cool, and seagulls dropped clams on the rocks, dive-bombing as they scooped up the morsels. We remembered all the beach-side barbecues we had had with the kids and dear friends, Pat and Jim Mulford, the Kellys, the Crolius's…but it was time to move on.

Time to move on to California.

As the furniture from Westport was unpacked in

Sherman Oaks, we realized that we needed more room. I had always wanted a dining room, and the dining table and chairs were pushed into a corner of the living room. Plus the master bedroom with its minuscule closet was woefully inadequate. So we took some of the money from the sale, contacted an architect, Nelson Fay, and proceeded with plans for an addition.

It was a true challenge for him. We wanted to keep the original feeling of the house, without any feeling of an add-on, yet we wanted a lot more room. He designed an upstairs bedroom that had a vaulted wooden ceiling, with exactly the same angle as that in the living room. It was directly over a dining room where a patio used to be. The bath off the bedroom had exposed beams and small-paned windows, so the "cottage" feeling was maintained, even though we had gained a lot of space.

We lived in the house while the work went on around us. Not an experience I would recommend, but it insured that everything was done exactly to our specifications, and we were pleased with the results.

So now we were truly Californians. And the family had, strangely enough, come together.

A few years back, when Michael won the Academy Award for *One Flew over the Cuckoo's Nest*, Doug had given a call to Bill suggesting that we all get together at his house to celebrate.

"If Diana isn't still mad at me, that is."

Bill assured him that I was happy to let bygones be bygones and that we would love to partake of the celebration. I think we were all a little nervous about getting together after almost five years of silence, and the cocktail hour was a little stilted even though the cocktails were strong. Joel was there, and Peter and Eric—the sons Doug had by Anne. At dinner, Anne served icy aquavit before the main course. Doug, being a great one for toasts and speeches, made a very touching one about his pride in Michael and his happiness that the extended family was all together.

I found myself profoundly touched by his generosity of spirit and his willingness to forget our differences in the past.

We all toasted enthusiastically, then Bill made a speech, then Anne, then I. By the time it got round to Michael, the aquavit had definitely got to him, and he weaved as he stood up.

Waving his glass in the air, he gave his toast.

"To my parents! For their extraordinary performance here tonight they surely deserve an Academy Award!"

That really broke the ice, we all howled with laughter and after that Anne and Doug and Bill and I had no trouble getting along and saw one another fairly often socially.

Mike had an almost uncanny sense of timing in the pictures he chose to produce, and when the Three Mile Island disaster struck just as *The China Syndrome* (which also dealt with a nuclear accident) was released, I wondered if he had inherited the Dill second sight.

Michael was refreshingly unimpressed by his rising fame and retained his common sense and his humor. I think the fact of having been exposed to the pluses and minuses of fame at an early age served as a sort of inoculation against a swelled head, and he has handled it all with ease and grace.

Speaking of the Dill second sight or paranormal proclivities, the combination of Irish feyness and the natural superstition of island folk had led to my being brought up amid spooky tales of my ancestors having visions of their dead relatives before the fact was known. Sea captains, dripping in seaweed, were reputed to stalk the halls of Newbold Place, announcing the fact of their demise to their widows and children.

Fan was fascinated by all the tales and announced that she had second sight. She may well have, she was able to predict when there was a crisis in the family even from halfway around the world. I, on the other hand, having heard so much on the subject, grew bored with it and eschewed anything to do with the supernatural. However something happened in 1972, and I have never been able to explain it. It may be that psychic forces were at work in spite of my disbelief.

Bill and I had cut short a skiing vacation in Kitzbuhel, Austria, due to snow conditions that were abysmal; roots, grass, and ice. We had had a week or so in Vienna, going to the opera and staying at a moat-surrounded castle called the Schloss Laudon, but still felt the need to explore more of Europe before heading home. Neither of us had ever been in Scotland so we booked a flight to Edinburgh.

The first thing I noticed about the city was the air. It smelled just like London had when I was a child, heavy with coal fires and coke. We checked into the George Hotel that night and planned our sightseeing itinerary for the next day. The morning dawned clear and beautiful, and we took a taxi up to Edinburgh Castle, watched the changing of the guard, and strolling on down the hill to Holyrood Palace.

As we stood before the door of the palace, I suddenly knew with a certainty what we were going to see inside. I grasped Bill's arm.

"What is it?"

"I know this sounds ridiculous, but there's a room upstairs where something terrible happened long ago, and I think they hid in the powder room."

Bill looked at me as though I had lost my mind.

"Powder room? Sweetie, they didn't have powder rooms in those days. They didn't have toilets for God's sake."

At the bottom of the stairs, we met a guide who ushered us up to the second floor. We followed him as he opened the door to a small room. I was suddenly so cold. I stopped at the door.

"This is the little supper room where Queen Mary's secretary, Rizzio, was murdered."

"I know," I breathed.

"And this," he said, gesturing to a door on the side wall,

"is where they would go to powder themselves before dining, their hygiene not being the greatest."

"And was it called the powder room?" I asked.

"Why, yes."

Bill threw a startled glance at me, and I held him back.

"In the next room, Mary's bedroom, there's going to be something humorous. Something she made. I don't know what." We stood at the threshold and looked around the Seventeenth-century bedroom. There was nothing unusual. Bill looked at me, and I shrugged. We walked to the window to look out at the courtyard. The guide's voice followed us.

"And this, Queen Mary embroidered herself."

We turned to see a needlepoint cushion that had been hidden from sight at the foot of the bed. On it were a cat and a mouse, both wearing crowns.

"As you see, the queen had a sense of humor. The cat represents Queen Elizabeth and the mouse, Mary"

Walking back to the hotel, we tried to figure out how I could have known what I did. I had always been a history buff and particularly intrigued with Mary, queen of Scots, but I don't remember ever reading anything about the particulars I'd witnessed. I'd never them in a movie. It was baffling.

That night, I couldn't sleep. After Bill fell asleep, I sat up in the bathroom, smoking cigarette after cigarette. Sometime around two, he knocked on the door.

"Are you okay in there?"

"I'm fine. Go back to sleep."

But I wasn't fine. Every time I started to drift off, strange melodies invaded my mind, tunes from another era. Ballads and galliards. I had a feeling of panic that if I slipped into sleep, I would wake up in another century.

So I sat and smoked till dawn.

When Bill woke up, I told him I wanted to leave Edinburgh immediately. He was startled, but complied, saying that I looked like death warmed over. Neither of us has ever been able to come up with a sensible solution to what happened, and, thank God, I haven't had any more supernatural experiences.

Before I leave the seventies, I must return to 1973, the year my dear mother died. It was right before we left for California. She was just short of ninety-three. She had managed to keep traveling well into her eighties, even though she was wheelchair bound and at one airport had been transported in a cattle hoist! Her good humor never failed her, and I looked forward to my yearly visits with her at Newbold Place. She presented me with a large needlework canvas that she had bought, but never started. I kept it in Bermuda working on it as I sat chatting with her, quite often over cocktails. It took me eleven years to finish it, and some missed stitches show where the second martini took effect.

In December of the previous year, I had paid her a visit, and for the first time, she had demurred at playing the piano for me. She was an accomplished pianist with a wonderful memory and delighted in playing songs from her girlhood such as "Floradora," "O Sly Cigarette," "Elsie from Chelsea," etc.

"I can't do it the way I used to," she said. "Sometimes I forget in the middle of a phrase, and I don't like that, so I shan't do it anymore."

"It'll come back, Mommy!"

"No, my darling child, it won't. It's gone, but that's all right."

Bless her, she was comforting me. She accepted life, and death, with a wonderful equanimity.

My nephew David recalled that shortly before she died she had said to him, "I long to come to the end of my journey."

In June of 1973, my sister Ruth called me in Vermont saying that the end seemed to be near, and Bill and I flew down to Bermuda. Fan and Jock had already arrived from England and were staying at Newbold Place, so Bill and I bunked with David and his wife, Mary Margaret.

Mother was in a coma and had not been conscious for

several days, but she seemed comfortable in her own bedroom with nurses round the clock. I held her hand and talked to her, this rewarded with a faint smile, but it seemed as though there was to be no return to consciousness. However, Mother had one more trick up her sleeve.

The night nurse, upon checking Mother's pulse, could detect no throbbing and thought that Mother had passed away. She put her head on Mother's chest to see if there was any heartbeat, whereupon Mother opened her eyes and said, "Boo!" Frightening the poor woman to death. She reeled across the room while Mother chuckled and lapsed back into unconsciousness. Twelve hours later, she died.

The funeral, on the twelfth of June, was held in Devonshire Church where we had attended services every Sunday. The pallbearers were Mother's grandsons, carrying the small coffin made of Bermuda cedar. The day was beautiful. Soft breezes wafted the smell of tropical foliage into the church, and the hymns were all of Mother's favorites. Bill said later that he got quite choked up watching her six children singing stalwartly "The King of Love My Shepherd Is."

If a funeral can ever be said to be a happy occasion, this was it. As we laid her to rest in Devonshire churchyard, we all felt a sense of continuity and of a good life…well lived. We all learned from her, though we could never do as well as she.

On New Year's Day 1980, our friends Alice Hirson and Steve Elliott were married after being together for some years. Both had grown children from previous marriages and many friends in the entertainment business. We all found the ceremony extremely touching, and the groom as well as most of the congregation were in tears by the end of it. We have remained good friends through the years.

We were all planning to be in Europe the following summer, so we made plans to meet at the end of our various journeys and take the Queen Elizabeth 2 from Southampton to New York. We had always found that more than half the fun of a trip was in the planning, and we had an enormous collection of travel books, clippings, and brochures over which to gloat during the winter months.

Fan and Jock were going to be away and made their house in Bagshot available to us. We decided to use it as a base, eagerly making our plans for 1980.

Chapter 16
THE EIGHTIES

Wow! What a summer that was!

First we made the long anticipated journey to Upper Chine. I was anxious to see what changes had been wrought in the forty-one years since I left the school, and Bill was interested in viewing a place that from my descriptions seemed like a poverty-stricken orphanage straight out of a Dickens novel.

As I related earlier, we were greeted by the acid Miss Pasmore in the driveway and taken immediately to see a perfect state-of-the art theatre named after her. I found this amusing, as she had only shown contempt for any of the arts.

The school uniforms were now quite glamorous. Nubile teenagers with flowing locks were sizing Bill up, twitching their scarlet-lined cloaks flirtatiously. They offered to show us the grass tennis courts and new swimming pool while Bill's eyes fairly bugged out.

"You lied," he said to me. "All your terrible stories about this place. It's a goddam country club!"

"But it wasn't like this, I swear."

"I'll bet."

I found that my English teacher, Miss Thomas, was living in a cottage in Shanklin village, and we went to have tea with her. Her complexion was still flawless, her manner gentle. She was charmed by Bill.

"Can Diana still recite Keats's 'Ode to a Nightingale' all the way through?" she asked him.

"I shall test her on the drive back."

He did, and I could.

We drove over to the village of Mottistone to see if we could locate the remains of my great-grandfather's ship in Mottistone Church. The place was deserted, the gravestones overgrown, and door to the vestry unlocked.

Tentatively, we pushed our way in and found ourselves in a lovely, small Norman chapel with needlepoint kneelers in front of the altar and a high, dark roof. I sniffed, but could detect no aroma of Bermuda cedar that my mother had told me to expect.

"This probably isn't the right place. There may be another church in Mottistone."

After a few contemplative moments in a pew, I rose to go. I was at the door when Bill called out.

"Wait! Come here! This is really spooky."

In a small side chapel, he had found a picture of the *Cedrene*, my great-grandfather's ship under full sail, with a plaque underneath giving her history. It stated that she had been wrecked off the Isle of Wight. The thing that had caught his attention was the fact that she had been launched at Shelley Bay where we had our first Bermuda cottage. The ship had been captained by Thomas Melville Dill, designed and built by the Outerbridges and Dills.

David's daughter Ruth Anne, is married to Douglas Outerbridge, so there we link up again—as do most of the families in Bermuda.

The interior of the Isle of Wight has retained its rural charm, and some of the small villages seem not to have changed in centuries in spite of high-rises filling the shoreline.

Back on the mainland, we took our time, driving slowly down to the West Country and through Somerset and Devon. Then into Cornwall. With its prehistoric menhirs, abandoned tin mines, and craggy cliffs, it has always held a mystical fascination for me. We climbed the ruins of Tintagel, clinging to the granite slabs high above the surf.

For a time I thought we were going to have to send for a helicopter to lift me off, as my acrophobia set in and my grip tightened on the rock. But Bill talked me down gently. Knees still shaking, I made it to the car and St. Ives.

Bill frequented the art shops and galleries at St. Ives, and I elected to go to St. Michael's Mount, the twin of Mont St. Michel. It's approached by a causeway that is underwater at high tide and, unlike its counterpart, has no tourist attraction. It has been in the same family since the eleventh century, and they are determined to keep all Disneyland aspects at bay.

Coming back through Devon, we stopped at the Manor at Moretonhempstead, a grand establishment. It's rumored that Goering planned to make it his home after the Reich conquered England. While there, we walked through the woods and came upon a fairy tale village, all thatched cottaged and blooming window-boxed, called North Bovey. We were entranced. When we saw a For Sale sign outside of one of the cottages facing the village green we became excited with the familiar real-estate lust.

As soon as we returned to Bagshot, we put in a call to inquire about the price. Fan and Jock had returned by this time and listened in astonishment as we made plans to return to Devon to inspect the property.

"I think you're both crazy," Jock announced.

He was right, but we had to satisfy our curiosity, and it was as well we did.

Next door to the cottage was a thirteenth-century inn with the charming name of The Ring of Bells. Either the Ring of Bells had no indoor plumbing or the locals just preferred to piss in the open air, but the alley behind the cottage was redolent with the fumes of urine. The inside wasn't much better. Mildew clung to the walls, and the attempts at renovation were charmless. And so we were saved from another mad real-estate venture. Back to California.

At home Cameron was growing apace and proving to be an interesting companion. I started taking him to museums and the theatre when he was about three. He fell asleep halfway through *The King and I*, but was entranced by *Peter Pan*, and pointed to one of the pictures on the nursery set just as Mr. Darling made his first entrance.

"Oh, look, Granny!" he shouted delightedly. "There is Humpty Dumpty!"

The actor in question was a little rotund and quite startled, so he blew his first line. Cameron then had his first lecture on the etiquette of the theatre. I bought him a set of miniature golf clubs and would take him to a local three-par course, where he was taught along with some other children by a golf pro named Dick Coogan. Coogan had been a star on a children's television show back in the fifties, and he had a wonderful way with the little ones, very encouraging and kind. Cam was making good progress and enjoying it, but then the decision was made for Michael's family to move back to New York. He never took it up again. I confess, I missed him dreadfully, and I'm sorry he missed out on some years with Bill.

Early in 1983, Bill came down with a bad case of hepatitis. He had been in New York dining at a rather fancy restaurant connected to Columbia and was served some bad oysters. They found out later that the fisherman had been harvesting them in some field known to be polluted, but close to shore. Eight people died in Manhattan as a result of this.

Bill at first thought he had a case of the flu and took to his bed, feeling rotten. While bringing him a breakfast tray, I detected a strong smell of sulfur all around him. Coincidently, our doctor Elsie Giorgi happened to call at the same moment, and I mentioned the sulfur smell.

"Put him in the car immediately!" she cried. "I'll meet you at the emergency entrance to St. John's."

"Thank God for your nose," she said to me later. "The sulfur smell was an indication that he was going into hepatitic shock and that would have been curtains."

He spent some time in the hospital, followed by a long recovery period at home. During this time, he was weak and often depressed. I scrounged around for all the travel brochures I could find and started to plan the trip to end all trips for the coming summer. Gradually his interest was aroused, and soon he was throwing out suggestions and ideas at a record pace.

We were to start in St. Tropez with Fan and Jock, then drive a rented car to Bellagio on Lake Como where the Howards would join us at the Grand Hotel Serbelloni. After a week there, we would all head north for Switzerland and the Jungfrau, probably finishing at Lake Annecy in the French Alps, the site of an enchanting village called Talloires.

Bill's recovery picked up momentum, and the trip was highly successful. The Serbelloni was redolent of a bygone era with potted palms, a string quartet playing show tunes from the thirties, and ancient English military types parked in deep club chairs. One of the endearing things about the Howards is their fascination with minutia. No gargoyle or flower escapes their attention. We almost missed the boat back across Como when Michael inveigled me into admiring some intricate rolls in a bakery, but we raced along the quay and fell onto the deck, laughing.

All went according to plan on our trip through Switzerland until we reached Talloires. There Michael Howard developed all the symtoms of a heart attack. We took him to the local doctor, who spoke no English. Unfortunately, Michael could speak no French, so I translated and hoped to God I was getting the symptoms right.

"Le vertige. Les palpitations," etc.

The doctor put him in the Annecy hospital for observation. There, he found that Michael, an asthmatic, had been using inhalants while in the high altitudes. I had remembered him using them quite often while we were on the Jungfrau slopes. Michael didn't know, and his stateside doctor had forgotten to warn him, about the dangerous reactions that the altitude could bring, such as palpitations and pain.

He was well enough to leave the hospital the next day, but elected to fly back immediately to the States. One could hardly blame him.

After dropping him and Betty off at the Geneva airport, Bill and I drove slowly up through Burgundy, ending up in Paris. There we met up with our great friend Richard Marquand, who was just finishing shooting a picture.

Richard and his wife Carole were gloriously happy. His career was booming, and she was pregnant with their second child. They were in love with each other and with the city of Paris. They delighted in showing us the secret bistros they had discovered. We covered a lot of the city on foot, and when it came time for us to leave, Bill had learned to know and love the City of Light.

On our last night in Paris, Bill and I decided to drop in to the Hotel Meurice for a simple supper. We ordered a filet mignon and salad, and when the sommelier approached with the wine list, Bill gave it a quick glance and indicated his choice. We went back to talking a blue streak, as was our wont, when I noticed the sommelier handling the wine bottle as though it were the Holy Grail—gently dusting off the cobwebs, easing the cork out in the way that one performs delicate surgery. Waiters hovered, transfixed.

"Darling" I said, "what was that wine you ordered?"

"I dunno…something I'd heard of somewhere. Cheval Blanc or something."

The sommelier reverently poured, and as Bill took a ceremonial sip, his eyebrows shot up.

"Yes, that will do," said Bill.

"I should certainly think so, Monsieur."

"It's really very good. May I look at the wine list again?"

"But of course, Monsieur."

As my glass was filled, Bill looked up from the wine list.

"You are not to pee for three days."

The wine had cost more than $200.

At home, my two sons were working on location in Mexico, on a movie called *Romancing the Stone*, which

Michael had been developing for some time. He brought Joel along as production manager, and his old buddy Danny de Vito was in the cast, so it should have been a comfortable, easy shoot. I gather it was anything but. The weather didn't cooperate, and the locations were in difficult terrain. However, with a couple of stellar performances from Mike and Kathleen Turner, they came up with a hell of a romantic comedy-adventure which did well at the box office.

He and Kathleen were to do two more films together: *Jewel of the Nile* and *The War of the Roses*, both successful, but never the great hit that *Romancing* was.

I auditioned for and got a plum role in *The Paper Chase*, a successful series starring John Houseman that had been running a couple of years. The role was that of a liberal-minded law professor, opposing Mr. Houseman's conservative bent. She had a sense of humor and was an expert at exploding bombast. As the series progressed, there was a hint of a possible romance between the two.

The possibility of a geriatric romantic entanglement made John very nervous.

"Most indecorous at my age. Don't you agree?"

I tried to think of a tactful reply.

"Well, there's always *Love among the Ruins*. That worked."

"You're not implying that I am a ruin?"

"Certainly not."

"All right, then. I suppose we might give it a try."

So, the writers were given their head up and eventually devised a scene where Norman Lloyd and John were vying for my affection. Very funny it was too.

I stayed with *The Paper Chase* until it went off the air two years later. In spite of the difficulty of learning legalese, I enjoyed it all thoroughly. John continued to amaze me with his knowledge, intelligence, and superhuman energy.

When we resumed shooting one fall, he asked me what I had done with my summer.

"Played Gertrude in *Hamlet* up at Solvang, and a play

called *Painting Churches*. And you?"

"Well," said he, "I directed an opera in Houston. Taught a master class in New York. Performed in the reading of a new play in London...which I think I may do...and went to Australia to check up on the acting company I founded."

"My God!" I said. "I hope you're able to sleep on the plane."

"Sleep? Good Lord, no. It's the best place to get writing done. No phones. No interruptions." He was, at this time, in his middle eighties. A great man. Sorely missed.

We had spent the summer in a rented house in Santa Maria. Bill wrote and I rehearsed and played *Hamlet* and *Painting Churches*.

Painting Churches turned out to be the more rewarding. I was working with an old friend, Barney Kates. I had known him since Woodstock days in summer stock, and our performances continued to grow so, that we felt compelled to repeat the production at the Town Hall in Bermuda in 1990.

However, on the evening of opening night in Solvang I had what is every actor's nightmare come true. We were living in Santa Maria where half the performances were played and would drive the thirty miles down to Solvang when performing at the open-air theatre there. Bill had left early to meet friends for a pretheatre dinner. After calling my understudy to assure her that I was healthy and on my way, I started the drive down.

The highway between Santa Maria and Solvang is one of the most deserted in California. There are no gas stations, no emergency telephones, no shopping malls, nothing. At least it was that way in 1985.

Halfway there the engine gave a cough, and the car glided to a stop. The gas tank was full. The engine wasn't overheating. The car was simply dead. I was due at the theatre in Solvang in twenty minutes. I got out and tried to wave several cars down, but none would stop for me. What I wouldn't have given for a car phone then! There was no point in trying to walk. Solvang was still a good ten to fifteen miles away. Panic was gripping me by the throat when a ramshackle truck slowed down.

In it were two of the most villainous-looking men I have ever laid eyes on. One was missing an eye, both had broken teeth and red bandannas tied around their heads, and both sported several days' growth of beard. Central Casting would have pegged them immediately as bandidos.

A rapid scenario ran through my head. My raped and mangled body was being laid to rest with friends and relatives standing by. Bill standing by the head of the grave saying, "But I always told her never to hitchhike."

I glanced at my watch, took a deep breath, and got in.

Luckily, one of the two spoke a little English.

"You pretty."

"Thank you."

Then speaking very clearly and distinctly, I said, "I am going to Solvang to meet my husband. He is waiting for me. If you could drop me at a gas station near…"

"You married, hey?"

"That's right. You don't have to go out of your way. I…"

"No, no. We take you where you want to go."

"Great. In that case would you take me to the theatre? I'll show you the way."

When we pulled up at the stage door, it was ten minutes late, and the stage manager was peering worriedly down the street.

Later the director stuck his head in the door.

"I understand you got a lift to the theatre, I hope you gave them tickets to the show."

"Tickets to the show? Are you mad? They really would have killed me. No, I gave them twenty bucks for beer, and we parted lifelong friends."

During intermission, I called Bill and told him my car needed to be towed.

Ominously, he asked, "…and how did you get to the theatre?"

"I hitchhiked. And, godammit, I don't want to hear

another word about it. Not a word!" He didn't say a word.

Wherever we went, Bill brought along his typewriter and kept to a disciplined schedule of writing. *Solomon Moon* had been published the previous year and was selling quite well. He always had a project underway. Either a screenplay, a drama, or a novel. Everyday he would glean articles from the *New York Times* that might trigger an idea. His active mind and imagination were magpielike, he was full of information. But he was never pedantic. His humor saved him from that. We had a good life—God I loved him!

Around this time, Michael and Joel came back from Morocco where they had been filming *Jewel of the Nile*. Joel confided that he had fallen in love with the French girl Patricia Reed, i.e. "Paddy," his assistant on the movie. He was determined to go back to Europe to woo her, even though she appeared to be engaged to someone else. Privately I didn't hold out much hope for him, but as an early nanny had remarked, he had a whim of iron. Once he set his mind to something, he would move mountains to accomplish it. We awaited the next development with interest.

Early the next year, he brought her to the States to meet the family. She was tall and beautiful with large, soulful eyes. She seemed very shy and retiring, but I put that down to unfamiliarity with the language and country. Her English was more than serviceable. They became engaged before she returned to France, and I gave him the diamond engagement ring that had belonged to my grandmother.

At this time, I was in rehearsal for *Hedda Gabler*, due to open at the Doolittle Theatre in Hollywood. I was playing the part of Aunt Julia. I was reflecting on the "biggies" that I was now too old to play, Hedda being one of them. I think the one I regretted most not having had a crack at was Rosalind in *As You Like It*. I think I could have done a credible job on that. Edwin Schallert, a critic on the *L.A. Times*, had said that I must do Hilda in *The Master Builder* after he had seen me in Major Barbara. Unfortunately by the time I got around to reading it, I was in my thirties and Hilda was a dewy eighteen.

I worked on Lady Macbeth in a scene class, using a friend of mine as a model, who was manic-depressive. In her manic phases, she was one of the most attractive people I have ever met, her enthusiasm knew no bounds. She could persuade anyone to do anything. Only to become almost catatonic in her depressive state. Sadly, she committed suicide before she was forty. It struck me that Marjorie's personality brought a certain logic to Lady Macbeth, much to the horror of the coach who was running the class.

"Wrong! Wrong! Wrong! Wrong!"

I had always considered class a place where there was no question of "wrong" or "right," only whether one fulfilled the intention one was after. It was the place to take chances, be outrageously bad, fall flat on one's face, and above all to stretch. This class, unfortunately, was about "networking," auditioning, and securing that first, important job. Very legitimate concerns to be sure, but not why I was there.

So, somewhat snottily, I said "I'm not interested in whether you think it was right or wrong. Did I convince you that I was manic-depressive? Did I do it without violating the character?"

He looked uncomfortable. He could sense the students getting restless and was used to his word being unquestioned. A bit of a "guru" he was.

"I don't think you are happy in this class."

"No. You're right. I'm not. I think I'll resign."

Evidently, this had never happened to him before. We went through endless meetings before he agreed that I didn't owe him for the coming year and asked me not to discuss my reasons for leaving. As he is still directing and teaching, I shall not mention his name. I still admire his quicksilver intuition and think he can be enormously helpful to those just breaking into the business, but networking is not what a workshop is for as far as I'm concerned.

When Cameron was five, I took him to Bermuda, just

the two of us. In the plane, I told him that there weren't going to be a lot of rules, but two had to be obeyed. He was not to go down to the road by himself, and he was not to go out on the slippery rocks by the bay. Other than that he had the run of the acreage around Ariel Sands. Of course, he had to test me, and the second day I spotted his tiny figure teetering along the slimy rocks with the waves splashing all around. I ran out and grabbed him, and he was grounded for the rest of the day.

After that, he discovered his cousin. Tom Moore was Fan's grandson. He was staying at Ariel with her. It was instant adoration. Tom was thirteen at the time and at first quite tolerant of his young relative. But Cameron clung to him like a shadow, following him everywhere, even into the bathroom. Tom's patience began to fray. Finally, a downcast Cameron leaned against my knee.

"Do you know what my cousin Tom called me, Granny? He said I was a bloody bore."

I bit my lip.

"Darling, everyone needs some privacy. You can't be with Tom all the time."

"But I like him!"

"I know, love, and he likes you. But sometimes he likes to be with people his own age."

"I don't see why."

It was too bad in a way that Cameron had no siblings. Though he seemed tough at times, he was at heart a lonely little boy. He seemed to relish being in the midst of the large Bermuda clan, though quite stunned at the noisy "sing-songs' in which my family indulged. When I was bellowing my way through a chorus of "Phil the Fluters Ball," I felt a tug at my sleeve.

"Granny," Cameron suggested, "Simmer down. Simmer down."

In 1986 "The Paper Chase" shot its final episode, and the summer opened up, free and clear. Joel announced that he and Paddy were going to be married in Nice in

September, so Bill and I planned an extensive trip that would end up in the south of France in time for the wedding.

We flew first to Zurich, and there I had my first view of the true horrors of drugs. In the park across from our hotel, there was open dealing going on day and night. One morning, I almost stumbled over a young man who was stark naked, syringe still in his arm. I thought for a moment that he was dead, but his chest was moving up and down. Bill spoke to a park policeman about it, but the man just shrugged. It certainly altered my view of the orderly and law-abiding Swiss.

We boarded a boat at Basel and spent a week going down the Rhine to Rotterdam. I had a Baedeker's guide with me, and someone had thoughtfully marked historic areas on the riverside to correspond to the history pages in the Baedecker. We sat on the top deck, drinking in the sights, and learning a hell of a lot at the same time.

In Amsterdam, we visited the small but exquisite Van Gogh museum, which held some of his more unfamiliar works. I had always assumed that the later paintings with their wilder brush strokes heralded his descent into madness, but was fascinated to see that some of his very last works were landscapes of orchards in bloom, serene and composed. One might almost say pretty.

After visiting Fan and Jock in Bagshot, we drove up to York, which, to my mind, ranks with Cracow as one of the most beautiful cities in the world. Then out to the Yorkshire dales.

When we returned to London we were invited to use Richard Marquand's flat in Iverna Gardens. This was to be the last time we would see him. Richard, a brilliant young director, died of a cerebral hemorrhage shortly before his forty-ninth birthday. He left behind a young widow and two toddlers, and a grievous sense of loss. Somehow he had always managed to be with us on our wedding anniversary, December 14. We always celebrated with much champagne and hilarity. Life lost a lot of its luster when he left us.

We were left instructions to drop the keys to the flat in the downstairs mailbox when we left, and we had hired a car and driver to take us to the airport for the flight to France. However, when we got to the ticket counter, we discovered that we were a day early, and all the flights were booked solid for the day. We looked at each other. The driver had been dismissed. Even if we went back to London, we wouldn't be able to get back into the apartment. What to do?

We booked ourselves into an airport hotel. After hiking around the uninspiring countryside surrounding Heathrow, we had a champagne lunch and spent the afternoon making love and watching old movies on television—an unexpected bonus to our holiday!

In the Loire Valley, we stayed at the Domaine des Hauts de Loire in Onzain. Rather expensive, but worth every penny. We did the expected tours of the chateaux Amboise, Chenenceau, Chambord, and the exquisite, small Cheverny, now given over to raising hounds. During World War II, it was the secret hiding place of the Mona Lisa. German officers were stationed in the chateau while hunts persisted nationwide in search of the missing treasures of the Louvre. They never found her.

Picnicking, and stopping at auberges, we made our way gradually south, taking the Route Napoleon down from Grenobles and arriving at destination in Villefranche to find that some of the wedding party had arrived ahead of us. My nephew, Sean Dill, was sitting in the lobby, looking forlorn. He had not told anybody that he was coming to the wedding so no accommodations had been arranged. We told him to take a nap and shower in our room while we contacted Joel. With that, ten or more of the Bermuda relatives showed up. All, thankfully, with reservations. Fan and Jock, with their son and daughter, Tom and Joanna were also on hand so our side of the family was well represented.

That evening, we met Paddy's mother, a delightful little

chipmunk of a woman, her Scottish uncle (Paddy's late father had been a Scot), and a very elderly great-aunt who spoke no English at all. She spoke French so slowly that I was able to carry on a conversation with her for about half an hour. I remarked to Paddy how thoughtful it was of her great-aunt to speak so slowly and clearly to a foreigner. Paddy laughed.

"Diana, my aunt is a very old lady. It takes her a long time to think of each word. She always talks slowly."

Paddy seemed radiant and much more confident than I had seen her in the U.S. Her sisters and small nieces and nephews were all chasing around, and it seemed like a warm, happy family, which eased some of my concern. Joel and Paddy planned to make their home in France, at least for the immediate future.

The wedding was spectacular. It was held in a beautiful old cathedral on the hills above Nice. The church and all the cars were decorated with flowers. Michael had arrived to be best man, accompanied by Diandra and her mother. The paparazzi were out in force recording the event, and Doug's youngest son, Eric Douglas, attempted to dictate the order in which we should enter the church. Evidently, that had not been thought out in advance, save the fact that Paddy would be last and unaccompanied.

"Okay," said Eric. "Joel, you accompany your mom and go first. Bill takes Paddy's mom. Okay, start up!"

Joel and I started down the aisle as all heads in the full church turned toward us. Suddenly a small, birdlike woman darted up the aisle waving her arms.

"Arretez! Arretez!" She called, then let out a torrent of French at Joel, none of which I understood.

"Shit," said Joel quietly. "She's the organist, and we were meant to wait for the processional music, but goddamed if I'm going to go back up the aisle and do it again. Chin up, Ma! Keep on going!"

They had had a difficult time finding a priest who would marry them. Joel was divorced, and Paddy was

Catholic, but they finally found one, adistant relative of Paddy's mother. He was so old he had to be held up by two acolytes during the service. Fan had an attack of food poisoning and threw up in the vestry, and Eric got a bit carried away with the drama in his reading from the Bible so that Michael's and Joel's shoulders were shaking with suppressed laughter. As weddings go, it was a lulu.

The only thing marring the occasion was a tension I sensed between my two sons over their plans for the Victorine Studios. Evidently Joel had moved ahead faster with plans to renovate the space than Michael was willing to commit to. They were both a little tight-lipped about it. As they had worked together successfully in the past, I prayed that this would resolve itself without a major blow-up.

During the winter of 1986, Michael decided to do a very special thing for Bill's and my thirtieth wedding anniversary. He rented a house at the Casa de Campo in the Dominican Republic and invited the Howards to join us with Pat, Diandra's mother, Diandra, and Cameron.

We had a glorious time, picnicking, swimming, and playing golf. But when the time came to leave, I had a glimpse of the downside of celebrity.

Upon boarding the plane, Michael had his hands full. Pat was nervous that she would miss her plane connections to Europe, Diandra was missing some luggage, and Cameron decided to have a full-fledged temper tantrum. In the midst of this, some tourists approached Mike for autographs.

"Please," said Michael, a squirming and screaming Cameron under one arm, "not now!"

"All right, Mr. Douglas, we're never going to go to one of your movies again!" The lack of simple humanity was appalling.

In 1986 Michael had made two major films. *Fatal Attraction*, in which he did perhaps my favorite performance, and *Wall Street*, for which he won an Academy

Award. On the night of the awards, Michael sent a limousine to pick us up and to meet him and Diandra at the Bel-Air Hotel. Bill looked quite smashing in his dinner jacket, and I was in a French designer dress that I had bought for Joel's wedding. Neither of them were ready when we arrived. Diandra had always had a shaky sense of punctuality, but this time, Michael seemed to have lost his shoes. After a frantic and fruitless search, the driver was sent to pick up a new pair, and we were on our way.

In the theatre where the ceremonies are held, the sheep and the goats are firmly divided. The stars are ushered up to be interviewed, their guests and families funneled down another route in order to meet up at one's seats in the theatre. Doug had elected not to come as he did not want to detract from Michael's triumph, which was gracious of him.

After the four of us were seated and the ceremonies had begun, Michael suddenly looked nervous.

"Mom!" he said. "Do you have a pencil or a pen?"

I checked my evening bag.

"Sorry, darling. What's the matter?"

"I gotta make some notes. Just in case."

"You mean you haven't prepared anything?"

He shook his head.

"Probably won't happen. But just in case."

I spotted Roddy McDowall in the row ahead of us and leaned over.

"Roddy, dear. You wouldn't happen to have a pen on you, would you?"

"Sure thing."

He handed it over, and Mike proceeded to write notes on his cuffs.

When his name was announced as the winner, he bounded up to the stage and made a warm and graceful speech, and if he referred to his notes it wasn't noticeable. A true pro.

The Governor's Ball, held immediately after the ceremonies, was a study in controlled hysteria. Hollywood loves a winner, perhaps more than in other businesses, and our table was awash with backslappers, pulling Michael this way and that. He coped beautifully, as usual, but I detected a trace of genuine fear in Diandra's eyes as the hordes moved in.

I had to leave early as I had a matinee the next day down in La Mirada, where I was doing *On Golden Pond* with Conrad Bain. I gather the festivities went on until morning.

Later in the year, it became evident that Bill's "hiatal hernia" attacks were coming with more frequency, and our internist suggested that he see a heart specialist. The doctor put him through a myriad of tests, then suggested we both come in for a consultation.

"You'll see," Bill said confidently, "I went through tests before, and it was absolutely nothing. Nothing at all."

But this time it was different.

Dr. Cohen explained it all carefully to us and said that a triple bypass should be done as soon as possible. There was some risk in surgery, but far more if it were neglected.

Bill was wonderfully matter-of-fact about it all and went about getting the dates set up with the surgeon like a true stoic while I sat silent with a little cold lump in my chest trying to keep an optimistic smile glued on my face.

The fortune-teller who had so accurately foretold Bill's future when he was sixteen, had also predicted a serious illness in middle age and death before his sixty-fifth birthday. He had indeed been very ill with hepatitis and was now sixty-four years old. Neither Bill nor I mentioned this before the operation, but it was there like an elephant sitting in a corner of the room as we waited for the day.

On the day of the operation, I sat in the waiting room with both my sons and Paddy. For five hours, we kept up mindless chatter, but my heart was in the operating room with Bill. Finally, one of my sons sensibly said that we should all eat something, and they both left to bring up some sandwiches.

A nurse poked her head around the door just before they got back.

"Mrs. Darrid?"

I steeled myself for the dreadful news. I grabbed Paddy's hand.

"Yes?"

"He is in the recovery room. You can see him in a few minutes."

"He made it? He made it?"

I burst into wild tears just as my sons got off the elevator. They assumed the worst and came racing up to comfort me.

All I could say was, "He made it! He made it!"

"God, Mom, that's not the right reaction at all. You scared the hell out of us!"

In the recovery room, Bill was hooked up to a maze of machines.

He was in a lot of pain, but bearing it with his usual stoicism. He gave me a wink.

"First time the fortune-teller's been wrong, huh?"

Going home in the car I figured it out. In 1939, when she made the prediction, there was no such thing as bypass surgery, and he would indeed have died before his sixty-fifth birthday.

A couple of days after his surgery, there was quite a severe earthquake. Bill had asked for a private room overlooking Santa Monica Bay. It had floor-to-ceiling windows. As they bowed in and out during the quake, Bill cursed himself for being so picky, but they held and there was little damage done to the hospital. During the bedlam, one of the patients managed to pull all the tubes out of his arms and dive under the bed, to the confusion of the nurses who couldn't figure out where he'd gone!

At home the electricity and telephones were out. I raced up the street to my friends, the Powers, and asked Jennifer to call Bill and tell him we were all right. In the meantime, I tried to get the car out of the garage without the remote. She reported that he was his usual calm, collected self, telling her to see that I didn't worry or drive too fast.

It's a strange thing in our profession, but a job always comes along at the most inopportune time. Plan a trip abroad and even if you haven't heard from your agents in months, sure as shooting, you'll get a call that will gum up the works.

With my husband in the hospital and the phones not working, I was due to start work on an episode of *Beauty and the Beast*, playing Roy Dotrice's wife, dying of pancreatic cancer. Roy was a joy to work with. He and his wife Kay became valued friends. Both he and Peter Medak, the director, were dear and sympathetic to the strain I was under, and all went well. It turned out to be one of the better episodes of the series.

When Bill came home again, I called on Jim Karen and Edward Power to help get him up the steps, as Edward was to do two times more for other vascular operations that Bill had. I'm lucky to have such friends and neighbors who never fail to jump in and help in an emergency.

Later that year, my nephew David came out to visit us and told us that Maggie Clark, a friend of Bayard and Clare's, was having a house built on Ariel Sands property. She was going to live in, and was it possible we might be interested in doing the same thing? We had previously owned property in Bermuda. The Shelly Bay house turned out to be a good investment as rental property, but was never vacant long enough for us to use it. We'd also owned a condominium at Whale Bay, an unmitigated disaster. Shoddy workmanship and continually rising maintenance fees made it impossible to justify. Ariel Sands sounded like the answer to a prayer. The club would maintain the property and rent it out, and we would use it one month a year. We put up half the building costs, and they put up the other half. It was agreed that we would get an 8 percent return on our investment.

We flew down to the island to inspect the site and finalize the arrangements, joined by John and Pam Blum and Michael and Betty Howard. While there, I heard that my sister Ruth was dangerously ill in a hospital in New Brunswick, New Jersey due to a botched colon operation. I flew there immediately and met with her three daughters, son, and husband. The word was not good, and though heavily sedated, she still seemed in a lot of pain.

I sat with her and sang the hymns and nursery songs that we had both remembered from our days at Newbold Place. She smiled a little at "Onward, Christian Soldiers!" and gave my hand a squeeze. It was the only recognition I was able to get.

I was glad that I had written her a few years back, thanking her for her extraordinary generosity. She had opened possibilities for so many of her relatives. She had sent Tommy's girls to boarding school and college, paid for my schooling at the American Academy when my parents were unable due to the pound-sterling block, and many more untold acts of kindness. One could always count on her to come through with sweetness and consideration. She was an innately joyful person, and it made me sad to see some of that joy leave her as her husband grimly found fault with all of her endeavors.

She died while I was there but I didn't stay for the services. I couldn't face talking to Phil, her husband. I was afraid of what I might say . I flew straight back to the coast.

The next year, Tommy died, but that was almost a relief. He had not been well, mentally or physically, for some time and had been quite a burden on his wife, Marge.

The whole family met in Bermuda at Christmastime. We moved into "Sea Change," our cottage at Ariel Sands situated on a hill overlooking the beach. Michael, Diandra, and Cameron as well as Joel and Paddy joined us there. Mary Lea, Ruth's eldest was there too, with her husband Marty Richards.

Mary Lea and Marty were sitting in the bar at Ariel

Sands watching television when the news broke about the Lockerbie air crash.

Mary Lea exclaimed, "My God! Joel!"

"What do you mean?" said Marty. "Were he and his wife on that plane?"

"No!" said Mary Lea. "I hadn't seen him in ten years, and there he is, sitting over there!" Marty heaved a great sigh of relief.

"Don't ever do that to me again!"

Clare had prepared Christmas dinner for twenty-five of us at Newbold Place. Following tradition, Bayard proposed a toast to the queen, and I saw Bill's eyes pop a bit at that. He gave me a "is he kidding?" look. I quickly frowned and shook my head, pressing his foot under the table. All solemnly raised their glasses, and Michael and Joel managed to contain their giggles. Sometimes being half British and half American gets one a bit schizoid.

That Christmas, Bill started a tennis tournament for friends and family, a sort of "round robin" with a lot of switching partners and laughter. Afterwards everyone would repair to our cottage for beer and then down to the clubhouse at Ariel for lunch. We kept up the tradition for the next four years he was alive, then I managed to continue it for two more. I must start it up again one of these days.

After Bill's death, I ordered a teakwood bench with a plaque that read "Bill's Bench," and it sits on the side of the court today.

Chapter 17
THE NINETIES

Having the house in Bermuda, we thought we would now investigate the possibilities of theatre down there. There were several amateur groups year-round, and the Bermuda Festival during the winter brought in ballet and string quartets from abroad along with some professional actors, usually in one man shows. The City Hall had a nice little theatre, seating around 300. The local drama groups were willing to pitch in painting scenery, etc. So we decided to bring *Painting Churches* there in the summer of 1990. Barney Kates was playing his original role, and we cast his actual daughter, Leah Kates Brown, as the daughter in the play.

We formed a company, Pyramid Productions, and joined with Donel Productions, a company that had been started by Don Gibson in Bermuda, still being run by his widow, Elsbeth. She had considerable knowledge of who to contact to get things done and was very helpful, but the available crew was a far cry from the professional Broadway bunch. Bill had his patience sorely tried as he coped with producing and directing, overseeing the light board, and God knows what else.

We had been warned that Bermuda would not sustain a two week run. It was midsummer, a time when a lot of the wealthier Bermudians were off the island and the rest preferred backyard barbecues or sailing in the long summer evenings to sitting in a theatre. July was the only time the theatre was available to us, so despite forces to the contrary we decided to plunge ahead.

The reviews were good, but a lot of the audience (and

most of the crew) professed bewilderment at the play. They didn't "get it," though I never found Tina Howes writing particularly obtuse. She doesn't follow a straight dramatic line, and this seemed to bother some people. Others found it challenging and exciting, but not enough, alas, to give us a hit. Beyond the glamorous opening night when the governor sat in the royal box toasting us with champagne, we limped along, and the audiences dwindled in the second week to a precious few.

Nevertheless, it was good work, and we were proud of the production. I remember the feeling of total bliss after we had closed and Barney and Leah had gone home. Bill and I lay by the side of the pool at Ariel, gazing out to sea, both conscious of a deep sense of satisfaction, of having used our talents well.

Later that summer, I flew over to England for the Oxford wedding of Nino (Nicky's and Bitten's son) and Fiona. Nino had been one of my favorites since he was three and asked me if I would be his girlfriend forever. Now he had grown up into an astoundingly handsome young man, about to go into Bayard's law firm. He gave a charming speech thanking his in-laws for the lovely gift of Fiona and saying that he "Could hardly wait to unwrap it tonight."

The ushers showed up wearing Bermuda shorts with their formal morning coats as a gag, but changed into formal, striped trousers for the actual ceremony. Bayard looked very distinguished in his top hat and many medals, and Laurence had flown over to play the organ at the ceremony.

After spending a few days with Fan and Jock, I decided to fly to Majorca. Michael and Diandra had bought some property with an ancient tower on it on the island where Diandra had spent a good deal of her girlhood. I was glad that I had seen it in its original state, for on my next visit three years later, it had been turned into a luxury estate. It was near the lovely old town of Valdemossa, where Chopin and Georges Sand had shacked up during a cold, wet winter in the 1800s. He'd died of pneumonia the following year. It's quite probable that Majorca weather did him in.

A letter from Joel awaited me when I got back.

Ever since his marriage, he had been urging us to take a canal trip with him and Paddy in a flat-bottomed motorboat called a "peniche." As opposed to the more popular barge trips, this one had only three staterooms and you ran it yourself. Joel and Paddy had spent their honeymoon on one and made several trips after. Paddy assured us that Joel was a very adept skipper.

As 1990 slipped into 1991, Joel called again.

"I'm hiring the boat for this June," he said. "If we keep putting it off, one of these days, it will be too late."

Bill was recovering from a second vascular operation on his legs, but we figured that by June all would be well. So, come the summer, we joined them with Paddy's mother in sailing from Narbonne up to Carcassonne and back. Joel manuevering the boat through the sixty-seven locks with expertise while Bill, Paddy, and I scrambled like monkeys, tying ropes and shouting directions as we leaped on and off of the locks, and generally having a whale of a time.

We would tie up at a local auberge for either dinner or lunch, having the other meal on board. Joel, Bill, and I were early risers, so Joel would get a pot of lethally strong French coffee brewing while Bill and I strolled along the towpath in search of a boulangerie, returning with piping hot croissants and baguettes. Then we would sit and admire the beauty of the morning on the canal and plot our next port.

The lovely medieval walled city of Carcassonne was a disappointment, however. From a distance, it was ethereally beautiful, but once inside the massive gates, it resembled Disneyland with booths selling junky souvenirs and tee shirts. Is there no corner of the earth where kitsch doesn't prevail? With worldwide communication, why is it that the Golden Arches of McDonald's and cans of Coca-Cola are the prevalent representation of America abroad? That, and blockbuster "disaster" movies.

We all got along fine on the voyage and parted with kisses. As we reached Narbonne again, Bill and I rented a car and headed north for the Dordogne and Brittany, stopping on the way at the most picturesque village of St. Cyr la Popie and the town of Brantome in the Dordogne.

It was pissing rain all along the Brittany and Normandy coast, but we climbed Mont St. Michel and happily overdosed on oysters in St. Malo. I called Fan and asked if we could pop over a bit earlier than planned, but it wasn't convenient for them, so we went straight to London to meet with Michael Redington.

A bit of backtracking here. Just before we went to Bermuda for *Painting Churches*, Dick Lewis, an old friend and producer had sent me a copy of the play *The Best of Friends*, which Michael Redington had produced in London with John Gielgud and Rosemary Harris in the cast. Dick thought that I would be very right for the part played by Rosemary, that of the Abbess of Stanbrook Abbey. At the time, my mind was solely on *Painting Churches*, but we promised to look up Michael Redington when in England, and, if there were a production, go to see it.

Michael said that there was indeed a production starring Dulcie Grey and her husband, Michael Dennison playing in Wales. So we tootled off to catch it, having by this time read the script, of course.

The play deals with the correspondence between George Bernard Shaw, Dame Laurentia McLachlan, and Sir Sidney Cockerell, the curator of the FitzWilliam Museum. All highly intellectual, opinionated folk

It made for an interesting evening, but one that must be followed closely. Dulcie Grey and Michael Dennison were both fine in their parts, as was the actor playing Shaw. However, the sets were heavy Victoriana, and the direction uninspired, the pace slow.

Bill and I compared notes after the performance, and both of us felt there was a worthwhile play there. A lot more fun could be had of it, the three were such disparate characters. It was amazing they spoke to each other at all, let alone remain lifelong friends. Actually, G.B.S. and Laurentia did not speak for a time until he thought she was dead and wrote a touching note to the convent, which she found hilarious. We were intrigued enough by the material to option it from Michael Redington for a tryout, with the possibility of bringing it to Broadway or Off Broadway.

We drove up to Worcestershire to Stanbrook Abbey, the convent where Dame Laurentia had presided. I asked permission to visit it to observe and absorb some of the atmosphere that had surrounded her. The present prioress, Sister Felicitas Corrigan, had kindly invited me to lunch. Laurence's daughter Susan was staying in a cottage near the convent, so we planned to stay with her for two nights while I did my research.

At 11:30, I arrived at the convent gates and was shown to a small room where, to my astonishment, the full garb of a nun was laid out on the bed. A novice explained to me that Sister Felicitas felt it might be helpful to me to be wearing vestments like those of Dame Laurentia while I explored her life. The pretty little novice giggled happily as she helped me into the heavy, black garments. She explained that the whole convent had been looking forward to my visit with great anticipation.

Sister Felicitas had been a friend of Laurentia's while she was alive and was able to fill me in on wonderful, very usable stuff. There was her directness and "no nonsense" attitude, her high intelligence and compassion, and one amusing side note—she didn't wear any underpants. She showed me portions of Laurentia's diary and handwritten letters from Shaw and Cockerell among others, then hung Laurentia's cross around my neck, put Laurentia's abbess ring on my finger, and insisted I stay for tea with all the nuns.

I was fascinated with the nuns, their artistic skills and knowledge, their appreciation and humor. There was nothing stuffy or dour about any of them. I thoroughly enjoyed myself throughout the tea, and, as I asked a question, I crossed my legs. Instantly, all eyes swiveled in my direction, and I uncrossed them hurriedly. It had never occurred to me before that nuns never cross their legs, at least not in the traditional habit. I studied the nun's walk, gliding as if on roller skates, heads bent demurely. When I attempted to copy it, Sister Felicitas roared with laughter.

"No, no, no!" she said. "Laurentia had a purposeful stride: head up! She moved so swiftly that the wind whipped her veil." The whole visit was enormously helpful and exciting. Sister Felicitas and I kept up a correspondence for years afterward to my delight.

Bill, who had been expecting me back right after lunch, had grown concerned as the afternoon wore on.

"I thought maybe you'd taken the veil," he said when I showed up around six.

It was tempting. The serenity and joy of the sisters was an inspiration.

On our return to the U.S., we went directly to the O'Neill Foundation, and asked George White who he could recommend as a bright young director. He mentioned Bill Partlan who had spent several seasons at the O'Neill and who had a small theatre of his own in Minneapolis called the Cricket. It had a good reputation and might be the ideal place to try the play out. We watched a production that Partlan had directed, had some discussions with him about the play, which he loved, too, and settled on a November opening in that coldest of cities, Minneapolis.

Meanwhile, Michael's company had secured the option of *Hart*, and he had a new partner, who was in charge of development. This partner employed a novice director aged twenty-five to work with Bill on changes felt necessary in the script. Bill was anxious to get the piece done after such a long time, so he went along with the changes, but was less than happy about them. He turned in one draft before we left for Minneapolis, only to be told that another one was required immediately. So during our rehearsal time, Bill was closeted away in the apartment, typing madly.

We had cast Michael Allinson as Cockerell and Vincent Dowling as G.B.S. Bill Partlan was directing, his wife Tina was doing the lighting, and a crackerjack young stage manager right out of Yale Drama named Mike Everett kept us on our toes, pouncing on any deviation from the script. A lovely, light, impressionistic set was designed. At dress rehearsal, it all seemed to be coming together. Bill was going to be seeing it for the first time, and I was nervous, but excited.

In my dressing room later that night was a note from him:

> Darling,
>
> As your husband I can only be pleased that you have not kept the chastity of your body intact. As what I hope is a fellow artist, I am tearfully proud of how you have kept your artistic chastity intact. I watch your sweet soul, your intensity of spirit on stage, and I bless the day we met. You are lovelier than you'll ever know.
>
> Please, please try to relax and enjoy the hell out of it. I love you. B.

We got uniformly good notices. "A blue ribbon cast in a highly articulate play." "For those who like their plays full of erudition and thought-provoking conversation, might I suggest *The Best of Friends*?" "Superb cast and staging make *Best of Friends* jolly good!" We were mentioned individually, all most complimentary.

We sent copies of the reviews to Gordon Davidson at the Mark Taper Forum, but he felt it was too "special" a piece for him. Some other theatres were contacted, but all seemed afraid that it might be too intellectual, so we came back to California with a fistfull of good notices, and nowhere to book the play.

One night, shortly before we left, we were walking back from the theatre. There had been near-blizzard conditions, and snowbanks were piled high with a narrow path on the sidewalks. I recall a slight feeling of apprehension as a young man brushed by me, too close for comfort, but we continued on in single file with Bill ahead.

Suddenly I heard running footsteps behind me, and my bag was being yanked by its shoulder strap. Instinctively, I yanked back. With that the young man pushed me down into the snowbank, but still I held onto the strap.

Bill, hearing the fracas, turned and came back to rescue me. The young man hauled off and hit him on the side of the jaw, drawing blood. With that, I let go of the strap, and he made off down the road with my bag where we could see accomplices awaiting him. Bill and I made our way to an apartment building where we phoned the police.

They drove us to the hospital protesting that "muggings never happen in Minneapolis. Very unusual. Not like New York or L.A."

Indeed.

Bill suffered from a sore jaw, but luckily nothing was broken.

Back in California, Bill turned in his draft of the screenplay *Hart*, but there were further meetings and nit-picking, and I could tell he was getting discouraged. His health had not been great after the two vascular operations on his legs, and his tennis game had slowed up a lot, much to his irritation. He grew quieter, and I sensed he was fighting off depression.

Suddenly, a new ailment showed up, an annoying and painful rash that started on his legs and feet, later spreading to his hands.

At first, none of us took it seriously. Doctors prescribed various ointments which we dabbed on, but which had little effect. They seemed to be at a loss as to how to diagnose it, but somehow a skin disease seemed less deadly than one affecting the internal organs, so we proceeded with our plans.

Vincent Dowling was very anxious to have *The Best of*

Friends play at his little Miniature Theatre in the Berkshires in the late summer, and in the absence of interest from other theatres, this seemed like a possibility. However, it was too far from New York to expect potential backers to make the journey up there.

We decided to make the commitment to him, but also to have a reading of it at the Players Club in New York in March. Bill had talked to Marty Richards of the Producers Circle who had expressed an interest, as had Lucille Lortel. We thought it might qualify for a Theatre Alliance project, so that was being looked into as well.

Meanwhile, I was cast in a TV pilot that was to be shot in New York in March so we would travel first class. Everything seemed to be falling into place.

We decided to ask our friends the Elliotts to join us in Bermuda after the reading for a short vacation and took off in the M.G.M. luxury airliner. There were few passenger seats and attentive attendants, whom I was to bless on our return flight.

The reading at the Players Club went off spectacularly, and Lucille Lortel said she wanted to have *The Best of Friends* at her White Barn theatre in the fall, with the possibility of bringing it into the former de Lys (now called the Lucille Lortel). I did my stint as an ancient lesbian in the pilot with Griffin Dunne, and all was going well except for Bill's rash, which was steadily growing worse.

Marty Richards said that he had a good dermatologist so we went to see him and finally had the condition diagnosed as "bullous pemphigoid," a rare disease for which there was no known cure, but one which could be kept under control with prednisone. I suggested we call the Elliotts and cancel the Bermuda trip, but the doctor said it wouldn't make any difference where he was, the treatment would be the same. If there was more discomfort, the Bermuda doctors could just put him on higher doses of prednisone.

I left it up to Bill, and he opted to go. He flew with the

Elliotts, while I was still shooting the pilot. When I joined them a few days later, he was definitely worse, though uncomplaining. We made visits to the doctor in Hamilton almost daily to have his painful blisters punctured, we cut large holes in his sneakers, and still walking was more and more difficult for him. After the Elliotts left, I wondered if we should have left with them, but Bill was adamant about sticking to our original plans. Perhaps I should have gone over his head, but as he was hanging on to every shred of dignity he could muster, I felt that I should comply with his wishes.

When the time came to leave, it was a nightmare. The airport personnel could not have been less helpful. Bill was in a wheelchair, as well as managing the baggage, customs, immigration, etc. It had to have been unbelievably difficult. Throughout, Bill was silent and stoic, though in considerable pain. We had called the dermatologist from Bermuda to get an immediate appointment and when he saw Bill, he recommended immediate hospitalization. He took Bill off all medication, including his heart medicine.

"Hell," said Bill, "if I'm going to be off my heart medicine, I damn well want to be near my cardiologist."

"Then you had better fly back to L.A. immediately," said the doctor.

I got on the phone while in the doctor's office and booked a reservation on M.G.M. airlines that was leaving within a couple of hours. While waiting in the small airport for the plane, the television was tuned to the Rodney King trial going on in California. The few passengers were glued to the set. When the infamous verdict came down and we knew that the police officers had been acquitted there was a universal groan.

The flight attendants helped me get Bill on board and were wonderfully solicitous on the flight out. As we started our descent into L.A., Bill nudged me.

"Look out the window! I've never seen so many fires in my life."

I looked.

"Oh, my God. It's that fucking verdict."

And there it was, the Los Angeles riots.

We had arranged for Nikki Grosso, Michael's loyal business manager, to meet us at the plane and book a room at the hospital for the morning. She was there, bless her heart, true to her word. She took us through back routes to our home in Sherman Oaks. Much of the city was blocked off due to the riots.

I made the mistake of muttering something about "the goddam cops."

"Watch it, kiddo," she said gently, "my husband is a cop."

I had forgotten. I apologized.

The next morning I took Bill down to St. Johns, and with a sense of relief turned him over to the medical team. Bill had fought his way back from so many illnesses, I was sure that he could come back out of this one too.

There were complications. The massive doses of prednisone he had been taking for the Bullous Pemphigoid were causing their own problems by weakening the immune system so they had to be decreased, but very gradually.

I would spend about four to five hours a day at the hospital, but Bill despised being "hovered over," so I started a new needlepoint project that enabled me to be there, but working on my stitching rather than being focused on him all the time.

Towards the end of May, there seemed to be improvement. The prednisone was being reduced with no ill effects. Bill encouraged me to go back to Massachusetts for Cameron's Grandparents Day at Eaglebrook. I was there for two nights.

Cameron and I had dinner together, and over coffee Cam asked. "Is Billy going to die?"

Cam and I have always been totally honest with one another. It's something I think he can count on.

I took a deep breath. He had forced me to think the

unthinkable.

"I don't know, Cam" and then "No! No, dammit, he is not going to die. He has always gotten better and he will this time, too."

"Okay, Granny," he said softly. "Okay."

And, indeed when I got back, the good news was that he was going to be allowed home in a week or two.

As usual, dear Edward Power helped him up the steps and I could see in his face the shock of Bill's appearance. Bill had aged perhaps ten years in the few months, but seeing him every day had made it less apparent to me. I made him comfortable in the guest room downstairs, so that he could move around on one level, and almost immediately he asked for his typewriter and wrote a letter to Phyllis Wender. She was a New York literary agent who had expressed interest in representing him. My spirits lifted, and I felt he was on the road to recovery.

We discussed plans for a solar system to be installed when a new roof was put on and went over catalogs of asphalt tiles trying to find the least offensive, as we were forced to give up our lovely wooden shake roof, being in a fire area.

Bill seemed to be gaining ground a little each day, and when I mentioned that I was going to call Vincent to find a replacement for me in *Friends*, he wouldn't hear of it.

"I'll be fine by then. I can tell. It'll be great being in the Berkshires, and I'll just take it easy."

A couple of days later, I heard a change in his voice. He sounded hoarse. I called his cardiologist, who suggested I bring him to his office. Neither of us anticipated that he would have to stay, so didn't bring any toiletries etc., but when the x-rays were developed, pneumonia showed up in both lungs. He was hospitalized immediately.

I wondered if it might be due to some neglect on my part, but the doctor said that his immune system had been so weakened by the massive doses of prednisone that he might have picked up the infection anywhere or from anybody. We both anticipated an early release from the hospital.

It wasn't until he was moved to another floor for longer-term care that the real sense of foreboding sank in.

Bill grew progressively weaker and less able to do things for himself. But he still struggled like the proud man he was. When he gave up going to the bathroom and accepted a urinal, I knew things were very grave. He had an oxygen mask on his face most of the time and spoke little. The last coherent word that he spoke was "Wimbledon!"

I had been unable to read his signals that he wanted the television turned on, so he tore off the mask in exasperation and croaked out his request.

I had alerted the boys and Bill's brother that he was in the hospital, but left it to our internist, Elsie Giorgi to keep them abreast of developments. Joel flew over from Monte Carlo just before Bill was moved to intensive care. In the past, Joel had had some problems with alcohol, and when I met him at the plane, I could tell he had been drinking on the way over, though he wasn't drunk. But knowing how fast the problem could escalate, I was blunt with him.

"If you're going to drink, I don't want you in the house. I've got all I can cope with."

I know the slip was because he was hurting, too, as he loved and relied on Bill. But, bless his heart, he quit immediately so as not to cause me any more anxiety.

As the move to intensive care was being planned, I told the staff that I wanted to keep the same nurses. Bill liked them and relied on them. I was told that, as there were special intensive care nurses, the insurance wouldn't cover the extra nursing care. Our funds were low, but I felt it was important that he have a sense of continuity with those he liked. I put in a call to Michael, who was in Spain for the summer Olympics, asking if I could borrow from him.

He assented immediately and said he would fly back if there were a turn for the worse. Bill, by this time, was on life-support machines, and septicemia had set in. We still kept hoping against hope, but the prospects looked dim. I called John, Bill's brother, and Michael Howard, his best friend, to say that if they wanted to see him before the end, perhaps they should think about flying out.

There was little response to their presence, though Michael Howard said he felt a pressure back when he squeezed Bill's hand. When Elsie Giorgi told me she thought it was a matter of days, Joel called Michael and he flew in. I watched him sitting by the bed, holding Bill's' hand and talking to him with tears streaming down his face. He had letters to Bill and to me from his twelve-year-old Cameron, full of encouragement and warmth, and he tried to read them through his tears.

Bill and I had both signed a living will stipulating no heroic measures, which included life support machines. Now came the time of decision as to when to turn them off. John felt we should keep them going more or less indefinitely. I felt Bill would not have wanted that, but it was too hard for me to give the order.

When the time finally came, I was alone at the hospital. Howard Cohen came into the waiting room and took my hand.

"It's time," he said, and led me to Bill's bedside.

"He is almost gone," he said. "But he might still be able to hear you." I sat holding his hand, telling him how much I loved him and thanked him for a wonderful life. I told him not to be afraid, while Howard slowly turned off the machines

He called the nurse in to remove the mask and paraphernalia so that Bill would look more normal when the boys arrived.

Later, he gave me a note that Bill had written earlier in case of his death:

> My dearest, darling girl,
>
> We all know that one day each of us has to go "through the trees." I have no intention of doing that yet but one never knows, do one? My life with you

has been such an extraordinarily happy one, you must promise me to mourn just a little and then squeeze the future years till the pips of joy cascade on you. Remember, I ain't gone, I'm just waiting to get together again and giggle through the clouds. I adore you!
     Me.

Bill died on July 11 1992.

Chapter 18

AFTER

Back in 1945, my mother did not attend my father's funeral. Her grief was so intense and private.

I suppose some of the same dynamics were at work within me directly after Bill's death. I felt that if I gave way at all, I would be hopelessly lost and would never be able to fight my way back to sanity. I put my head down and butted my way through, immersing myself in a myriad of details.

Bill's brother, John, sent me a poem he had written which, to me, captured the essence of Bill. He called it "Sweet William":

> Comatose. She woke to say "I do not want to die."
> Only Bill heard her. He told me long ago.
> Not long ago he told me: "Do not go gentle…"
> He liked the sound of Yeats
> But left in quiet grateful for love.
>
> He'd had none from a father.
> Not mother, sister-twin, brother could
> Ease that deprivation.
> Diana did.
>
> Paternal spurning bred the rage
> He said he shared with Yeats. He didn't really
> But he hurt.
>
> It's inside sadness makes great clowns,
> They entertain to mask the feeling.
> Bill held his audience, gave joy,

Costumed rage in glee, spent it with energy as love.

Now images:
Child—small, freckled boy exuding mirth
Imp, so mother called him
Youth—blue eyes beguiled the gentle sex,
Jaunty style in speech and dress.
Man—vigor in stride, motion on court,
Quick typed fluency.
A couple of jiggers end the day.
"Fuck all!" announcing the time for play.

Now remains ache tinged with laughter.
Love judges not; brother knew brother so well.

Michael and Joel took care of informing friends and relatives, as I didn't trust myself on the phone. Mike brought me catalogs to choose the urn that would contain Bill's ashes. Though Bill had wanted to will his organs for transplants, due to his many illnesses, none were in good enough shape to warrant it.

We had decided long ago, after my mother's funeral, that we would be buried together in Old Devonshire churchyard in Bermuda. So I phoned Nicky Dill, Bayard's son, and asked him to arrange it and provide a simple plaque saying "He brought such joy."

Vincent Dowling called to express sympathy, but with an undertone of anxiety in his voice. I assured him that I would be at his theatre for rehearsals the first week in August and would arrange to fly down to Bermuda with Bill's ashes the week before.

There was a memorial service at the Writers Guild with about 800 in attendance. Howard Cohen spoke, as did Walter Seltzer, Chuck Heston, Jim Karen, Steve Elliott, and Doug. Michael and Joel even managed to inject a little humor into their memories of Bill, and afterwards we went to Kate Mantalinis, a nearby restaurant to have the party that Bill had stipulated in his will. "For God's sake, not to be confined to cheese and white wine!"

Lydia Heston reminisced amusingly about a production of *The Hasty Heart* that she had been in with Bill and in which the entire wardrobe of the Scot was missing. They had ad-libbed their way through, describing the outfit, until it came to the sporran. This, she decried as "That big, hairy thing that hangs down in front." Whereupon they both giggled their way through the rest of the play.

Paddy and Diandra flew in for the ceremony, and friends and relatives were dear and supportive, but I couldn't let down my guard, save for some hot and secret tears in the privacy of my room. Later, Michael was to refer to my "stuffing my feelings," which indeed was true, but it was the only way I could cope without flying completely to pieces.

In Bermuda, I met with the bishop of Bermuda, who had agreed to do the service in Old Devonshire church. Bill was the first Jew to be buried there, and I insisted that a segment of his writing having to do with Judaism and his feelings about it be incorporated into the ceremony. It was.

"I grew up without any knowledge or insight regarding my own past. Although my parents were Jews, they rejected the religiosity, the traditions, the teachings, the historic culture of a Jew and I grew up uninformed. I did not relate to being a Jew; indeed, when first confronted as a child by anti-Semitism, I resented being a Jew. As a boy, an adolescent, a young man, I had never been in a temple or synagogue, never participated in any Jewish ceremony or festival, and never gave much thought to what being a Jew was.

I think it was not until World War II when I served in the army for almost five years, that I was forced to examine my own position, my feelings on the matter. Anti-Semitism was virulent. There was no way to escape it. One had to confront it head on. Having been taught that disputation should be settled with reason I, at first, tried to combat hatred with logic. But on one snowy night in a quonset hut in Alaska, the superficial calm which I wore like a protective cloak was gone in a sudden burst of rage. I tried to kill a man who vilified me as a Jew.

Although I am, of course, glad that I was unsuccessful, I felt a huge relief at finally taking a stand. The moment provoked me to at least try to discover what a Jew was. I'm still not sure. There are those who say that one isn't a Jew unless one embraces the religion of a Jew. I am unable to embrace any religion. At best, I suppose, I'm a reluctant agnostic. Reluctant only because it must be nice to have a specific faith that one can accept without question. But what was important, is important, is that one doesn't have to embrace the religious aspect of Judaism to feel like, to be, a Jew. By history, tradition, culture and blood I am a Jew. It has taken me many years to examine the background and I am the richer for it. I love the traditions, the ceremonies, the kind of mysticism one encounters. Somewhere in the book *Solomon Moon* I say that one derives comfort from ritual and myth. I believe that's true. I believe all of us respond to it. It doesn't make any difference whether the solace comes from Judaism or Zen, Catholicism, or a solitary walk in the woods. I think all of us need to relate to a kind of inexplicable mystery which is part of our lives. In a way which I am unable to intellectualize I think it is this very mystery which contributes deeply to our sense of community and which, in today's world, has moved people to search for more than the mundane.

On another subject, accommodations. I feel strongly, both from personal experience and from the observation of others, that it is painfully easy to fall into the trap of accommodation. The phenomena of accommodation occurs on many levels; in our relationships with our parents, our lovers, our wives and husbands, our children, our employers or employees, our schools, our very government. How many times have we been instructed to "make do" or to recognize the need to compromise. To settle, as it were, for less than what is wanted. Make no mistake. I think perfection is imaginary. But possibilities are not. Our accommodations strip us of possibilities, and in so doing, erode our spirit. Such circumstances and choices lead to frustration and, finally, a build-up of anger which can explode in unfocused rage. It is what happened to Solomon Moon.

The roots of the book, the above, I suspect, explains why I was interested in telling the story of a man who discovers his past and, in the discovery, re-examines his life. As to accommodations, it is an area that is universal and something we had all better deal with before we wither on the vine."

The bishop agreed readily and suggested readings from the Old Testament that might be appropriate as well. He was open, pragmatic, and unstuffy. A true man of God. He asked me to make some notes about Bill, as he had never had the pleasure of knowing him. I wrote:

> About Bill. He was one of the most ethical, deeply moral men I have ever met. People were drawn to him because they could trust him, as well as enjoying his warmth, intelligence and humor.
>
> He loved life, and fought hard and courageously against many illnesses, but in the end his body could take no more.
>
> It's fitting that his urn is made of Vermont marble, as he loved that state, and we lived there for a time. But, I think, even more he loved Bermuda—its beauty, its climate, but most of all, its people. He loved the kindness and gentleness and humor he found here, and, if I had gone first, he said he would move here. He found the way of life compatible and enjoyed all the generations of the family, as well as his friends among the staff at Ariel Sands.
>
> He will be terribly missed, but Lord, we were lucky to have him in this world for a time. He was

rare. He was compassionate. He brought out the best in everyone.

I thank God for thirty-six years of love, laughter and high adventure."

David asked to borrow the notes after the bishop had read them, then he used them in his tribute during the service. The urn was buried at the top of the hill against the wall of the graveyard, the plaque fastened to the wall. My brother Bayard, in fragile health himself, insisted on climbing the hill to the burial site. The sight of his dogged, but faltering step nearly did me in. For some reason it reminded me of the gallantry in *The Bridge over the River Kwai*.

At the wake at Newbold Place Laurence played the piano, and we had the proverbial Dill "sing-songs," some of the more sentimental lyrics hitting a bit too close to home, and I saw tears streaming down the cheeks of both my brothers. I realized that mine were wet too.

I had a long, lively conversation with my sister-in-law, Marge, and thought I had never seen her looking so well, but two days later when I had returned to the States, I had a call that she had died unexpectedly. It was almost too much to take.

Michael's driver drove me up to the Berkshires. It was a drive that took about three hours, so I had time to mentally and emotionally shift gears, and prepare for the work situation ahead. I knew that it would take all my strength and concentration and hoped that I was up to it.

The driver dropped me off at a farmhouse high in the hills, with cattle grazing in the fields below. Vincent had told me that I would be alone in the house, but that it was "a healing place." The other actors were quartered in a farm about a half-mile distant, and it was about a four-mile run to the theatre. There was no sound but the wind and the lowing of the cows. I had all the privacy I needed.

Down at the theatre, Bill Partlan and Matt Everett had arrived from Minneapolis to help restage the piece on a much smaller stage. Rehearsals went along easily until the moment when, as Laurentia, I recall Shaw's death. Then I couldn't stop the tears from flowing.

Dear Matt said, "Thank God. Your coolness and control were getting kind of eerie. It was as though Bill was still here."

Bill Partlan had to leave for another engagement halfway through rehearsals, so Kenneth Tigar took over and brought some fresh and interesting insights to the relationships. No wonder we all love the rehearsal. It is a time of discovery and renewal, of digging deep and finding surprises.

There was a small kitchen in my house, so I would invite members of the cast and crew for dinner quite often. Shopping and preparing the meal gave me a sense of continuity, and the company helped stave off the terrible emptiness that was always waiting to take over.

I remembered my mother taking in a paying guest after my father's death, much to the chagrin of the family who thought it beneath her. But mother knew what was right for her.

"It gives me something to get up for," she said.

Indeed, her life had been structured round my father and her family, and suddenly, she was adrift.

I was luckier, having a career to concentrate on, but you don't get over grieving until you go through it, as I was to find out. Michael said later that it disturbed him that whenever he called, I said I was "fine." When he knew damn well I wasn't.

The opening went well, and the *Berkshire Eagle* gave us a rave review, a copy of which I sent to Marty Richards's office in the hope that he would come up and take a look, but no dice. John and Pam Blum came down from Vermont and the McCormick clan came up from Connecticut, as did the Howards, but no one that could move the production to New York.

The reading at the White Barn Theater did not go well.

338 In The Wings

Vincent was upset and uncomfortable with the new space and complained a lot. Michael blew his top and told him to "fucking well get on with it!" and when it came to performance time, they had used up all their energy. It played like a dirge, both of them getting slower and lower. I tried to pick it up and kick it along, but it was like swimming through molasses, and Lucille Lortel's disappointment was evident when we met after the show. She was polite, but there was no more talk of booking her theatre in New York.

I stayed the night with Margot and Mason Adams in Westport, then drove over to Whitney Street the next day to check on our old house. It was exactly the same; white clapboard with black shutters and red barn, willow trees in the back where the boys used to play. Some wistful moments to be sure. But nostalgia was not for me.

Time to get on to New York and find a future for the play.

I met with Marshall Purdy, whom Bill had hired as general manager for the show, to look into the availability of theatres even though we had yet to find backing. My preference was for the Promenade, to my mind the tops of the Off-Broadway houses. I was ready to lay out the down payment to secure it if I had a guarantee from Marty that The Producers Circle would come in.

Marty said that he was interested, but would make no definite commitment unless, perhaps, Michael might be interested in co-producing with him. When I checked with Mike, he said that it was a good possibility, but we would have to meet with his company accountant and that certainly nothing could be done about it in the coming fall.

So I went back to California.

My friends were dear and invited me out for dinner a lot, but sometimes hopelessness threatened to overwhelm me. An ominous little poem kept running through my brain:

> He first deceased.
> She, for a little tried

> To live without him
> Liked it not, and died.

I took French lessons and painting lessons, and I was somewhat obsessive, I fear, while Michael and Marshall were trying to keep the project alive, but they were patient and dear. By Christmastime, Marshall had secured the Westside Theatre for a March opening. Michael and Marty had agreed to co-produce.

They were used to mammoth budgets, to them the $400,000 needed to produce *Friends* seemed like small potatoes. They had their regular investors, then friends bought shares, as did Doug and Anne. Of course I bought some too.

Late one evening, I was sitting with Michael after a session with the accountant. He took my hand and said, "Mom, I really wish you would go to a grief therapy group. You really need it. You've got to stop stuffing your feelings."

"Darling, I know you want what's best for me, but, trust me, I couldn't stomach pouring out my guts to a host of strangers. I just couldn't do it."

"Well, you gotta do something. Some kind of therapy. Believe me, you need it."

He gave me pause for thought. I had thought I was coping so well, but the shell of self-possession was wearing thinner all the time, and I was tense and jumpy. And sleepless. The next day I called the Screen Actors Guild and asked if they covered therapy under their medical plan. They did, and I saw an intelligent and caring woman therapist for the next few months. She truly helped me to gain back some perspective on my life.

The first sessions released all the held-back tears, and it was a relief to be able to weep and grieve openly, to let all the pain show without shame. Next, she gently cautioned me that I might be "deifying" my dead mate, imbuing him with qualities he didn't have. This made me furious, and I told her off in no uncertain terms. It was only much later that I realized that she was channeling my anger and guilt into a release. She mentioned that I must not use Bill for a criterion for future relationships, for no one could ever measure up.

"Future relationships! What, are you crazy?"

"I'm only saying that you should leave yourself open. It would not be the same, of course and you should not expect it to be. But I pity the poor man who must measure up to the brightest, funniest, warmest, most ethical man in the world."

"Shut up! Just shut up!" I sobbed.

And so it went. But bit by bit, I was beginning to see past the pain, I was able to sleep through the night again and make plans for the play without being quite so obsessive.

Christmas was spent in Santa Barbara with Michael, Diandra, and Cameron. Not the easiest of times as Mike and Dia seemed to be having marital difficulties, and Cameron was pissed off at having to be in boarding school. Long walks on the beach helped to clear my head.

In January we were in Bermuda to celebrate my seventieth birthday and Susan's (Laurence's adopted daughter) wedding to Rod Attrick-Sterling, a bright young lawyer whose mother was Mexican and father, a black Bermudian. Even a generation ago, such a union would have caused raised eyebrows, and it was heartwarming to see how Bermuda and the family had progressed. It was a relaxed and joyful occasion, and I had some good, long talks with Lucy, Rod's mother, who had a like interest in Amnesty International.

Michael was still going through his own period of grieving for Bill. He had spent time in a rehab center the previous fall. I have no doubt that part of the problem was due to his feeling of loss. Here in Bermuda, where Bill is buried, he had to cope with it all over again. He came back from a long walk just at dawn, having gotten up at two and walked straight across the island ending up at Bill's gravesite. He had had a rather profound spiritual experience he told me.

He and David arranged a bang-up birthday party for me

at Edey's Hill. It was dear and heartwarming and helped with the healing process. Vincent Dowling had informed me that he did not want to be part of the New York production as it would interfere with his teaching job in Massachusetts. so I had contacted Roy Dotrice, who was shooting a series in Jamaica, to see if he would be free and interested in playing G.B.S. It turned out that he would, so I was looking forward to the start of rehearsals in New York with great anticipation.

I had arranged to sublet a studio apartment from Eric Douglas in the Manhattan Plaza complex, which was in the same block as the Westside Theatre.

Michael's involvement turned out to be a big publicity bonus for the show, and he was terrific about putting time and effort into the production as was Marty Richards. There was a certain amount of dickering around with the script. Roy wanted some other letters of Shaw incorporated, and there was some pruning of Sidney's and Laurentia's speeches. They were all, of course, submitted and approved by Hugh Whitemore. I think it made for a livelier production, though some of the lyricism was lost.

Roy was great fun to work with, mischievous and discerning as G.B.S. I loved his freshness of approach, his willingness to try new things. Michael Allinson was less happy with it, preferring to go by the book. To set a performance and leave it set. He was excellent in the part and totally reliable, but I relished the give-and-take between Roy and me. We would prepare small surprises for one another, nothing changing the play, just slight changes of attitude or reading that kept us alert and investigative.

We played a couple of weeks of previews to appreciative audiences, but cuts and changes went on clear up to opening night.

What an opening that was! Fan and Joel flew in from Europe, the Elliotts from California. My dressing room was so filled with flowers, I could barely get in, some arriving without cards. So to this day I owe some "thank you" notes to a few generous, anonymous souls. The opening night party was at Sardi's, filled with friends and family. Cameron came down from Eaglebrook, sporting a Douglas tartan tie I had given him years before.

The first review was in the Gannett Newspapers and was read out to the throng. It was a rave, and jubilation was rampant. Next came Mel Gussow of the *New York Times*, who was laudatory toward the actors, but felt the piece was "less a play than an elaborate platform reading." However, he wrote: "Diana Douglas, the most poignant of the three, conveys the intellectual curiosity as well as the moral weight of the woman Shaw labeled 'the enclosed nun with the unenclosed mind.'" So I felt I had not done too badly by Laurentia.

And I felt we had given the play a good production. Both Michael Redington, the English producer, and Hugh Whitemore agreed.

"Billy my darling, we pulled it off," I murmured.

The rest of the reviews did not come out until the following morning. They were mixed, but had good, quotable stuff. Enough to mount a publicity campaign, and plans were made to take a half-page in the *New York Times* the following Friday. It would use up a lot of our budget, but as we had little in advance bookings, we felt it would kick the run off to a good start.

My friend Carole Shelley came to see the show shortly after opening and gave me a lovely piece of business that only a fellow actor could come up with. When, as Laurentia, I filled some little bags with lavender, some would invariably spill on my lap. I had either ignored it or brushed them away.

"Wrong!" said Carole. "She would carefully save every sprig, hunting them down."

I love actors.

Late Thursday night, the mother of all blizzards hit New York. When I woke on Friday morning, it was eerily still, and when I looked out the window at Tenth Avenue, there was nothing stirring. No cars, no cabs, no buses, no pedestrians. Nothing but the wind-whipped snow flying horizontally toward the Hudson.

I turned on the TV, and the news was full of the worst storm to hit the Eastern seaboard in decades. Many trains had stopped running, and I wondered how Michael Allinson was going to make it in from Larchmont. Soon I had a call from Marshall Purdy who was also worried about it and had called a rehearsal for Michael's understudy just in case.

It wasn't until I was walking to the theatre that afternoon, seeing the piles of soggy, undelivered newspapers that I thought of our large and very expensive ad in the *New York Times*. My heart sank.

Edwin McDonough, Michaels' standby, was well prepared and did a very creditable job for an audience of twenty-nine valiant souls who had struggled through the snowdrifts. At the end of the performance, the cast gave them all a hand for having made it, and Roy gave a graceful little speech.

Audiences were minuscule all through the weekend. Plays all over New York suffered, but many had healthy advances to see them through. We had no more money in the budget to pay for future advertising and were hoping that a photo shoot that Michael and I had done for *Life* magazine, fifty years after the original cover, might give us a boost. Alas, that and a favorable *New Yorker* review came out after we closed three weeks later.

Five other shows closed the same week, but that was little comfort to us. At the final curtain, I started weeping and couldn't stop. Saying good-bye to the crew, wardrobe people, and cast, then all the way out to Seward Johnson's house in New Jersey, I wept on behind dark glasses. Occasionally I would see the chauffeur give worried glances in the rear view mirror, but I went on like a veritable Niagara.

I managed to pull myself together before arriving, but that evening, an opera star friend of theirs launched into a ballad, and, to my horror, they started up again. Later I realized that the closing of the play was like yet another death. It was something that had linked me so close to Bill and now would have to be relinquished.

Perhaps I've gone on long enough about grieving, but the steps I have taken might be useful to another widow. Of course, every loss is different. I came across notes thrown into my desk drawer charting my progress or lack thereof. Work had saved me, helped me get through the first months, but then, when I returned to our home in California, the prospect of empty days filled me with terror. I entered a period of over structuring myself.

I joined a golf club so that I would be forced to play every Tuesday. Took Spanish lessons three evenings a week at Valley College. A life-drawing class.

March 8th 1994.
Oh God, today was Bill's birthday and grief hit me again with a force I didn't believe possible. I begin to think that this almost physical pain in my chest will never go away, yet I know there have been days when I haven't had it. When I have trouble controlling my tears while buying garden hose in a hardware store, I know that recovery is still far away.

Yet I'm having lunch with some new women acquaintances, who may turn out to be friends, to discuss the possibility of an Oxford seminar this summer. If I continue to put one foot in front of the other maybe one day I'll be marching instead of limping one day to the next.

I'm trying to turn outward and not be taking my emotional temperature continually, but sometimes I don't know if I can go on without him. I look at my friends, many of whom have husbands who are old or ill and think I'd gladly change places with them, but I know I would not have the freedom of choice that I have now. I know that Bill with his fighting spirit would have been increasingly miserable as an invalid, but God I miss that wonderful sense of invulnerability we had as a couple. We truly felt we could tackle any problem as long as we had each other, and oh how I miss his wise advice, his compassion and clarity of thinking.

It's been over a year and a half since Bill died and I guess I'm inching my way toward recovery, though sorrow lies just below the surface and I can never tell what will bring sudden tears—a piece of music, an old photo, the sight of snow on the mountains that brought us such delight.

Even up to his last illnesss we never lost a sense of childlike play, leaving funny notes for each other or setting up surprises for each other. We were each other's best audience and careful listener and didn't give much of a damn whether or not we saw anyone else. "Two loners who found each other," Bill called us.

He was smarter than I, and warmer. The friends I have now came to us through him. They turned to him like plants to the sun because they sensed he really listened, really cared. Now he's gone. I'm trying damn hard to make a life for myself and I hope when I look back a year or so from now the pain will have eased.

An old lover called this morning and wants me to meet him in Albuquerque next month. He asked if he should book separate rooms or one. It's terrible. I miss the touch, the feel, the smell of a man. It's like a hunger but I'm in no shape to make any commitment and I don't want my independence compromised. I hurt this man once before when I left him and I don't want to do it again.

"We are responsible for those we tame...," said the Little Prince, and I know that I am not ready to take on that responsibility.

March 10th 1994

The night of Bill's birthday I lost it. The Karens had invited me to dinner with Morgan Freeman and Michael Griffith and I must have had a glass too many of wine. After dinner Alba showed me the latest quilt she was working on and among the scraps she pointed out a shirt of Bill's that she had incorporated into the design. For some reason that undid me. I made it out to the balcony before I burst into tears, so the other guests were unaware, but Alba followed me out and was very upset. Christ, I wish I knew when it was going to hit. I'd better stop with the second glass.

Having dinner with the Elliotts the next night I was angry to hear that they had been discussing my emotional state with Jim and Alba. I know it's unreasonable of me and I know they are concerned friends, but I hate to be gossiped about. Ridiculous pride? Perhaps, but I find sympathy to be my undoing. I can forge ahead with the minutia of life and make plans for the future, but any fingering with the pain in my soul sends me spiraling into depression. I find it hard to concentrate and tend to lose things.

The prospect of giving a dinner party alone scared me to death. Bill was a marvelous raconteur and host, and our dinners were always fun and lively. However, I realized I couldn't go on accepting from our dear and loving friends forever without reciprocating, so tentatively I began inviting a few people over. Husbands invariably pitched in on bar-tending, and soon I began to feel more confident. I don't know what I would have done without supportive friends at this time. The Elliotts, the Seltzers, the Karens, George and Phyllis Jenkins, and the Bevans wove me into the fabric of their social lives and forced me to interact. God bless them.

Then came two large changes in my life. The first was the arrival of Maggie, my dog. Alice Elliott called me in tears one day, saying that a stray dog had been brought to her house and that she couldn't keep it as it had scared all her cats, who in turn fled up into the trees. I didn't plan to have a pet. Bill and I had decided after Penrod's demise that we wanted to be free to travel and work without the worry of an animal, and I was inclined to feel that way still, but I told Alice that I would keep it until a good home could be found to place it.

This was the fall of '93 when fires were rampant all over

the southland, and many pets were running free. So the shelters were overloaded, as I found when I started to make some calls in an effort to place the dog.

I picked Maggie up, and I wish I could say it was instant love, but it was far from it. She was and is a pretty looking dog with a black muzzle and the pointed ears of a shepherd, with legs a bit too short for true beauty. The main problem was that she was hysterical after having been abandoned.

She crapped on my sofa, and when I attempted to confine her to the laundry room, tried to chew her way through the doors so splinters and blood were everywhere. She had no sense about cars, and if the door was opened, would dart out into the street. She would leap in the air and set off the burglar alarm…in short, had me going crazy. I took her to the vet's to have her shots, and he thought that because of the configuration of hairs on her belly, she probably been spayed. When I detected spots of blood on the living-room floor and realized she had no cuts on her, I knew she had come in season.

I think this was the first time I made contact with her. As I wiped up the blood, I showed it to Maggie, and I swear she looked embarrassed, like a teenager with her first period. I think it was then I decided to keep her. I arranged to have her spayed and then had the entire boundaries of the property electrified with a battery in her collar to prevent her straying into the street.

Shortly after that, in January of '94, the second event happened. The Northridge earthquake.

Maggie had been sleeping on a pad in my bedroom, but she must have sensed something before the first massive jolt, for when I turned on the flashlight she was nowhere to be seen. I got out of bed while the rocking was still going on, pictures falling from the bedroom walls, and made my way out onto the landing. There a mound of books four feet high blocked my way, and I could hear her whimpering.

I was afraid she had been caught underneath when the books fell out of the bookcase, but then I saw her eyes gleaming at me from inside my little office. Naturally I was afraid, but dealing with her helped stifle real panic.

I wanted to get us outside before an aftershock hit, but she didn't want to move from the safety of my kneehole desk. I started to go down the stairs to get a leash, then realized that the steps were covered in glass from the fallen pictures in the stairwell. I remembered that in earthquake preparedness articles, one thing that was stressed was the importance of sturdy shoes, so I went back and put on some clodhoppers.

Even with the leash, she wouldn't move, so I picked her up and carried her outside—all fifty pounds of her. By this time, neighbors were gathering on the street, listening to car radios and trying to assess the damage. I stayed and talked with then for a time, then decided to go up the road to the Powers' house to await the dawn with them. Little Lilian Power and I sat under a doorway with Maggie as a few aftershocks rocked us, and she amazed me with her sangfroid.

"Auntie Di," she said, "I was at Disneyland yesterday, and when the quake started I thought I was dreaming that we were on the roller-coaster ride. What a surprise! By the way, what are you going to do about Maggie's paws with all the glass around?"

"Gosh, I don't know, Lilian."

"Well, I know what to do. I'll lend her my socks. We will stuff them with Kleenex and then fasten them with rubber bands."

"Great idea!"

And, as Edward Power and I walked back to my house in the dawn, Maggie padded ahead of us, looking like Chaplin's tramp, her feet splayed out in Lilian's socks.

The devastation to my house was frightening. Part of the front porch had collapsed, and as we made our way inside we could see that the chimney in the den had fallen, taking the back wall with it. The whole house had tilted to one side, and the chimneys to the living room and bedroom had broken off and were lying in a gable.

"First," said Edward, "we have to turn off the gas."

"Right," I said. "Bill had a wrench tied to the gas line."

But it didn't seem to reach the right spigot.

"Must be the other spigot," we surmised, and it wasn't until a week later that we discovered that we had turned off the swimming pool heater and gas was still pouring into my house.

Thinking I had no gas, I opened the earthquake kit we had stashed under the bed and took out a Sterno can to make some soup. I was damn lucky I didn't blow myself and my house to kingdom come, but whatever leak there was was small.

To my surprise, our swimming-pool man showed up at his appointed time. The pool had sustained no damage whatsoever. Amazing, since it was built in 1954, but if it had gone, it would have taken the house with it, being on a higher level. We would have ended up down on Ventura Boulevard!

George took one look at the chimneys resting on the roof.

"You had better get those down in a hurry. Another shock and they'll come right through the roof."

"Oh, God," I said. "Do you know of anyone who does that?"

"A friend of mine, Polish too. He has a crew. His name is Artur Okienewski." And the next day dear Artur with a crew of four stalwart Polish young men arrived. They had not only the chimneys, but plaster and all, cleaned up and hauled away by the end of the day.

"If you decide to rebuild," Artur asked, "would you consider hiring me?"

Would I!

I got word that the city was sending around inspectors who were "red tagging" buildings that they felt should be condemned and demolished. I feared for my home with its obvious damage. I felt it was mandatory to get an engineer in as quickly as possible to see if it could be saved.

Luckily Michael had used an engineer in Santa Barbara when he was renovating his house, so, with the help of Nikki, I was able to persuade Les Grant, the engineer to drive down and inspect my house.

The timing was perfect. No sooner had Mr. Grant arrived than "tagger" showed up at the door. I introduced them, and as Mr. Grant had all the proper credentials, the "tagger" said he would delay condemnation until the engineering reports were in. Les went all over the house, donning a pair of overalls to crawl underneath while we both prayed that there would be no aftershocks. He determined that the living-room wall was weakened, so recommended that I sleep downstairs as it was the main support for the upstairs bedroom, but he said that it would be safe for me to stay in the house, though not too comfortable.

He felt that it would be a difficult job, but the house could be saved and, indeed, was worth saving due to having been built in a time when detailed workmanship was the norm. He wrote up his report to present to the insurers.

A note on this: I had remembered a conversation that Bill had had with Don Bevan about whether it was worthwhile to keep having earthquake insurance, as we had been paying premiums for eighteen years without a tremor. The day of the quake, I made my way down to the bank in fear and trembling to look into our safe deposit box, praying he hadn't canceled it. Thank God, he hadn't.

I spent the next year in altercations with the representatives of Allstate who wanted to tear the house down and build me an entirely new one. They seemed stunned that I wouldn't jump at the opportunity. I finally had to bring in three outside engineers to work with Artur and prove that the house could be anchored safely. It would involve jacking the entire house up off its foundations, poring cement pilings down to and into bedrock, and then lowering the house back down onto new foundations and anchoring it.

In April, Michael persuaded me to move out of the

house and move in with him. He had rented a house with a guesthouse on Woodrow Wilson Drive, close to Warner Brothers Studio where he was starting a film with Demi Moore called *Disclosure*. Maggie and I moved into the guesthouse and relished living in a palatial estate. In addition, Michael and I have always enjoyed hanging out together, so it worked out well, as we'd meet for coffee and a gossip in the mornings.

It was around this time that I ran into my friends Norman and Peggy Lloyd at an art gallery, and they persuaded me to join them on a trip to Poland and the Czech Republic, sponsored by the Eugene O'Neill Foundation. It was all to do with theatre, opera, and meeting opposite numbers in the business. After ascertaining there was nothing further I could do about the house at this juncture, I signed on.

We all met up at Kennedy Airport in New York. We included the Lloyds, Barbara Poe Levee, and myself from the West Coast, Max Showalter—the leader of the group—David Wayne, Woody Broun, and several academics from the East Coast. A total of twelve in all. In Warsaw, we were joined by others who had flown in from Russia, so we numbered about twenty.

The first four days in Warsaw were spent at the Drama Academy where we watched with fascination the exercises that the four-year students were put through. They were so adept physically that the language barrier became almost nonexistent. We were told that, having lived under two repressive regimes, German and Russian, that would allow only "safe" classics or mindless pap performed, the actors developed a secret code with the audience that was closely attuned to their body language. It was in this way that they could get across all sorts of subversive information under the eyes of the authorities.

The versatility of the young people put our two year curriculum to shame, and we watched in awe. We saw a glorious production of *Fedora* at the opera house, had a piano recital all Chopin at his family home, and watched in amusement as Woody Broun (Heywood Broun, Jr) and David Wayne tried to outdo one another in raunchy theatre stories. Our Polish hosts and hotel guests listened in puzzlement while the two old actors had us holding our bellies in laughter.

Cracow is perhaps the most beautiful city on earth. Its eleventh-century charm was preserved during WWII because, ironically, it was the headquarters for the officers stationed at Auschwitz, forty miles away. The Lloyds, Barbara, and I wanted to visit the concentration camp but our guide tried strenuously to discourage us, so we hired a taxi and took off on our own.

Auschwitz, one feels immediately, is a holy place sanctified by the blood of all who passed through there. It is the small, personal things that tear at the heartstrings. Eyeglasses, suitcases with the labels still on, baby clothes, and the cloth made from human hair. It was shattering, and tears seemed too small a tribute to pay. As I stood by the gate to leave, an attendant motioned me to take a picture of the camp. I shook my head. It didn't seem right to treat this as a tourist attraction. He urged me again, and reluctantly I raised my camera. I focused and...it jammed. Somebody, or something didn't want me to take it. It gave me goose pimples. I gestured to him and left.

We took the overnight train to Prague, and suddenly I needed to be away from the group. We were put up at a club in the Old Town, and while everyone else was napping, I crossed the Charles Bridge and found a riverside market. While there I bought some wooden tulips and strolled along the embankment. It was a relief not to be told what to see, but just to take in whatever happened to be passing. While in Prague, we saw some interesting avant garde theatre, but the language barrier posed more problems than in Poland, for some reason.

On our way back, Barbara and I were dumped at Amsterdam. Due to a misunderstanding, overbooking, or whatever, the plane filled up with our stalwart leader on board to be told there were no more seats. That we would have to spend the night in Amsterdam courtesy of KLM, which had taken responsibility for the error. Barbara was due to catch a connecting plane back to L.A. at Kennedy, and I had planned to stay overnight with the Howards in Brooklyn, so we wanted out.

Crises in travel bring out the basic character in everyone I have found, and Barbara was the perfect companion to have in a disaster. Giggling like a couple of inane schoolgirls, we raced through the gates, lugging our baggage, and managed to get ourselves rerouted via Heathrow onto a Virgin Airlines flight. I have enjoyed her friendship ever since. She is a fine artist and a delightful lady.

Back in L.A., I found that negotiations with the insurance company were still going on with very little progress made. Michael has said that at this time I got a slightly insane look in my eye.

He said, "Mom, have you considered that maybe this shouldn't be? That maybe you should move to a nice condominium or something? Perhaps God is trying to tell you something."

"Well, if He is, I'm not listening. Because He is wrong, and you're wrong!"

Mike sighed patiently, but backed off.

When Michael's movie was completed, I moved into small house off Ventura Boulevard with a six-months' lease, and the proviso that I was to move out if it were sold. Meanwhile, Artur and I were going over plans of possible improvements that could be made once the insurance was approved. I knew that they would not be covered by insurance, but felt that while the house was undergoing renovation anyway, now was the time to make them. Four feet were added to the downstairs bedroom so that it could accommodate twin beds, a window in the den was installed where the fireplace used to be, and a Franklin stove added. An "entertainment center" fit into an unused closet in the den and a bathroom next to the pool house.

Finally their engineers and ours agreed, and the first payment to start work was issued in January, exactly a year after the quake.

A lovely bonus popped up at this time. My niece, Elaine Wold, Ruth's daughter, invited me to join her family on a Caribbean cruise on their private yacht, flying me there and back first class. The timing was ideal. We sailed from St Marten to St. Barts and then up to the Virgin Islands, all six of us, with help to wait on us. Elaine's husband Keith, her daughter, Diana, son-in-law, and granddaughter aged twelve. We snorkeled, ate ourselves silly, played poker, read, and lounged. It was a perfect holiday, spending Christmas and New Year's on board. Ruth's children, Elaine and Seward, inherited her joyful generosity, which enhances life for the rest of us lucky relations!

Joel had undergone hip replacement surgery in November and was making a slow, painful recovery. Things had not been going well between him and Paddy for some time. They seemed to have many problems, some to do with her inability to conceive. She had been in treatment for in vitro fertilization and had been given massive doses of hormones to induce pregnancy, which seemed to send her normally volatile personality out of control. She hated being in the United States, even for a short while, and proceeded to make Joel's life miserable while he was recuperating in the hospital. In the end, she went back to France, much to everyone's relief. She never returned.

Michael was due to start another movie, *The American President*, so he decided to rent an enormous mansion in Bel Air with room for Joel and me. Just in time, as my rented house had been sold. Joel had been released from the hospital, but was still on crutches, so he had quarters downstairs. Maggie and I had a suite over the garage, and Mike was in the master bedroom. It was the first time we had all been together since Michael left for prep school at fourteen, but it worked out well. We respected each other's privacy, but were there for each other. I cued Mike through his scenes in *American President*, counseled Joel through Paddy's abusive phone calls, and on occasion we all left notes for one another. Mike saved one from me:

> "Gentlemen, when you have your midnight snacks it would be nice if you cleaned up after yourselves. Thank you. Mom."

Meanwhile, work was finally about to begin on the reconstruction of my house. Then the rains came. Torrents poured down day, after day and when the pilings were due to be poured, it was discovered that the water table had risen above the bedrock, so there was a steady stream only sixteen feet down. Waiting until the dry season would entail another six to nine month delay.

So another engineer joined the forces. This was one who specialized in building piers and was adept in anchoring foundations through water. Work began again.

I had stressed to Artur that I wanted to keep the authentic "cottage" feel of the building, and he worked with me closely every step of the way, finding antique-looking hinges for doors, tile that matched the original, and sending to Maine for the Franklin stove. His workmanship was superb, and I blessed the day that George sent him to me.

Now, I had an invitation from another George. George White, of the Eugene O'Neill Foundation. He and Betsy, his wife, as well as her sister and brother-in-law were all going to Russia in a sort of cultural-exchange program. He asked me if I wanted to join them and perhaps bring another couple. Immediately I thought of the Howards, who quickly accepted.

My house would not be habitable until August, and we had to vacate the Bel Air house by May, so it seemed like the perfect time to visit a country that I had yearned to see. Joel kindly put me up in his cottage until the departure date. I am lucky that my relationship with both my adult sons is easy and companionable. They sure are nice fellows.

Funny and loving, and always there for me.

This trip was very different from the one to Poland the previous year. George had been "persona grata" since his first exhange trip to Russia in 1980, when it was still the Soviet Union. Our group was small, and we were promised visits to palaces normally off limits to tourists, lunching with the minister of culture in Moscow etc.

After spending overnight at the Savoy Hotel in Moscow, we were taken by bus north through Yaraslavl (only recently opened to foreigners because of a big military base nearby). Stopping in a local church, we came upon four singers in the shadows of a side chapel chanting a capella the lovely, sad Russian church music. It was a mystical moment, wherein one felt that one had touched the soul of Russia.

Shelakova, our destination, had long been a summer retreat for actors under the Soviets. Here George had decided to do his latest experiment. He had had Russian actors visit the O'Neill many times, I don't know how he incorporated them into the work as I was not at the O'Neill at that time. This time he had decided on doing a play bilingually, part in Russian, part in English, with an American director working with a translator. He had brought over three American actors, male, and they had been rehearsing for two weeks.

The second project was to be an American play, set in the Virgin Islands, spoken totally in Russian by Russian actors.

Shelakova, never luxurious under the Soviets, had fallen into disrepair under the present regime despite it being the home of one of their most famous playwrights, Ostrovski. Our accommodations were spartan. There were small hard cots for sleeping and plumbing that made one shudder, but the overall feeling for creating art and reaching out across language barriers made the heart leap. I imagine the atmosphere was very like the Group Theatre in its beginnings.

On our first evening there, a large party took place in a

summer house with much toasting of vodka and singing. One of the Russians, a man of perhaps sixty, kept making eye contact with me while raising his glass and smiling. I toasted him back and turned to resume my conversation, but I was conscious that his eyes never left me. At the end of the party, he grabbed my hands and started kissing them. As he worked his way up to my elbows and tried to pull me toward him, I realized he was pretty drunk and I had better get the hell out of there. So with international gestures of shrugs and waves, I extricated myself from his embrace. In the next few days as I watched rehearsals, he tailed me, nodding and smiling as though we shared some secret, which made me acutely uncomfortable.

The bilingual play did not work for me. It was a heavy-handed propoganda piece about two soldiers observing the first atom bomb tests, one speaking Russian while the other spoke English. Given the theme, I could see why it had been chosen, but the long soliloqies left part of the audience in the dark. The acting was excellent, and I was particularly struck with one spectacularly beautiful actress who was highly talented. I remarked to George that she would go far. He laughed.

"She is one of the most famous film and television stars in Russia, but they all jump at the chance to come here and work out."

What a difference from Hollywood!

The second play, spoken in Russian, was somehow more intelligible than the first. The acting and intentions were all so clear. I congratulated the actors in halting Russian.

"Bolshoi robote. Spasiba." Great work. Thank you, and we all embraced.

On the anniversary of Ostrovski's death, a service was held at his grave in the local churchyard. The priest, bearded and dressed in glittering robes, waved incense, speaking first in falsetto, then a deep bass voice.

I inquired as to the reason. Normally, I was told, there

are two priests doing the ceremony, but as this is a poor, small church, they can only afford one. He plays both parts.

On the day we were to leave, my admirer came running up the path (still reeking of vodka), grabbed my hands, and started in kissing them again, talking a blue streak. I looked around desperately for our translator.

"Oh my God, is he asking me to marry him and move to Siberia? What is it all about?"

She smiled.

"He says that he has been trying to tell you for days how much he admires Michael's work."

So much for my career as a femme fatale. Michael has a lot to answer for.

On the way back to Moscow, we stopped at the monastery at Kostroma where there is a museum devoted to the late royal family. Charming sketches by the czarina, family photos, personal notes and diaries, all denoting a warm and loving family. George said that as little as two years ago such an exhibit would have been impossible, but things are changing rapidly. For some, there is a nostalgia for the Czarist era, and now the royal family have been reburied with Peter the Great in St. Petersburg.

The hostage taking in Chechnya had been happening while we were away, and on our return to Moscow, we were startled to see several army tanks rumbling around, their crew looking an average age of sixteen. Riots had been expected, and the army was ready, just in case.

Just outside Red Square, a sort of impromptu market was set up. Women sold personal household items, bunches of wildflowers, anything to bring in a ruble. One of our party stopped to take a picture and was greeted by loud shouts of protest and some tears. Our translator explained that the woman felt shamed, she was a professor and intellectual and did not want any record of how low she had fallen.

The intellectuals and the elderly seem to have fared worse under the new regime, whereas an ex-K.G.B. member had opened up a series of "American" clubs, with names like "Beef and Bourbon," joining the ranks of instant millionaires. Capitalism is not without many victims. A young woman who had been a translator and guide for Charlton and Lydia Heston a few years back came to visit me and have tea at the hotel. She desperately wanted a job in the States, partly to support her aged parents who she feared would starve to death on their meager pension. I told her that I would contact the Hestons on my return to see what they could do, but sadly I had no job to offer.

We had lunch with the minister of culture. He and George signed several documents, and everybody toasted in champagne. Then we were invited by the curator of Kolomenskaya to visit the grounds where Peter the Great had built an enormous wooden palace on the banks of the Volga (later Catherine the Great had it torn down), and we were greeted by a host of singers in native dress to be rowed up the river by two stalwart oarsmen. It was obviously very special treatment for the foreigners, and many citizens watched with puzzled frowns on their faces.

Michael Howard and I made a special visit to Stanislavski's home, which has been preserved as a museum. We found it deeply touching. I half expected Michael to genuflect as he is an up-to-date interpreter of the Method.

We were warned that the night train to St. Petersburg was known for crime and were warned to keep our valuables and passports close by, but I found it clean and comfortable with no untoward incidents. As we approached the city, however, I was fascinated to see the difference in the skyline. Instead of onion domes, most churches here had spires. When we alit at the station, I was aware that the people looked different. Gone were the wide, flat Slavic cheekbones. There one saw more of a Scandinavian look, long heads, blond hair.

In our very modern, luxurious hotel, American and British businessmen were applying hard-sell tactics in the lobby on skeptical Russians, or so it appeared. We saw the "disputed art" at the Hermitage, the newly uncovered Impressionists that the Germans claimed had been stolen by Russia. The colors were astonishingly vivid, more so than others I had seen in galleries. I was told that it was because they had been hidden so long and not exposed to light, they had kept their original colors. The small Catherine Theatre in the Hermitage is a veritable gem. George said he wanted me to do a play he was writing on Catherine the Great and Voltaire in the space. I would love to. I hope he hurries up and finishes it before I get too old!

The summer palace is a miracle of restoration, from the exquisite Mon Plaisir to the gigantic formal palace. The Germans had systematically wrecked it while they waited for Leningrad to fall, stabling their horses in Mon Plaisir and burning the panels of chinoiserie. Obviously it had taken many years to bring it to this glittering state, and I questioned our guide as to why the Soviet Union would be so anxious to restore a symbol of the monarchy.

"We had to show the Germans that it could be done. That they could not defeat us. And we used German prisoners of war to rebuild it."

Nice touch.

Actually, a thing that impressed me while in Russia was the care they took of their theatres, museums, and churches. The streets outside may be dirty, but inside the gold leaf shone. Nothing wrong with their priorities.

It was a great trip and one I wouldn't have missed for anything, but now I was suddenly anxious to get back home to see how Artur had progressed on my house as well as introduce Maggie to her new surroundings. We had moved so many times since the quake that now she was completely bonded to me. And I to her, if the truth be told.

Just before I went on the trip, I had attended an auction. The house next door, owned by a dear elderly couple named the Shamoons, was irreparably damaged. The foundation cracked right in two, and it had been condemned. The lot was about the same size as mine, and I was afraid that a developer would put up a massive structure like the one on my uphill side. So I asked Michael if he would go in with me to buy the lot, putting it in trust for Cameron. This would give me a good-sized garden. He did, and I bless him every day as we sit and watch Maggie and her dog friends cavort on the lawn.

Now it was time to start the landscaping and fencing. Maggie and I couldn't move in until the whole property was fenced as she was still fairly dumb about traffic. One fine day in August about year and a half after the quake, my furniture came out of storage, Artur put on some finishing touches, and I was home again!

BACK HOME

Maggie and I spent the first night in the newly enlarged guest room, a strange experience for both of us; listening to eerie noises, prowling around in the shadows, searching for a comfortable, familiar space.

I've found it useful to park myself in a guest room to see what future guests will have to contend with and, indeed, I found the mattresses too hard and put "egg crates" on top of them. Closet space, lighting, and TV were fine, so I moved back into the upstairs bedroom I had shared with Bill.

I had only been in a week when I was summoned to Nantucket by Seward and Joyce Johnson to celebrate Fan's eightieth birthday. In keeping with their generosity, they had sweetly flown her daughter, son, daughter-in-law, and grandchildren over from England for a big family get-together, so there was no way I could refuse. Alma, my cleaning lady, spent nights in the house to care for Maggie, but the poor dog was sad and confused as I left.

I had never visited Nantucket before and was intrigued by the open beauty of its moors and seashore. We were all put up in a converted motel that Seward and Joyce had bought and now used as a guesthouse, and it worked well. We all had our privacy as well as a priceless view across the bay and a dock where we met for cocktails. Fan was in seventh heaven with all her brood around her, and I think she found it immensely comforting after the loss of Jock the previous year. She coped with her widowhood with great courage.

I invited her with her daughter Joanna and her granddaughter, Alice, to come to California for a few weeks to join in the housewarming party I was planning. I included everybody who had worked on the house and grounds and all friends and neighbors for a giant celebration. I hired bartenders and extra help, and it was a great success, though the landscaper was disturbed that people would see his work in such a raw state. However, he described in detail so they could visualize what it would become.

I had not been getting calls for auditions for some time now. My agents said that they were submitting me, but I didn't seem to fit into any known category. So I had to face the fact that my acting career was at a standstill and might be over, much as I hated the thought. I began the process of structuring, perhaps overstructuring, my life to combat the fear of not knowing what I was going to do when I got up in the morning.

Monday was for tennis with Barney and two other chaps; Tuesday was for golf with the womens club; Wednesday I volunteered at a day-care center to care for one year olds. Thursday was tennis again; and Friday, a life-drawing class in Santa Monica. Saturday and Sunday there were films being shown at the academy. Most days I tried to spend some time on these memoirs. It all helped give some form to my days now that the two mainstays of my life, my husband and my work, were gone.

In January of 1996, I went for my usual mammogram, and a suspicious lump was found.

I was inclined to put off the surgery as my health had always been excellent, and I was due to go to New York for Marty Richards's Red Ball at the Plaza, but the radiologist was insistent even though the tumor would probably turn out to be benign. That was the opinion of the surgeon too. But the lab found a malignancy, and I had to be operated on again to see if the lymph nodes were involved.

My initial reaction was one of shock that this could happen to me. Other people got ill, but me? Never! I felt a cold chill around the heart as I faced the possibility of leaving this earth before I was ready. I missed being able to turn to Bill for comfort, and though Joel and Alice Elliott came with me on the day of the operation, we were all doing a minuet of falsely cheerful chatter.

Thank God, the lymph nodes turned out not to be involved, and I was told that radiation should take care of any cancer that was left. Of course, I was immediately taken off Premarin and put on Nolvadex to leach the estrogen out of my system, with the result that I went through all the symptoms of menopause at a ridiculously late age.

I went through seven weeks of radiology with no ill effects and feeling quite optimistic about a total recovery. But when a second lump was discovered later that year, I had two days of frozen fear until the biopsy showed that it was benign.

While waiting for the results, I have never felt more alone.

I have good friends, but I have never had the gift of easy intimacy that Bill had, and I couldn't discuss my pain with them or my sons, who have their own problems

Later that year when an offer came up to play Mrs. Higgins in *My Fair Lady*, I grabbed it. Howard Keel was to play Henry Higgins, and he was a friend of the Elliotts and as such was instrumental in persuading the producer that I was right for the part of his mother, even though he was five years my senior.

Our first booking was in St. Louis, an outdoor auditorium that seated 12,000 people. Our second was in Atlanta, where the lovely old Fox Theatre on Peachtree Street seated a mere 5,000. The dancers in the chorus were rehearsed separately, so we didn't get together until about a week before opening. When we did, I was stunned at the precision and grace they displayed. It was up to the best of Broadway standards. I gather that St. Louis has a plethora of ballet schools, and the training shows.

Leslie Dennison was our Eliza and a fine one she was,

graceful and talented with a lovely singing voice and great professional composure on stage. This she needed, as Howard was a little fuzzy as to giving correct cues. She and Raye Birk, who played Pickering, had the most to cope with. My part as Henry Higgins's mother, is a dream part for any actress. There are a few short scenes with crisp lines that always get a laugh and a pretty surefire exit applause.

I wore a white wig and had thought that Howard would color his white hair and mustache to look younger, but this he disdained to do and in the review the *St. Louis Dispatch* reporter remarked that we "made a very handsome couple." but I doubt that was what Shaw had in mind.

I really enjoyed working with Howard, who was a great-spirited man. He must have been nervous as hell dealing with the precision of the lines and lyrics written in such a British vernacular, but he was always cheerful, affectionate, and "up." The audiences adored him, even if he did play fast and loose with some of the dialogue.

Opening night, rain threatened, and we had a few sprinkles just before the entrance of Freddy with his great song, "On the Street Where You Live." The producer was in the wings in a nervous sweat wondering whether to cancel and refund the money or to take a chance and go on. Finally he crossed his fingers and pushed Freddy onstage. The stage was slippery, and a couple of the dancers fell in the Ascot number, but were not hurt and continued on.

The other thing that the weather did was to screw up our body mikes. Mine went out completely for a time and in a 12,000-seat house, that's serious. However, I projected as best I could, and there were no complaints.

I had never been in St. Louis before and took full advantage on my free time to be a goggle-eyed tourist. There was the Arch, of course, and then lots of time spent at the zoo and the fabulous art museum. I discovered a German sculptor I had never heard of before, but whose work I found immensely moving, by the name of Anselm Kiefer. He specialized in grotesque, antiwar figures.

Then it was on to Atlanta, where I had played *Gigi* and *Once More with Feeling* thirty years earlier. The same producer, Chris Manos, was in charge and congratulated me on not forgetting how to get my laughs, a nice feeling of continuity in the theatre. Atlanta was gearing up for the summer Olympics and was getting ever more crowded. An immense Gay Parade trundled down Peachtree Street on our final Sunday, led by "Dykes on Bikes." A bunch of the toughest looking lesbian motorbike riders I have ever seen were followed by some outrageous drag queens. The gay chorus members in our group were cheering madly, and I saw one or two wipe away a tear. I suddenly realized how important that recognition was for them, whereas before I had always felt a vague impatience with the need to "come out." My feeling being that whatever one does in the privacy of the bedroom is fine, as long as it's not hurtful. Why the need to advertise? These guys made me stop and think about how affirmation is necessary to all of us.

I guess I'm still in the process of learning, which will go on until I leave this earth, as things evolve and change constantly. Coming back to L.A., I realized that once again work had saved me, had put the past into perspective and opened up the possibility of a future. I started dating some men, but only on a friendship basis. Suddenly things changed.

In the next year and a half, I became involved in an intense love affair, one that I let dominate my life. It had to be kept secret as the man in question was married with an incurably ill wife, but the secrecy only fanned the flames higher. My emotions, kept strictly under wraps since Bill's death, threatened to overwhelm me. I fell deeply in love.

I had been rather proud of my independence and hadn't realized that I was lonely until he came into my life, and then I seemed to experience all the pangs of young love. I was stunned that passion could be as immediate in our seventies as it was in our twenties. I waited for his phone calls, checked my machine avidly for his dear and funny messages. The sound of the scrape of his car on my driveway sent my heart racing. I gave myself to him completely, and all decisions were made with him in mind.

It was a time of great aliveness, great joy, and my love was reciprocated for some time.

Then came a time of conflicting attitudes from him, sometimes ardent, sometimes cool. It had me confused and off guard.

Eventually, the truth came out. He had fallen in love with someone else.

The devastation was total.

I cursed myself for becoming that vulnerable. In the years following Bill's death, I had successfully warded off male attentions, confining them only to friendship. Indeed, our relationship had started that way until he had pressed for more.

I could not cope. It was as though I had lost all resilience and felt unable to make plans or carry them through for everything seemed to be tied to him. A trip to New York, which I used to find exhilarating, was now flat and grey. The future seemed without hope. I was back to the sleepless nights I had experienced after Bill's death, and waking only brought searing memories.

I finally faced the fact that the depression was not lifting and that I was at a loss as to what to do. So I asked my doctor for the name of a therapist, preferably male, as I felt that perhaps a man could bring me some insight into what had happened. He was helpful in getting me to stop being angry at myself, for not seeing the signals of waning love from my lover, and for still loving him.

With the passage of time, it is becoming a bearable memory, but I'm still working on regaining the equilibrium and independence I had before I met him..

This morning I woke up with the sense that I had started to recover from a long illness. I looked out at my garden and saw planting that needed to be done. Sometimes the small things can lead one back to health.

I remembered back, fifty years ago, after Doug and I were separated. My life was in a similar turmoil with many decisions to be made. Male friends of Doug's began calling and asking me for dinner dates that I suspected would lead to other things. Female friends of mine were offering all sorts of advice on how to lead my newly bachelor life. My head was spinning.

Suddenly, I realized it was Halloween. My children expected a jack-o'-lantern, trick or treats. The works. While carving the pumpkin, I sensed a slowing down of my heartbeat, a calming of the senses, a beginning of perspective. And that will come again as one becomes involved in the minutia of living, I know.

While my star-crossed romance was going on, Michael and Diandra separated. I believe this time it's for good, so we have all been going through our private hells. Cameron included. We are all finding our various ways of working through them.

For my seventy-fifth birthday, my sons gave me a dinner celebration at Spago, a fashionable restaurant to which many of my old friends were invited, including Doug and Anne. It was a bittersweet moment, for then I sensed that my love affair was coming to an end though I did not know why. My sons both gave loving tributes. Then Doug got up to make a speech full of affection and humor, speech slightly slurred from the stroke he had suffered two years ago. The gallantry with which he faced the afflictions of old age brought tears to my eyes.

There will probably never be another man in my life, and as mankind tends to move in couples, like Noah's Ark, I have to revise the travel plans I cherished in order to find interesting and exciting things to do on my own.

The family is a great solace.

At the end of 1998, members of the Dill clan gathered from all over to celebrate Thankgiving and Laurence's ninetieth birthday at Ariel Sands in Bermuda. Elaine and Keith Wold flew in from Florida and their grandaughter from

Switzerland. Fan came, as did her son Ian from England. There were over eighty of us there for the celebration.

A choir sang four of Laurence's compositions before dinner, and even the newest babies in the family were quiet as they listened. The warmth was palpable. The next day I made my usual pilgrimage to Bill's grave. It is a peaceful and beautiful site, one that invites contemplation, and when I am in Bermuda, I often sit there remembering the joy that Bill and I shared. Later I found out that Michael, Joel, and Cameron had also paid their visits, bringing flowers. I hope that Cameron will bring his children here in the future and find a sense of peaceful continuity.

There are still adventures ahead, and I intend to take advantage of all of them so to live each day to its fullest before I go to my personal happy-hunting ground.

For death is waiting—perhaps sooner, perhaps later. I hope to be able to face it with as much grace as my mother did. I am glad that my ashes will be in Devonshire churchyard next to Bill's and a stone's throw from her grave. It seems fitting. It seems right.

Michael asked me to write these memoirs for Cameron, and I wish I had great words of wisdom to impart after my long time in this world, but my dictum is fairly simple. Be compassionate, be courageous, and, for God's sake, have fun!

So Cam, this is your Granny, warts and all. Now you probably know me better than anyone, and I hope I don't disappoint you. Have a great life.

Carpe diem!

—30—

Index

A Cook for Mr. General, 223
A Whistle at Eaton Falls, 158
Abbott, George, 92
Abbott, Judy, 92, 106
Adams, Margot, 338
Adams, Mason, 338
Adler, Luther, 126, 138
Albee, Edward, 257
Algiers Naval Station, 95, 98
Alida (cousin, d. of Helen), 37
Allen Stevenson school, 153-54, 184, 201
Allinson, Michael, 321, 341, 343
Ameche, Don, 252
American Academy of Dramatic Arts, the, 9, 63, 156, 313
American President, The, 354, 355
Andersonville Trial, The, 221, 223, 226, 230, 231, 233
Andrews, Lois, 177
Angeli, Pier, 194
Anouilh, Jean, 163, 171-72
Arvenides, John, 247
As You Like It, 157
Attrick-Sterling, Rod, 64, 155, 302
Bacall, Betty, 242
Bachelor Born, 69
Bagetta, Vincent, 267, 273-74
Bain, Chris, 44
Bain, Conrad, 190, 310
Bain, Whit, 44
Barclay, Steve, 84
Barry, Philip, 40, 144-45, 150
Bauman, Dick, 263
Beatty, Warren, 276
Beauty and the Beast, 312
Beerbohm-Tree, 144
Ben Casey, 241, 245
Benedek, Lazlo, 160
Bennett, Eddie, 48
Berghof, Herbert, 231
Bernstein, Leonard, 111
Best of Friends, The, 318, 321, 323
Bevan, Don, 54, 350
Birk, Raye, 366
Blanchard, Susan, 123
Blooding, The, 273, 279
Blum, Edith, 210
Blum, John, 210, 242
Blum, Morton, 210
Blum, Pam, 313, 337

Bohnen, Roman, 122
Boland, Mary, 169
Booth, James, 281
Borgnine, Ernest, 158
Bowman, Lee, 84
Brackett, Rogers, 136
Brando, Jocelyn, 121
Breit, Harvey, 204, 215
Bridges, Lloyd, 158, 206
Brooks, Norman, 84-85
Brooks, Phyllis, 84
Broun, Heywood (Woody), Jr., 351-52
Brown, Leah Kates, 315
Brown, Tom, 136
Bruce, Carol, 253
Burghley, Lord, 113
Burns, Bobby, 232
Bushnell, Bill, 280
Buydens (Douglas), Anne, 193, 195
Cactus Flower, 242
Caine Mutiny, The, 180
Cantor, Eddie, 24
Carmichael, Hoagy, 84
Carmichael, Ruth, 86
Carousel, 113
Carpenter, Carleton, 158
Carroll, Nancy, 54
Carter, Jimmy, 276
Caruso, Paul, 125
Cast a Giant Shadow, 240
Cedars of Lebanon Hospital, 128
Champion, 10, 134, 136
Champlin, Charles, 263
Chaplin, Michael, 142
Chaplin, Charlie, 140-143
Chaplin, Oona, 141-42
Charleson, Leslie, 267
Chatterton, Ruth, 183-84
Chevalier, Maurice, 29
China Syndrome, 286
Cilento, Diane, 219
Circle Theatre, 140, 154
Clark, Maggie, 312
Clark, Marilyn, 154
Cochran, Steve, 191
Cockerell, Sir Sidney, 328, 332
Cohen, Alex, 223
Cohen, Howard, 334
College of the Seven Seas, 226
Collier, Constance, 140-41, 143-44

Index

Comden, Betty, 111
Conwell, Jack, 271
Coogan, Dick, 296
Cooper, Irving, 232
Coote, Robert, 82
Corrigan, Sister Felicitas, 319
Corso, Judy, 272
Corso, Mary, 125
Corwin, Norman, 160
Cotton, Joseph, 187-89
Cowan, Ronnie, 147, 151
Cowan, Warren, 137, 147
Coward, Noel, 84, 132-33
Cowboys, The, 269
Critic's Choice, 234
Crockett, Phil, 87, 103
Cromwell, John, 188
Crosby, Jerry, 8, 30
Cukor, George, 94
D'Angelo, Aristide, 56, 67
Dabney, Augusta, 258
Dana, Leora, 267
Daniels, Gibson, 209-10
Darnell, Linda, 120, 163-67, 170, 180
Darrid, Bill, 276-81, 283-90, 293-298, 300-302, 307-312, 320-29, 331-333, 335-340, 342, 344-346, 349-50, 363, 365, 367-68, 370
Davidson, Gordon, 321
Davis, Jim, 269
de Gilderode, Michael, 245
de Liagre, Alfred, 145
De Rochemont, Louis, 158
De Toth, Andre, 198
de Vito, Danny,271, 299
Death of a Salesman, 154-55
Defenders, The, 241
Demsky, Byrna (Kirk's mother), 11
Demsky, Harry (Kirk's father), 11
Dennison, Leslie, 365
Dennison, Michael, 318
Deutche, Armand, 130
Diestel, Emil, 63
Diggins, Peggy, 75
Dill, Bayard, 14, 18-19, 21, 34, 113, 211, 248-50, 312, 316, 332, 336
Dill, David, 248, 250, 289-90, 294, 312, 336
Dill, Fan, 14, 16, 18, 21, 27-38, 43-46, 55, 60, 82, 159, 179-80, 207, 235, 275, 286, 289, 291, 295, 297, 304-6, 308, 316, 318, 341, 363, 370
Dill, Laurence, 13, 14, 18
Dill, Nicky, 248-50, 316, 332
Dill, Ruth, 18, 29, 34, 39, 45-8, 56-8, 62, 66, 68, 72-77, 84, 87, 94, 101-9, 151, 154, 156, 182, 204, 210, 226, 275, 288, 294, 313
Dill, Susan, 235, 319, 340
Dill, Thomas Melville, 16, 294
Dill, Thomas Newbold, 17
Dill, Tommy, 18, 313
Disclosure, 7, 351
Disenchanted, The, 196, 204
Dobbs, Florrie, 49
Dotrice, Roy, 312, 341
Douglas, Cameron, 12, 231, 280, 282, 295-96, 303-4, 308, 313, 325, 328, 340, 342, 361, 369-70
Douglas, Diandra, 141, 276-77, 279-80, 282, 307-9, 313, 316, 333, 340, 369
Douglas, Joel Andrew, 107, 129-30, 133, 136, 143, 154, 156-59, 165-66, 189, 193, 195-96, 200, 202, 207-210, 215-18, 226-231, 236, 238-39, 261-63, 268, 271-73, 280283, 285, 299, 302, 306-9, 313-14, 317, 327-28, 332, 341, 354-55, 365, 370
Douglas, Kirk (Doug), 9, 11, 54, 66-72, 75, 91-131, 134-137, 140, 144-151, 159, 161, 163-65, 183, 192-202, 206-211, 216-17, 228, 235, 244-47, 254, 260, 262, 270, 273, 276, 285-86, 294, 307, 309, 332, 338, 342, 369
Dowling, Vincent, 321-22, 332, 341
Drummond, Paddy, 354-55
Duchess of Devonshire, 249, 250-51
Duff, Howard, 200
Dunholme Manor, 35
Dunne, Griffin, 325
Ederle, Gertrude, 169
Edwards, Blake, 265
Edwards, Vince, 243
Elliott, Steve, 290-332
Engel, Sam, 122
Englund, George, 156
Englund, Pat, 154
Epstein, Jerry, 140, 142
Ernst, Bud, 81
Ernst, Gwynne, 81
Escuria, 245
Eugene O'Neill Foundation Theatre, 246
Everett, Matt, 336
Everett, Michael, 321
Everything in the Garden, 257
Fan's children, Ian, Tom, Joanna, 180
Fatal Attraction, 308
Ferrer, Jose, 232
Fetigan, Dorothy, 251
Fitzgerald, Barry, 141
Fjeld, Julianna, 282
Fletcher, Louise, 271
Flynn, Errol, 71, 76, 176
Fonda, Henry, 123, 234
Fonsigrives, Lisa, 90
Ford, John, 120-22, 269
Foreman, Carl, 135
Forever Amber, 125
Forman, Milos, 270-71
Francis, Ann, 158
Freeman, Morgan, 345

Index

Friderichson, Birgit, 59
Furness, Lord and Lady, 36
Furness-Withy Line, 36
Gabel, Martin, 186
Gam, Rita, 280
Gardner, Ava, 277
Geary, Alex, 140
Geer, Will, 234
Gethers, Steve, 233
Gibbs, Sir Peter, 113
Gibson, Don, 317
Gibson, Elsbeth, 317
Gielgud, John, 318
Gigi, 254
Gilmore, Virginia, 234
Giorgi, Elsie, 298, 327
Gish, Dorothy, 158
Gish, Lillian, 81
Goddard, Dick, 91
Godfather, The, 241
Goodman, Benny, 131
Granlund, Nils Thor, 85
Grant, Les, 350
Gray, Emmy, 38
Green, Adolph, 111
Gregory, Angela, 95
Grey, Dulcie, 318
Griffith, Micheal, 345
Grizzard, George, 220
Grossman, Esther, 118
Grossman, Milt, 115
Grosso, Nikki, 325
Grover, Lorraine, 188
Guare, John, 258
Gudefin, Georges, 91
Gunn, Moses, 269
Gussow, Mel, 342
Gutterman, Morty, 119
Gwynne, Fred, 234
Hadley, Leila, 155
Haller, Ernie, 174
Hamilton, Murray, 158, 181
Hampden, Walter, 255
Hansen, Harald, 59
Happy Time, The, 183-87
Hardy, Oliver, 72
Harris, Pat, 197
Harris, Rosemary, 222, 318
Hartford, Huntington, 84
Hartley, Mariette, 234
Hasty Heart, The, 136
Hawkins, 268
Hay, Ian, 69
Healey, Myron, 163
Heaven Can Wait, 112
Hebo, Hafdan, 156
Hedda Gabler, 302
Heflin, Frances, 131

Heflin, Van, 119
Henry, Sweet Henry, 251
Hepburn, Katharine, 40, 42, 83, 140, 144, 155
Here Comes Mr. Jordan, 112
Heroes of Telemark, The, 245
Heston, Charlton, 332, 359
Heston, Lydia, 333, 359
Highest Tree, The, 225, 228
Hill, Arthur, 268
Hill, George Roy, 255
Hiller, Wally, 263
Hirson, Alice, 290
Holden, William, 266
Horowitz, Israel, 258
Horsfall, Bill, 42
Horsfall, Dr. and Mrs., 42
Horsfall, Emily, 42
Horsfall, Frances, 42
Horst, 93
House of Strangers, 11, 126, 137
Houseman, John, 299
Howard, Michael, 184, 187, 297, 328, 359
Howes, Tina, 316
Humphries, Millie, 255
I Walk Alone, 125
Indian Fighter, The, 197-98
Inherit the Wind, 199, 204
Irving, Henry, 144
Jackman, Margaret "Jacko," 41
Jackson, Sybil "Tiddles," 41
James, Mary, 206
Jehlinger, Charles, 63
Jenkins, George, 346
Jenkins, Phyllis, 346
Jessell, Georgie, 177
Jewel of the Nile, 299, 302
Johnson, Bobby, 24
Johnson, Elaine, 29, 354
Johnson, Georgann, 234
Johnson, Mary Lea, 28, 57
Johnson, Seward, 18, 45, 343, 363
Johnson, Seward, Jr., 29, 34, 354
Jorgensen, Susan, 261-62
Judd, Forrest, 163
Karen, Jim, 258, 312, 332
Karloff, Boris, 54,
Keel, Howard, 365
Keeper of the Flame, 84
Kennedy, Arthur, 155
Kent, Atwater, 130
Kerr, Mary, 235
Kiefer, Anselm, 366
Kilburn, Terry, 140
Kirchner, Irv, 263
Kirkland, Pat, 54
Kiss and Tell, 92, 106, 108
Knot's Landing, 281
Knox, Alexander, 134

Index

Knox, Doris, 139
Kopit, Arthur, 268
Krakower, Arnold, 147, 196
Kramer, Stanley, 135
Kung Fu, 271
Laire, Judson, 269
Lancaster, Burt, 125
Lancaster, Norma, 125
Langner, Lawrence, 155, 191, 225
Lawrence, Paula, 181
Leachman, Cloris, 154, 191
Lear, Norman, 141-42
Lehr, Tom, 257
Let's Live Again, 135
Levee, Barbara Poe, 351
Levin, Peter, 267
Levine, Barbara, 156, 164
Levine, Win, 156, 164
Levitt, Saul, 221
Lewis, Dick, 318
Liebling, Bill, 209, 220, 283
Life and Times of Eddie Roberts, The, 281
Light Up the Sky, 161, 171, 187
Limelight, 143
Little Foxes, The, 183
Lloyd, Norman, 200, 283, 299
Lloyd, Peggy, 351
Lord, Marjorie, 200
Lortel, Lucille, 323, 338
Los Angeles Actors Theatre, 280
Love Is a Many Splendored Thing, 265, 268
Loving, 263
Luker, Diandra, 141, 276, 279
Lupino, Ida, 82
M.C.A., 236, 254
M.G.M., 84, 119, 135, 223-4, 323-4
Maharajah of Kaputhala, 174
Major Barbara, 140-42, 144, 302
Malden, Karl, 266-7, 271
Malone, Fred, 239
Mankiewicz, Joseph, 11
Manos, Chris, 367
Marcovicci, Andrea, 267
Marcus, Ann, 265, 281
Marley, John, 168
Marquand, Carole, 300
Marquand, Richard, 298, 305
Marshall, Armina, 155, 191
Martinelli, Elsa, 198
Mary of Scotland, 42
Maschio, Connie, 84
Maschio, Johnny, 87
Master Builder, The, 302
Matthau, Walter, 201, 241
Maxwell, Marilyn, 136
Mayer, Lyle, 38
McCarthy, Glenn, 176-77
McCormick, Dr. Frank, 196, 228, 283

McDonough, Edwin, 343
McDowall, Roddy, 136, 309
McGuire, Dorothy, 100
McKay, Scott, 188,
McKenna, Kenneth, 224
McLachlan, Dame Laurentia, 318
Medak, Peter, 312
Meisner, Sandy, 52, 237
Merrick, David, 114
Merrill, Dina, 237
Meyer, Johnny, 73, 176, 178
Meyer, Lloyd, 212
Miani, Count, 178-79
Miller, Clare, 263
Mills, Donna, 267
Mills, Gordon, 188
Modern Primitive, 180
Monsieur Verdoux, 142
Monsoon, 163
Moore, Billee, 35
Moore, Colonel, 35
Moore, Demi, 351
Moore, Jock 19, 35
Moore, Tom, 304
Moore, Vera, 35
Morley, Robert, 141
Mulford, Pat, 284
Muni, Paul, 199
My Darling Clementine, 120, 122
My Fair Lady, 365
Nader, George, 163
Native Uprising, 200
Neighborhood Playhouse, 162, 237, 258
Nelson, Fay, 285
Nesbit, Cathleen, 190
Newland, John, 235
Nicholson, Jack, 268, 70, 276
Northcross, Sam, 259
Okienewski, Artur, 349-50, 353, 355, 360
Old Times, 280
On Golden Pond, 310
On the Town, 112
Once More with Feeling, 243, 367
One Flew over the Cuckoo's Nest, 270, 284
Painting Churches, 300, 317-18
Palicio, Fernando de, Jr., 47
Paper Chase, The, 299, 304
Partlan, Bill, 320-21, 336-37
Partlan, Tina, 321
Pascal, Gabriel, 139
Pasmore, Miss, 41, 293
Patton, Frank, 152
Pearman, Jim, 19
Peters, Susan, 134
Petrie, Dan, 220
Phelps, Eleanor, 156
Philips, Margaret, 150
Pickford, Mary, 81

Index

Pinter, Harold, 280
Playwrights company, 187
Plummer, Christopher, 233
Posse, 268
Potter, Hank, 187
Power, Edward, 267, 312, 326, 348
Power, Jennifer, 311
Power, Lilian, 348
Power, Susie, 267
Power, Tyrone, 207-8, 211
Preminger, Otto, 180, 234
Pressman, David, 220
Prince, Nicky, 208
Purdy, Marshall, 338
Quine, Richard, 134
Quinn, Anthony, 181
Quinn, Catherine, 125
Quinn, Tony, 125
Raitt, John, 112
Randell, Ron, 140
Reason, Rex, 160
Reclining Figure, 186
Redford, Robert, 224
Redington, Michael, 318-19, 342
Reed, Patricia, 302
Reed, Rex, 263
Renoir, Jean, 163
Richards, Marty, 313, 323, 337, 341
River, The, 163
Robards, Jason, Jr., 219
Roberts, Mark, 168
Robertson, Cliff, 183
Robinson, Edward G., 11, 64, 137-38
Robinson, Francis, 95
Rogers and Cowan, 137
Rogers, Ginger, 40
Romancing the Stone, 298
Rosenstein, Sophie, 75
Russell, Rosalind, 64
Sabrina Fair, 187, 223
Saidenberg, Eleanor, 219
Saint, Eva Marie, 263
Saks, Dr. Herbert, 238
Sargent, Herb, 154, 156, 160, 164-65
Saroyan, Carol, 241
Schallert, Edwin, 302
Schary, Dore, 223, 227-28
Schdanoff, George, 121
Schneider, Batami, 137
Schneider, Benno, 134
Scott, George C., 231-33
Second Threshold, 40, 144, 150
Segal, George, 263
Seltzer, Frank, 137
Seltzer, Michael, 121
Seltzers, the, 128, 270, 273-74, 346
Shaw, Artie, 150-51
Shaw, George Bernard, 35, 140-42, 160, 318-19, 337, 341-42, 366
Shearer, Norma, 35
Shelley, Carole, 258, 342
Showalter, Max, 351
Shulberg, Budd, 196, 204, 215, 220
Sign of the Ram, 133
Siodmak, Robert, 158
Skerritt, Tom, 266
Solomon Moon, 256-57
Solt, Andrew, 160
Sound of Music, The, 229
Spewack, Bella, 121
Spewack, Sam, 121
Spiegelglass, Leonard, 132
Stanhope, Lady Blanche, 34
Stanley, Kim, 265
Stanwyck, Barbara, 119
Stewart, James, 268
Storm Over Tibet, 160
Straight, Beatrice, 258
Strange Love of Martha Ivers, The, 114
Streetcar Named Desire, 154
Streets of San Francisco, The, 267
Sullavan, Margaret, 187-88, 190, 234
Sunrise at Campobello, 223
Thiess, Ursula, 163
Thomas, Michael, 264
Three Steps to Heaven, 167
Tigar, Kenneth, 337
Tites, the, 22-24
Tone, Franchot, 123
Tors, Ivan, 160
Tracy, Spencer, 64, 84
Trio, 106, 110
Trojan Women, The, 281
Truscott, Laurie, 251
Turner, Kathleen, 299
Twig Is Bent, The, 121
Tynan, Kenneth, 227
Universal Pictures, 236, 254
Vacarro, Brenda, 268
Van Middlesworth, Dick, 67, 71-2, 77-8, 84
Van Sleet, Barbara, 110, 156
Van Sleet, Bill, 71, 156, 161
Venuta, Benay, 130
Vining, Jimmy, 175
Voight, Jon, 237
Von Luckner, Erich, 14
Vye, Murvyn, 181
Wadlington, Clare, 21
Waite, Ralph, 280
Wall Street, 308
Wallace, Jean, 123
Wallis, Hal, 114, 117, 125
War of the Roses, The, 299
Wasserman, Lew, 236, 253-54
Watson, Douglas, 234
Wayne, David, 351-52

Index

Weaver, Fritz, 283
Wender, Phyllis, 326
West Point Story, The, 204
Westmore, James, 158
White, Betsy, 355
White, George, 246, 320, 355
Whitehead, Commander, 240
Whitemore, Hugh, 341-42
Whitty, Dame May, 134
Widmark, Richard, 106
Wild Rovers, 265
Wilde, Cornel, 130
Williams, Emlyn, 183
Williams, Tennessee, 175
Wilson, Langford, 260
Wilson, Paul, 66
Wind Is Ninety, The, 110
Winsor, Kathleen, 147-150
Winter's Tale, The, 234
Wold, Elaine, 354
Wold, Keith, 354
Wold, Ruth, 354
Woman Bites Dog, 121
Women's Strike for Peace, 247
Wood, Audrey, 209, 235-36, 283-85
Woodruff, Dick, 84
World of Henry Orient, The, 251
Wouk, Herman, 180, 182
Wrightsman, Irene, 145
Wyatt, Jane, 122
Zanuck, Darryl, 120-22